CAMBRIDGE MONOGRAPHS ON APPLIED AND COMPUTATIONAL MATHEMATICS

38 **The Christoffel–Darboux Kernel for Data Analysis**

87173480
6814370
87173480
45790
310
1160
1160
310
1160
45790
7360
310
110
7360
619370
87173480
6814370
87173480

The *Cambridge Monographs on Applied and Computational Mathematics* series reflects the crucial role of mathematical and computational techniques in contemporary science. The series publishes expositions on all aspects of applicable and numerical mathematics, with an emphasis on new developments in this fast-moving area of research.

State-of-the-art methods and algorithms as well as modern mathematical descriptions of physical and mechanical ideas are presented in a manner suited to graduate research students and professionals alike. Sound pedagogical presentation is a prerequisite. It is intended that books in the series will serve to inform a new generation of researchers.

A complete list of books in the series can be found at www.cambridge.org/mathematics.

Recent titles include the following:

22. The mathematical foundations of mixing, *Rob Sturman, Julio M. Ottino & Stephen Wiggins*
23. Curve and surface reconstruction, *Tamal K. Dey*
24. Learning theory, *Felipe Cucker & Ding Xuan Zhou*
25. Algebraic geometry and statistical learning theory, *Sumio Watanabe*
26. A practical guide to the invariant calculus, *Elizabeth Louise Mansfield*
27. Difference equations by differential equation methods, *Peter E. Hydon*
28. Multiscale methods for Fredholm integral equations, *Zhongying Chen, Charles A. Micchelli & Yuesheng Xu*
29. Partial differential equation methods for image inpainting, *Carola-Bibiane Schönlieb*
30. Volterra integral equations, *Hermann Brunner*
31. Symmetry, phase modulation and nonlinear waves, *Thomas J. Bridges*
32. Multivariate approximation, *V. Temlyakov*
33. Mathematical modelling of the human cardiovascular system, *Alfio Quarteroni, Luca Dede' Andrea Manzoni & Christian Vergara*
34. Numerical bifurcation analysis of maps, *Yuri A. Kuznetsov & Hil G.E. Meijer*
35. Operator-adapted wavelets, fast solvers, and numerical homogenization, *Houman Owhadi & Clint Scovel*
36. Spaces of measures and their applications to structured population models, *Christian Düll, Piotr Gwiazda, Anna Marciniak-Czochra & Jakub Skrzeczkowski*
37. Quasi-interpolation, *Martin Buhmann & Janin Jäger*

The Christoffel–Darboux Kernel for Data Analysis

JEAN BERNARD LASSERRE
LAAS-CNRS, University of Toulouse, CNRS

EDOUARD PAUWELS
IRIT, University of Toulouse, CNRS

MIHAI PUTINAR
University of California, Santa Barbara

CAMBRIDGE
UNIVERSITY PRESS

University Printing House, Cambridge CB2 8BS, United Kingdom

One Liberty Plaza, 20th Floor, New York, NY 10006, USA

477 Williamstown Road, Port Melbourne, VIC 3207, Australia

314–321, 3rd Floor, Plot 3, Splendor Forum, Jasola District Centre,
New Delhi – 110025, India

103 Penang Road, #05–06/07, Visioncrest Commercial, Singapore 238467

Cambridge University Press is part of the University of Cambridge.

It furthers the University's mission by disseminating knowledge in the pursuit of education, learning, and research at the highest international levels of excellence.

www.cambridge.org
Information on this title: www.cambridge.org/9781108838061
DOI: 10.1017/9781108937078

First published 2022

A catalogue record for this publication is available from the British Library.

ISBN 978-1-108-83806-1 Hardback

Contents

Foreword

Francis Bach, INRIA

Characterizing and analyzing probability distributions through their moments has a long history in probability, statistics, optimization, signal processing, machine learning and all related fields. Christoffel–Darboux (CD) kernels are well-studied mathematical objects which were originally introduced for very different purposes. They turn out to benefit from interesting properties within a moment-based analysis context leading to interesting applications.

The theory of CD kernels and their relationship to moments is more than a century old, and is still an active field of mathematical research. The motivations for studying such objects arose from fundamental mathematics, with orthogonal polynomials and approximation theory, and have remained quite disconnected to applied disciplines centered on inference from data. Yet CD kernels turn out to have several appealing properties from an empirical inference perspective. They can be defined from moments, requiring only conceptually simple numerical operations. Furthermore, theory shows that many subtle properties of the underlying distribution can be obtained from the CD kernels of increasing orders, such as its support.

This book demonstrates the potential of CD kernels as an empirical inference tool in a data analysis context. It investigates the consequences of the favorable properties of CD kernels in a statistical context where one only has access to empirical measures and empirical moments. This original thematic positioning naturally leads to questions at the interface between applied statistical inference and the CD kernel literature. These include statistical connections between empirical Christoffel functions and its large-sample limit, quantitative estimates and bounds, and consequences for applications.

Interestingly, the Christoffel–Darboux kernel is a reproducing kernel for a space of polynomials, a notion that is now common in statistics and machine learning. The construction is, however, very different with a sample dependency of underlying scalar product and norm, which are adapted to the empirical measure. This contrasts with more usual machine learning applications where the scalar product is fixed and given, and provides an efficient basis for polynomial estimation with a natural interpretation for increasing degree orders.

Many aspects of the theory of Christoffel functions and the associated Christoffel–Darboux kernels are well established and have become classical in the polynomial approximation literature. This book provides a unified and clear exposition of the main tools and algorithms, with a strong focus on data analysis applications. It shows in particular how the new polynomial kernels can be efficiently used for many relevant tasks, such as support estimation, outlier detection or experimental design.

Symbols

$\mathbb{N}$	the set of natural numbers
$s(d)$	$\binom{n+d}{n}$
$\mathbb{Z}$	the set of integers
$\mathbb{Q}$	the set rational numbers
$\mathbb{R}$	the set of real numbers
$\mathbb{R}_+$	the set of nonnegative real numbers
$\mathbb{C}$	the set of complex numbers
$\mathbf{A}$	matrix in $\mathbb{R}^{m\times n}$
$\mathbf{A}_j$	column j of matrix $\mathbf{A}$
$\mathbf{A} \succeq 0$ ($\succ 0$)	$\mathbf{A}$ is positive semidefinite (definite)
x	scalar $x \in \mathbb{R}$
$\mathbf{x}$	vector $\mathbf{x} = (x_1, \ldots, x_n) \in \mathbb{R}^n$
$\boldsymbol{\alpha}$	vector $\boldsymbol{\alpha} = (\alpha_1, \ldots, \alpha_n) \in \mathbb{N}^n$
$\vert\boldsymbol{\alpha}\vert =$	$\sum_{i=1}^n \alpha_i$ for $\boldsymbol{\alpha} \in \mathbb{N}^n$
$\mathbb{N}^n_d \subset \mathbb{N}^n$	the set $\{\boldsymbol{\alpha} \in \mathbb{N}^n : \vert\boldsymbol{\alpha}\vert \leq d\}$
$\mathbf{x}^{\boldsymbol{\alpha}}$	vector $\mathbf{x}^{\boldsymbol{\alpha}} = (x_1^{\alpha_1} \cdots x_n^{\alpha_n})$, $\mathbf{x} \in \mathbb{C}^n$ or $\mathbf{x} \in \mathbb{R}^n$, $\boldsymbol{\alpha} \in \mathbb{N}^n$
$\mathbb{R}[x]$	ring of real univariate polynomials
$\mathbb{R}[\mathbf{x}] = \mathbb{R}[x_1, \ldots, x_n]$	ring of real multivariate polynomials
$\Sigma[\mathbf{x}] \subset \mathbb{R}[\mathbf{x}]$	set of sum-of-squares (SOS) polynomials
$\mathcal{P}(\mathcal{X})_d$	space of polynomials of degree at most d, nonnegative on $\mathcal{X}$
$(\mathbf{x}^{\boldsymbol{\alpha}})$	canonical monomial basis of $\mathbb{R}[\mathbf{x}]$
$V_{\mathbb{C}}(I) \subset \mathbb{C}^n$	the algebraic variety associated with an ideal $I \subset \mathbb{R}[\mathbf{x}]$
$\sqrt{I}$	the radical of an ideal $I \subset \mathbb{R}[\mathbf{x}]$
$\sqrt[\mathbb{R}]{I}$	the real radical of an ideal $I \subset \mathbb{R}[\mathbf{x}]$
$I(V(I)) \subset \mathbb{C}^n$	the vanishing ideal $\{f \in \mathbb{R}[\mathbf{x}] : f(\mathbf{z}) = 0\, \forall \mathbf{z} \in V_{\mathbb{C}}(I)\}$
$V_{\mathbb{R}}(I) \subset \mathbb{R}^n$	the real variety associated with an ideal $I \subset \mathbb{R}[\mathbf{x}]$

$I(V_{\mathbb{R}}(I)) \subset \mathbb{R}[\mathbf{x}]$	the real vanishing ideal $\{f \in \mathbb{R}[\mathbf{x}]\colon f(\mathbf{x}) = 0, \forall \mathbf{x} \in V_{\mathbb{R}}(I)\}$
$\mathbb{R}_n[\mathbf{x}] \subset \mathbb{R}[\mathbf{x}]$	real multivariate polynomials of degree at most n
$\Sigma_n(\mathbf{x}] \subset \mathbb{R}_{2n}[\mathbf{x}]$	set of SOS polynomials of degree at most $2n$
$\mathbb{R}[\mathbf{x}]^*$	the vector space of linear forms on $\mathbb{R}[\mathbf{x}]$
$\mathbb{R}_n[\mathbf{x}]^*$	the vector space of linear forms on $\mathbb{R}_n[\mathbf{x}]$
$\mathbf{y} = (y_\alpha) \subset \mathbb{R}$	moment sequence indexed in the canonical basis of $\mathbb{R}[\mathbf{x}]$
$\mathbf{M}_n(\mathbf{y})$	moment matrix of order n associated with the sequence $\mathbf{y}$
$\mathbf{M}_{\mu,n}$	moment matrix of order n associated with a measure μ
$\mathbf{M}_n(g\,\mathbf{y})$	localizing matrix of order n associated with the sequence $\mathbf{y}$ and $g \in \mathbb{R}[\mathbf{x}]$
$P(g) \subset \mathbb{R}[\mathbf{x}]$	preordering generated by the polynomials $(g_j) \subset \mathbb{R}[\mathbf{x}]$
$Q(g) \subset \mathbb{R}[\mathbf{x}]$	quadratic module generated by the polynomials $(g_j) \subset \mathbb{R}[\mathbf{x}]$
$\mathcal{M}(\mathbf{K})_n$	space of finite sequences $\mathbf{y} \in \mathbb{R}^{s(n)}$ with a representing measure on $\mathbf{K}$
$\mathcal{P}(\mathbf{K})_n$	space of positive polynomials of degree at most n, nonnegative on $\mathbf{K}$
$\mathscr{B}(\mathbf{X})$ (resp. $\mathscr{B}(\mathbf{X})_+$)	space of bounded (resp. bounded nonnegative) measurable functions on $\mathbf{X}$
$\mathscr{C}(\mathbf{X})$ (resp. $\mathscr{C}(\mathbf{X})_+$)	space of bounded (resp. bounded nonnegative) continuous functions on $\mathbf{X}$
$\mathscr{M}(\mathbf{X})$	vector space of finite signed Borel measures on $\mathbf{X} \subset \mathbb{R}^n$
$\mathscr{M}(\mathbf{X})_+ \subset \mathscr{M}(\mathbf{X})$	space of finite positive Borel measures on $\mathbf{X} \subset \mathbb{R}^n$
$\mathscr{P}(\mathbf{X}) \subset \mathscr{M}(\mathbf{X})_+$	space of Borel probability measures on $\mathbf{X} \subset \mathbb{R}^n$
$L^p(\mathbf{X}, \mu)$	Banach space of functions on $\mathbf{X} \subset \mathbb{R}^n$ such that $(\int_{\mathbf{X}} \lvert f\rvert^p d\mu)^{1/p} < \infty$, $1 \leq p < \infty$
$L^\infty(\mathbf{X}, \mu)$	Banach space of measurable functions on $\mathbf{X} \subset \mathbb{R}^n$ such that $\lVert f\rVert_\infty := \text{ess sup } \lvert f\rvert < \infty$
$\sigma(\mathcal{X}, \mathcal{Y})$	weak topology on $\mathcal{X}$ for a dual pair $(\mathcal{X}, \mathcal{Y})$ of vector spaces
$\nu \ll \mu$	ν is absolutely continuous with respect to μ (for measures)
$\nu \perp \mu$	measures ν and μ are mutually singular

Preface

Among the many positive-definite kernels appearing in classical analysis, approximation theory, probability, mathematical physics, control theory and more recently in machine learning, the Christoffel–Darboux (CD) kernel stands out by its numerical accessibility from raw data and its versality in encoding/decoding fine properties of the generating measure. Indeed this unique feature was recognized very early and was exploited over a century and a half via surprising developments. One can safely draw a parallel: just as the power moment problem is the quintessential inverse problem, the CD kernel is the prototypical positive-definite reproducing kernel. While the computationally oriented practitioner may think that dealing with real monomials brings instability, we argue that complex monomials restricted to the unit circle or higher-dimensional tori are the very stable ubiquitous Fourier modes.

The CD kernel has a particular property that enables us to identify the underlying reproducing kernel Hilbert space (RKHS) inner product with a bilinear form induced by a given measure over a finite-dimensional function space. This feature allows us to develop a rich theory describing the relation between the Christoffel–Darboux kernel and the underlying measure in a data analysis context. Our aim in this book is to explain this property and its application in data analysis and the numerical treatment of statistical data. Another of our goals is to make it straightforward for the non-expert reader to obtain further insights about the role of the Christoffel function in function theory, approximation theory and the spectral analysis of dynamical systems, as well as sketching some possible extensions (e.g. to Lebesgue $L^p(\mu)$ spaces).

Since the Christoffel function and the Christoffel–Darboux kernel have a long mathematical history, we confine ourselves on the one hand to describing in a streamlined manner their classical theory and on the other to giving an up-to-date collection of results that provide a theoretical basis for such applications. Examples of these include:

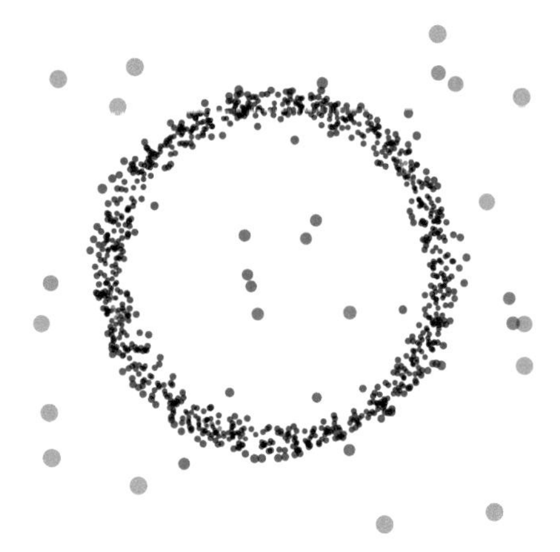

Figure 1 $N = 1040$ and $n = 8$; points with size and color proportional to the value of $1/\Lambda_n^{\mu_N}$.

- *outlier detection*, where $\Lambda_n^{\mu_N}$ provides a simple test to decide whether a point $\mathbf{x}$ of the cloud can be considered as an outlier;
- *density estimation*, when μ_N is the empirical measure μ_N on a cloud of points drawn for some unknown probability distribution μ on $\mathbf{\Omega}$, with a density with respect to Lebesgue measure on $\mathbf{\Omega}$;
- *manifold learning*: when the cloud of points is supported on a subset of a manifold (e.g. the sphere) or on an algebraic variety, can we detect the manifold (or algebraic variety) and its dimension?

To better appreciate the simplicity of the approach, consider the cloud of two-dimensional points shown in Figure 1. Most points are in an annulus and the color and size of a point ξ is proportional to the value of $\Lambda_n^{\mu_N}(\xi)^{-1}$ at this point. Therefore all points ξ with "color" $\Lambda_n^{\mu_N}(\xi) \leq \tau$ (for some threshold τ) are declared potential *outliers*. In Figure 1 one clearly sees that points with colors close to pink, red, or brown, are "outside" the annulus.

Of course, when μ_N is the empirical measure supported on a sample drawn from some distribution μ on $\mathbf{\Omega}$, to obtain rigorous asymptotic results on the unknown μ and $\mathbf{\Omega}$, it is expected that one has to carefully scale the degree n with the size N of the sample. This issue is clearly particular to data analysis because one uses an empirical measure μ^N on a typically *finite* sample. We show how such asymptotic results can be rigorously justified in this data analysis framework.

By its nature, our text interlaces distant themes, over-simplifies most of the theoretical background and sacrifices fine tuning for wide accessibility and utility. We are aware that balancing such opposite tendencies leads to brutal omissions. The story does not end here. We apologize in advance to the neglected parties and invite them to take our essay as a basis for exploring novel ramifications of Christoffel–Darboux analysis.

Having said all that, we have to recognize the lasting creative power of the two founders of the theory. The genius of E. B. Christoffel emanates from every page of the astounding collection Butzer and Fehér (1981). Darboux's innovative brilliance was recognized by all leading figures of the mathematical landscape (Lippmann et al., 1912). His eulogy in Hilbert (1920) is as fresh and accurate now as it was at the time of its publication a century ago.

Acknowledgements: The first and second authors gratefully acknowledge financial support from **ANITI** (Artifical & Natural Intelligence Toulouse Institute), coordinated by the Federal University of Toulouse within the framework of the French Program "Investing for the Future C PIA3" under the grant agreement ANR-19-PIA3-0004. The third author was partially supported by a Simons Foundation collaboration grant for mathematicians.

1
Introduction

To get a glimpse of the main theme of the book, consider an arbitrary cloud of N points $\mathbf{x}_i = (x_i, y_i) \in \mathbb{R}^2$, $i = 1, \ldots, N$, in the plane, dense enough to form some geometric shape. For instance in Figure 1.1 the shape looks like a rotated letter "T"; similarly in the frontispiece, the cloud of points is concentrated on the letters "C" and "D" (for Christoffel and Darboux). Then we invite the reader to perform the following simple operations on the preferred cloud of points:

1. Fix $n \in \mathbb{N}$ (for instance $n = 2$) and let $s(n) = \binom{n+2}{2}$.
2. Let $\mathbf{v}_n(\mathbf{x}) = (1, x, y, x^2, x\,y, \ldots, x\,y^{n-1}, y^n)$ be the vector of all monomials $x^i y^j$ of total degree $i + j \leq n$.
3. Form $\mathbf{X}_n \in \mathbb{R}^{n \times s(n)}$, the design matrix whose ith row is $\mathbf{v}(\mathbf{x}_i)$, and the real symmetric matrix $\mathbf{M}_n \in \mathbb{R}^{s(n) \times s(n)}$ with rows and columns indexed by monomials such that

$$\mathbf{M}_n := \frac{1}{N} \mathbf{X}_n^T \mathbf{X}_n.$$

4. Form the polynomial

$$\mathbf{x} \mapsto p_n(\mathbf{x}) := \mathbf{v}_n(\mathbf{x})^T \mathbf{M}_n^{-1} \, \mathbf{v}_n(\mathbf{x}).$$

5. Plot the level sets $S_\gamma := \{\mathbf{x} \in \mathbb{R}^2 : \; p_n(\mathbf{x}) = \gamma\}$ for some values of γ, and in red for the particular value $\gamma = \binom{2+n}{2}$.

As the reader can observe in Figure 1.1, the various level sets (and in particular the red one) capture quite accurately the shape of the cloud of points.

The above polynomial p_n is associated with the cloud of points $(\mathbf{x}_i)_{i \leq N}$ only via the real symmetric matrix $\mathbf{M}_n$ in a conceptually simple manner, the main

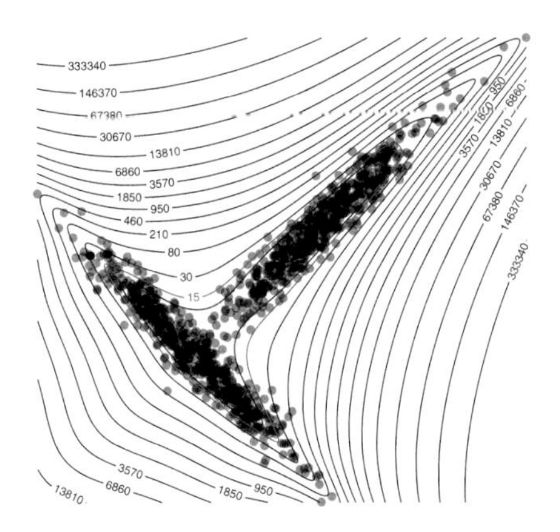

Figure 1.1 $n = 4$; $N = 1000$; level sets S_γ $\left(\text{in red for } \gamma = \binom{2+4}{2}\right)$.

computational step being matrix inversion. It turns out that $\mathbf{M}_n$ is called the *moment matrix* associated with the empirical probability measure

$$\mu_N := \frac{1}{N} \sum_{k=1}^{N} \delta_{\mathbf{x}_i}, \tag{1.1}$$

where $\delta_{\mathbf{x}}$ is the Dirac measure at the point $\mathbf{x}$, and $\mathbf{M}_n = \frac{1}{N} \sum_{i=1}^{N} \mathbf{v}_n(\mathbf{x}_i)\, \mathbf{v}_n(\mathbf{x}_i)^T$.

The reciprocal function $\mathbf{x} \mapsto \Lambda_n^{\mu_N}(\mathbf{x}) := p_n(\mathbf{x})^{-1}$ is called the *Christoffel function* (say of *degree* n as p_n is polynomial of degree $2n$) associated with the empirical measure μ_N. It depends only on the moments of μ_N, up to order $2n$.

In mathematical terms, the level sets S_γ in Figure 1.1 depict the shape of the *support* of the measure μ_N. This striking property is not an accident for this particular cloud. Indeed in Figure 1.2 we have displayed other clouds of two-dimensional points with various shapes and the corresponding level sets S_γ for various values of γ and n. Again, remarkably, the level sets S_γ approximate to high precision the shape of clouds even for a relatively small value of n. The same observation applies for the picture on the book cover where the shape of the "C" and "D" letters is very well approximated by level sets S_γ of the bivariate Cristoffel polynomial p_{10} of degree 20, and in particular by the one with boundary in red.

It turns out that in fact this property holds in the general framework of the Christoffel function Λ_n^μ associated with an abstract measure μ on a compact set $\mathbf{\Omega} \subset \mathbb{R}^d$. This time one replaces the empirical moment matrix $\mathbf{M}_n$ with

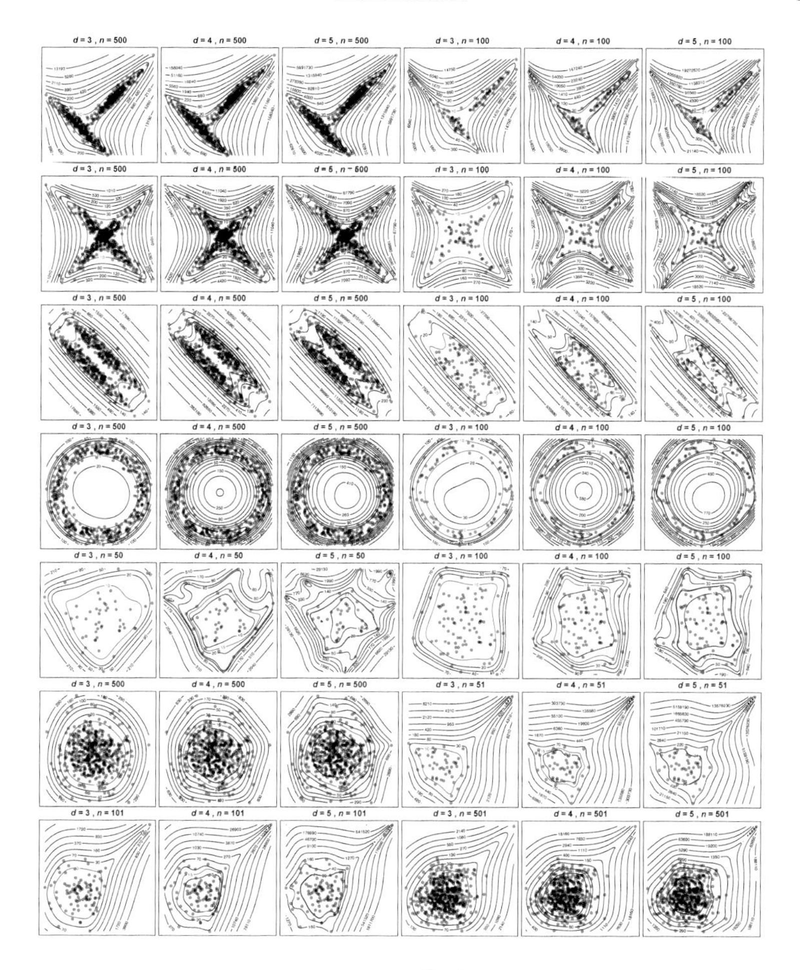

Figure 1.2 Level sets S_γ (in red for $\gamma = \binom{2+n}{2}$) for various clouds and various values of n.

the *exact* moment matrix $\mathbf{M}_n(\mu)$ associated with μ. For instance for $\mathbf{\Omega} \subset \mathbb{R}^2$, $\mathbf{M}_n(\mu)$ now reads

$$\mathbf{M}_n(\mu) := \int_{\mathbf{\Omega}} \mathbf{v}_n(\mathbf{x}_i)\, \mathbf{v}_n(\mathbf{x}_i)^T\, d\mu(\mathbf{x}),$$

where the integral is understood coordinate-wise. Notice that the empirical probability measure μ_N in (1.1) could have been obtained from a sample of N points $(\mathbf{x}_i)_{i \leq N} \subset \mathbf{\Omega}$, drawn from some probability distribution μ on $\mathbf{\Omega}$.

This property has been known for a long time in various related domains of mathematics, for example approximation theory, orthogonal polynomials, potential theory, reproducing kernel Hilbert spaces, function theory, spectral analysis, statistical mechanics, to cite a few. However, most works in these areas have been concerned with the asymptotic analysis of Λ_n^μ (appropriately scaled) when $n \to \infty$, and proportionally much less attention has been paid to the study of $\Lambda_n^{\mu_N}$ for fixed n, when μ_N is some empirical measure μ_N supported on a cloud of points, not to mention the clear benefits and potential applications in data analysis.

We know sketch out the structure of the book. It is divided into three rather distinct parts:

Part ONE consists of four chapters and focuses on historical and theoretical background. After introducing the key concept of a *reproducing kernel Hilbert space* (RKHS), classical results pertaining to Christoffel–Darboux kernel in the univariate case and separately the more involved multivariate case are recorded. More specifically:

Chapter 3 recalls classical results referring to the univariate Christoffel function (either in complex setting $\mathbb{C}$ or in the real line). Familiar results, sometimes several decades old, offer a necessary comparison basis for multivariate analogs. The latter are sometimes much more involved, still under investigation, or simply do not exist.

Chapter 4 focuses on the real multivariate Christoffel function for a measure on a compact set $\mathbf{\Omega} \subset \mathbb{R}^d$ and introduces both qualitative and quantitative asymptotics results. Several key theorems are stated without proofs due to intricate ingredients or necessary vast preliminaries (such as, for instance, pluripotential theory). Such important details fall beyond the scope of the present book. For the interested reader we provide some historical notes, technical statements and their sources. The level of depth and sophistication of recent advances in the multivariate theory of Christoffel–Darboux is barely suggested by our brief comments.

Chapter 5 is concerned with CD kernels associated with measures supported by a real algebraic variety. Think for instance of data points located by their very nature on a subset of the Euclidean sphere or a torus. In the singular support situation we fully exploit the concept of localized Hilbert function spaces. In spite of its theoretical flavor this is the natural framework for manipulating a structured moment matrix. To be more precise, it is quite remarkable that the degenerate moment matrix $\mathbf{M}_n$ (already described in the introduction above in dimension 2 and easily accessible from observed data) encodes profound analytical and geometrical characteristics of the generating measure.

Part TWO develops the motivation of this book, namely the utilization of the Christoffel–Darboux kernel associated with the empirical measure supported on a cloud of data points as the central carrier of structural information. How to decode this information into qualitative geometric, analytic or probabilistic features is our main task.

Chapter 6. As is typical in statistics and data analysis, a finite sample of size N is drawn independently from some unknown distribution μ with compact support $S \subset \mathbb{R}^d$. As detailed in the introduction, this provides an empirical version of the Christoffel function, related to the empirical measure supported on the finite sample. As expected, a generalization trade-off occurs at this point. For small values of n and large N the empirical Christoffel function is close to its population counterpart related to μ. On the other hand, for large n, the empirical Christoffel function has a trivial behavior which does not depend at all on μ. As described in Chapter 4, the population Christoffel function captures information on the underlying measure μ and its support S provided that the degree n increases. Therefore, in order to benefit from this phenomenon and avoid the trivial behavior of the empirical Christoffel function, it is crucial to relate the degree n of the Christoffel function. This chapter exposes recent results about statistical concentration for the Christoffel function and joint asymptotics in (n, N) under certain restrictions related to relative growth of n and N. Furthermore, in the context of singularly supported population measure μ with support contained in an algebraic set (which can be described by polynomial equations) we describe a finite-sample convergence phenomenon. Namely, under technical assumptions, the intrinsic rigidity of algebraic sets allows us to prove that, beyond a certain sample size N_0, with probability 1 the information contained in a finite sample is sufficient to fully characterize through the moment matrix the underlying algebraic set, that is, the set of equations describing it.

Chapter 7 illustrates the theory and expands on occurrences of CD kernels and Christoffel functions in statistics, for example the empirical CD kernel constitutes a higher-degree generalization of the well-known Mahalanobis distance. First in a parameteric regression setting, it turns out that the CD kernel has a natural interpretation in terms of predictive variance. This view allows us to make a direct connection with well-established quantities, such as leverage scores, and to discuss the problem of optimal design of experiments through the prism of the Christoffel function. Beyond parametric regression, the statistical results developed in Chapter 6 are illustrated on support inference problems for which we provide Christoffel function based estimators which benefit from the conceptual simplicity of the CD kernel, the main computational step being matrix inversion. This chapter also reports empirical results which were obtained for singularly supported densities on an algebraic set (sphere, torus), a situation that occurs for certain types of data (orientation, angles, positions on earth). We also provide results related to the motivating example of this introduction with outlier detection problems where we consider unsupervised network intrusion detection.

Part THREE contains a representative selection of complementary topics.

Chapter 8 focuses on two applications: one in basic approximation theory of nonsmooth functions, the other in the spectral analysis of certain ergodic dynamical systems. The clear advantages of treating such fundamental questions of mathematical analysis with techniques originating in the study of a CD kernel are simply stunning.

Chapter 9 deals with recent advances of immediate relevance to the topics of the book: stability under perturbations of Christoffel–Darboux kernels and a noncommutative, matrix analysis scheme of isolating the dense cloud from scattered and possibly *embedded* outliers of a 2D point distribution.

Chapter 10 is concerned with some spectral characterization as well as extensions of the Christoffel function. A first extension is to depart from the standard and classical $L^2(\mu)$ Hilbert space associated with the underlying measure μ and rather consider standard $L^p(\mu)$ Banach spaces. Another extension is to consider some natural convex cones of polynomials (positive on the support of μ) rather than "squares" in the variational $L^2(\mu)$ formulation of the Christoffel function. This yields alternative Christoffel-like functions with their own properties. Finally, when viewing the standard Christoffel function as single-point *interpolation*, it is also natural to investigate its natural *multi-point* extension.

The year appearing in cross references, for instance Hilbert (1953) or Marcel Riesz (2013), does not reflect the date of the original publication, but rather the year of a reprint edition.

PART ONE

HISTORICAL AND THEORETICAL BACKGROUND

2

Positive-definite Kernels and Moment Problems

This chapter contains a few definitions of key concepts used throughout the book. Besides positive-semidefinite kernels, their reproducing feature in an adapted Hilbert space and some essential examples, we touch on some aspects of the classical moment problem. We do this for two reasons: behind the scene of any moment problem there is a lurking Hilbert space carrying a finite-dimensional filtration of subspaces, and, in their turn, the reproducing kernels of this very chain of subspaces are the Christoffel–Darboux kernels, our main characters.

2.1 Hilbert Space with a Reproducing Kernel

Throughout this text all Hilbert spaces are defined over the complex field. In most cases of interest, the Hilbert spaces will also be separable. Although some applications are naturally formulated in real Hilbert space terms, as soon as we depart from the realm of linear self-adjoint operators, spectral analysis can only be developed on complex Hilbert spaces.

While the Lebesgue space $L^2(\mu)$ associated with a positive measure is the quintessential Hilbert function space, in general it does not carry bounded point evaluations. However, certain subspaces of it possess bounded point evaluation functionals. Their structure is encoded in a *reproducing kernel*, a concept of constant interest for about a century and a half, since the dawn of the theory of orthogonal expansions. We briefly recall in this section some facts and examples of Hilbert spaces with a reproducing kernel.

Let X be a set and $K\colon X \times X \longrightarrow \mathbb{C}$ a *hermitian kernel*, that is,

$$K(\mathbf{x}, \mathbf{y}) = \overline{K(\mathbf{y}, \mathbf{x})}, \quad \mathbf{x}, \mathbf{y} \in X.$$

The kernel K is called *positive semidefinite* if

$$\sum_{i,j=1}^{n} K(\mathbf{x}_i, \mathbf{x}_j)\, c_i \overline{c_j} \geq 0,$$

for any finite selection of mutually distinct points $\mathbf{x}_1, \mathbf{x}_2, \ldots, \mathbf{x}_n \in X$ and complex scalars $c_1, c_2, \ldots, c_n \in \mathbb{C}, n \in \mathbb{N}$. The kernel K is called *positive definite* if the equality sign

$$\sum_{i,j=1}^{n} K(\mathbf{x}_i, \mathbf{x}_j)\, c_i \overline{c_j} = 0$$

is attained only for $c_1 = c_2 = \cdots = c_n = 0$.

Since the matrix $[K(\mathbf{x}_i, \mathbf{x}_j)]_{i,j=1}^{n}$ appearing in the above definitions is positive semidefinite, the Cauchy–Schwarz inequality holds true. More precisely, for every choice of scalars $c_i, d_i \in \mathbb{C}, 1 \leq i \leq n$, one has

$$\left| \sum_{i,j=1}^{n} K(\mathbf{x}_i, \mathbf{x}_j)\, c_i \overline{d_j} \right|^2 \leq \left(\sum_{i,j=1}^{n} K(\mathbf{x}_i, \mathbf{x}_j)\, c_i \overline{c_j} \right) \left(\sum_{i,j=1}^{n} K(\mathbf{x}_i, \mathbf{x}_j)\, d_i \overline{d_j} \right).$$

As a matter of fact, more can be said. And the following is the beginning of our story.

Lemma 2.1.1 (Kolmogorov, 1941) *Let $K\colon X \times X \longrightarrow \mathbb{C}$ be a positive semidefinite kernel. There exists a Hilbert space H and a function $\phi\colon X \longrightarrow H$, such that*

$$K(\mathbf{x}, \mathbf{y}) = \langle \phi(\mathbf{x}), \phi(\mathbf{y}) \rangle, \quad \mathbf{x}, \mathbf{y} \in X. \tag{2.1}$$

Moreover, if the range of ϕ spans a dense linear subspace of H, then the pair (ϕ, H) is unique up to a unitary transformation.

Proof Fix $\mathbf{y} \in X$ and denote by $K(\cdot, \mathbf{y})$ the scalar function

$$\mathbf{x} \mapsto K(\mathbf{x}, \mathbf{y}), \quad \mathbf{x} \in X.$$

The vector space V spanned by these functions has a typical element of the form

$$f(\cdot) = \sum_{i=1}^{n} c_i\, K(\cdot, \mathbf{y}_i),$$

where $\mathbf{y}_i \in X, c_i \in \mathbb{C}, 1 \leq i \leq n, \; n \in \mathbb{N}$. We define an inner product on V as follows:

$$\left\langle \sum_{i=1}^{n} c_i\, K(\cdot, \mathbf{y}_i), \sum_{j=1}^{n} d_j\, K(\cdot, \mathbf{x}_j) \right\rangle = \sum_{i,j=1}^{n} K(\mathbf{x}_j, \mathbf{y}_i)\, c_i \overline{d_j}.$$

In short, we extend by sesqui-linearity the convention

$$\langle K(\cdot, \mathbf{y}), K(\cdot, \mathbf{x})\rangle = K(\mathbf{x}, \mathbf{y}), \quad \mathbf{x}, \mathbf{y} \in X.$$

Since the kernel K is positive semidefinite, the Cauchy–Schwarz inequality assures that the set

$$N = \{f \in V : \langle f, f\rangle = 0\}$$

of null elements is a vector subspace of V. Then V/N is a pre-Hilbert space and the function

$$\phi(\mathbf{x}) = K(\mathbf{x}, \cdot) = \overline{K(\cdot, \mathbf{x})} \pmod{N}, \quad \mathbf{x} \in X$$

satisfies

$$K(\mathbf{x}, \mathbf{y}) = \langle \phi(\mathbf{x}), \phi(\mathbf{y})\rangle, \quad \mathbf{x}, \mathbf{y} \in X.$$

Denote by H the completion of V/N to a Hilbert space. This proves the first part of Kolmogorov's Lemma.

For the uniqueness part, assume that (ϕ_1, H_1) and (ϕ_2, H_2) are two pairs meeting the minimality constraint in the statement. Then the map

$$U\left(\sum_{i=1}^{n} c_i\, \phi_1(\mathbf{x}_i)\right) = \sum_{i=1}^{n} c_i\, \phi_2(\mathbf{x}_i)$$

is well defined due to the identity

$$\left\|\sum_{i=1}^{n} c_i\, \phi_1(\mathbf{x}_i)\right\|_1^2 = \sum_{i,j=1}^{n} K(\mathbf{x}_i, \mathbf{x}_j)\, c_i \overline{c_j} = \left\|\sum_{i=1}^{n} c_i \phi_2(\mathbf{x}_i)\right\|_2^2,$$

and as a matter of fact it is linear and isometric. In view of the density assumptions, $U: H_1 \longrightarrow H_2$ turns out to be a unitary transformation. □

The Hilbert space factorization (2.1) is called *minimal* if the Hilbert space H is spanned by the vectors $\phi(\mathbf{x}), \mathbf{x} \in X$, as in the second part of Kolmogorov's Lemma.

While Hilbert spaces of the same dimension (i.e. cardinality of an orthonormal basis) are all equivalent in an abstract manner, the above construction ties the Hilbert space to the generating positive-definite kernel in a natural way. To be more precise, using the notation in the proof of Kolmogorov's Lemma, we first single out a subset of X outside which the kernel K does not vanish identically:

$$X_0 = \{\mathbf{x} \in X : \ K(\mathbf{x}, \mathbf{x}) = 0\}.$$

Owing to the positivity of K, we infer

$$K(\mathbf{x}, \mathbf{y}) = 0, \ \ \mathbf{x} \in X_0, \ \mathbf{y} \in X.$$

Let $X_1 = X \setminus X_0$. For $\mathbf{x} \in X_1$, we have $K(\mathbf{x}, \mathbf{x}) > 0$. In general, for an element $f \in V$, the very definition of the inner product yields

$$f(\mathbf{x}) = \langle f, K(\cdot, \mathbf{x}) \rangle, \quad \mathbf{x} \in X.$$

This reproduction (of value) formula is not altered by summands from the null subspace N, and consequently, for every element $h \in H$, one can define without ambiguity a function

$$[h](\mathbf{x}) = \langle h, K(\cdot, \mathbf{x}) \rangle, \quad \mathbf{x} \in X.$$

Note that $[h]$ vanishes identically on X_0, and moreover $[h](\mathbf{x}_1) = [h](\mathbf{x}_2)$ for all $h \in H$ holds only if $K(\cdot, \mathbf{x}_1) - K(\cdot, \mathbf{x}_2) \in N$.

All in all we have constructed above a Hilbert space of functions defined on X. These functions may not separate the points, but on the core subset X_1 they do satisfy a remarkable inequality which will be the guiding light for the whole book. Specifically, for a point $\mathbf{x} \in X_1$, the Cauchy–Schwarz inequality implies

$$|[h](\mathbf{x})| \leq \|h\| \, \| K(\cdot, \mathbf{x}) \|, \quad h \in H.$$

Since

$$\| K(\cdot, \mathbf{x}) \|^2 = K(\mathbf{x}, \mathbf{x}) > 0,$$

we find

$$\frac{1}{\sqrt{K(\mathbf{x}, \mathbf{x})}} = \inf\{\|h\| : [h](\mathbf{x}) = 1\}. \tag{2.2}$$

The minimum is attained by a multiple of $K(\cdot, \mathbf{x})$.

Corollary 2.1.2 *Let $K \colon X \times X \longrightarrow \mathbb{C}$ be a positive-definite kernel with minimal Kolmogorov factorization (ϕ, H). Then H can be identified with a space of complex-valued functions defined on X which separate the points of X and satisfy* (2.2).

The mirror image of the preceding construction leads to the following definition.

Definition 2.1.3 A *reproducing kernel Hilbert space* (RKHS) is a Hilbert space H of complex functions defined on a set X, with the property that all point evaluations

$$h \mapsto h(\mathbf{x}), \quad h \in H, \ \mathbf{x} \in X$$

are linear continuous functionals on H.

Assume this is the case. The Riesz Lemma implies the existence of a vector $k_{\mathbf{x}} \in H$, satisfying

$$h(\mathbf{x}) = \langle h, k_{\mathbf{x}} \rangle, \quad h \in H.$$

Then $K(\mathbf{x}, \mathbf{y}) = \langle k_{\mathbf{y}}, k_{\mathbf{x}} \rangle$ is a positive-semidefinite kernel on X, and we are right back at the beginning of this section.

Assume that H is separable and that $e_n(\mathbf{x}), n \in \mathbb{N}$, is an orthonormal basis of the Hilbert space H with reproducing kernel K. The orthogonal projection onto the finite-dimensional subspace H_n generated by $e_0, e_1, \ldots, e_n$ is

$$P_n = \sum_{j=0}^{n} e_j \langle \cdot, e_j \rangle ,$$

hence it is represented by the hermitian kernel

$$\Pi_n(\mathbf{x}, \mathbf{y}) = \sum_{j=0}^{n} e_j(\mathbf{x}) \, \overline{e_j(\mathbf{y})} \, .$$

More specifically, for every $f \in H$, one finds

$$(P_n f)(\mathbf{x}) = \langle f , \Pi_n(\cdot, \mathbf{x}) \rangle \, .$$

Note that the norm of H is *not* represented by an integral against a measure defined on X. One step further,

$$f = \lim_{n \to \infty} P_n f \quad \text{in norm.}$$

Thus one can say that

$$f(\mathbf{x}) = \lim_{n} \langle f , \Pi_n(\cdot, \mathbf{x}) \rangle , \quad \forall \mathbf{x}, \tag{2.3}$$

and infer

$$f(\mathbf{x}) = \left\langle f , \sum_{n=0}^{\infty} e_n(\cdot) \, \overline{e_n(\mathbf{x})} \right\rangle , \quad \forall \mathbf{x} \, . \tag{2.4}$$

Hence the specific Riesz Lemma element is

$$k_{\mathbf{x}} = \sum_{n=0}^{\infty} e_n(\cdot) \, \overline{e_n(\mathbf{x})}.$$

In particular,

$$K(\mathbf{x}, \mathbf{x}) = \|k_{\mathbf{x}}\|^2 = \sum_{n=0}^{\infty} | \, e_n(\mathbf{x}) \, |^2 < \infty ,$$

and hence the reproducing kernel is represented by the absolutely convergent series

$$K(\mathbf{y}, \mathbf{x}) = \sum_{n=0}^{\infty} e_n(\mathbf{y}) \, \overline{e_n(\mathbf{x})}. \tag{2.5}$$

Note that the projections P_n and their functional kernels Π_n depend on the choice of basis, but the reproducing kernel $K(\mathbf{x}, \mathbf{y})$ is intrinsic to the

Hilbert space and its embedding into functions defined on X. In general, fine properties of the Hilbert space H are encoded into the function theory behavior (asymptotics, zero location) of the convergent series above.

2.1.1 Examples

Finite-dimensional Subspaces of $L^2(\mathbb{T}, d\sigma)$: An important example stands out. Let $\mathbb{T} = \{e^{it}, -\pi \le t < \pi\}$ denote the torus = unit circle in the complex plane, endowed with the normalized arc length measure $d\sigma = \frac{dt}{2\pi}$. The Fourier modes e^{ikt}, $k \in \mathbb{Z}$, form an orthonormal basis for the Lebesgue space $L^2(\mathbb{T}, d\sigma)$. This is a Hilbert space of classes of equivalence of functions defined on the torus. Point evaluations do not make sense in L^2, as we can deduce from the divergence of the series

$$\sum_{n\in\mathbb{Z}} e^{in(t-s)}.$$

However, a reproducing kernel restricted to the subspace of trigonometric polynomials of degree less than or equal to d is well defined and represented by the finite series (Dirichlet kernel)

$$\begin{aligned}\Pi_d(t,s) &= \sum_{j=-d}^{j=d} e^{in(t-s)} = \frac{\sin\frac{(2d+1)(t-s)}{2}}{\sin\frac{t-s}{2}} \\ &= 1 + 2\cos(t-s) + 2\cos 2(t-s) + \cdots + 2\cos d(t-s).\end{aligned}$$

The divergence of $\lim_d \Pi_d(t,t)$ is a clear indication of the missing bounded point evaluations in this Hilbert space. More on such truncations in the next section.

Hardy Space: The picture changes dramatically if we allow only nonnegative frequencies, leading to the *Hardy space*:

$$H^2(\mathbb{T}) = \left\{ \sum_{n=0}^{\infty} c_n e^{int}, \sum_{n=0}^{\infty} |\, c_n \,|^2 < \infty \right\}.$$

This is a closed subspace of $L^2(\mathbb{T})$ and every $z \in \mathbb{C}$, $|z| < 1$ is a bounded point evaluation. Indeed, if $f = \sum_{n=0}^{\infty} c_n e^{int} \in H^2(\mathbb{T})$, we can define the function

$$F(z) = \sum_{n=0}^{\infty} c_n\, z^n$$

by the respective absolute convergent series. It is clear that F is an analytic function in the unit disk $\mathbb{D}$ and moreover

$$F(z) = \int_{\mathbb{T}} \frac{f(t)d\sigma(t)}{1 - ze^{-it}}, \quad |z| < 1 .$$

By a theorem of Fatou,

$$\lim_{r \to 1} F(re^{it}) = f(e^{it}), \ \ d\sigma\text{-a.e.}$$

where a.e. stands for 'almost everywhere' and it is customary to denote by the same symbol f the analytic function F.

In conclusion, the Hardy space $H^2(\mathbb{T})$ is a reproducing kernel Hilbert space consisting of analytic functions defined in the unit disk. It has an orthonormal basis formed by the complex monomials $1, z, z^2, \ldots$, endowed with the norm

$$\left\| \sum_{n=0}^{\infty} c_n z^n \right\|^2 = \sum_{n=0}^{\infty} | c_n |^2 .$$

The reproducing kernel is

$$S(z, w) = \frac{1}{1 - z\overline{w}}, \quad z, w \in \mathbb{D},$$

and bears the name of *Szegő's kernel*. The orthogonal projection $\Pi : L^2(\mathbb{T}) \longrightarrow H^2(\mathbb{T})$ is

$$(\Pi f)(z) = \int_{\mathbb{T}} \frac{f(e^{it})d\sigma(t)}{1 - e^{-it}z}, \quad f \in L^2(\mathbb{T}), \ \ |z| < 1 .$$

Polynomial Subspaces of $L^2(\mathbf{\Omega}, \mu)$: Let $\mathbf{\Omega} \subset \mathbb{R}^d$ be compact, μ a finite Borel measure on $\mathbf{\Omega}$, and let $L^2(\mathbf{\Omega}, \mu)$ be the real Hilbert space of square-integrable functions. The vector space of all real polynomials is dense in $L^2(\mathbf{\Omega}, \mu)$ and the vector space $H := \mathbb{R}_n[\mathbf{x}]$ of polynomials of degree at most n is an RKHS with reproducing kernel

$$K_n^{\mu}(\mathbf{x}, \mathbf{y}) = \sum_{\alpha \in \mathbb{N}_n^d} P_\alpha(\mathbf{x}) \, P_\alpha(\mathbf{y}), \quad \mathbf{x}, \mathbf{y} \in \mathbb{R}^d,$$

where $(P_\alpha)_{\alpha \in \mathbb{N}^d}$ is an orthonormal polynomial basis of $L^2(\mathbf{\Omega}, \mu)$. This is by definition a Christoffel–Darboux kernel, as we shall see in more detail in the next section.

Non-uniqueness: A reproducing kernel Hilbert space is not necessarily tied to a single "geometric support". For instance, a nonempty open subset of the unit disk $U \subset \mathbb{D}$ carries the positive-definite kernel

$$S_1 : U \times U \longrightarrow \mathbb{C}, \ \ S_1(z, w) = \frac{1}{1 - z\,\overline{w}}, \quad z, w \in U,$$

which obviously possesses the Hardy space factorization

$$S_1(z,w) = \int_{\mathbb{T}} \frac{d\sigma(t)}{(1-e^{-it}z)(1-e^{it}\overline{w})}, \qquad z,w \in U .$$

By the uniqueness principle for analytic functions, the family of functions

$$t \mapsto \frac{1}{1-e^{it}\overline{z}}, \qquad z \in U$$

is dense in $H^2(\mathbb{T})$. Whence the construction of a Hilbert space in Kolmogorov's Lemma yields the full Hardy space $H^2(\mathbb{T})$, although we started with a tiny part of the reproducing kernel S.

2.2 The CD kernel and the Moment Problem on the Real Line

In this section we relate the CD kernel to the important and celebrated classical *moment problem*. We narrow our discussion to positive Borel measures on the real line that are rapidly decreasing at infinity, and their power moments. A wide array of inverse problems can be reduced to the reconstruction or approximation of such a measure from its moments. Without aiming at completeness we touch on a few relevant observations.

Let μ denote a positive measure on $\mathbb{R}$, possessing all moments

$$s_j = \int_{\mathbb{R}} x^j \, d\mu(x), \quad j \in \mathbb{N}. \tag{2.6}$$

The positivity of the measure implies

$$\sum_{k,j=0}^{n} s_{k+j}\, c_k \overline{c_j} = \int \left| \sum_{j=0}^{n} c_j\, x^j \right|^2 d\mu(x) \geq 0,$$

for every finite selection of complex numbers $c_0, c_1, \ldots, c_n \in \mathbb{C}$. A celebrated theorem due to Hamburger asserts that, conversely, the positive semi-definiteness of the Hankel kernel $(k,j) \mapsto s_{k+j}$ is also sufficient for the infinite sequence $(s_j)_{j=0}^{\infty}$ to represent the power moments of a positive measure on the line (Akhiezer, 1965).

In all its forms, the moment problem assumes that the sole available data is $s_0, s_1, \ldots, s_n$ with the degree n finite or not. As we have remarked, the necessary positive semi-definiteness condition of the Hankel kernel/matrix $(s_{k+j})_{k,j=0}^{n}$ is assumed. Exactly as in the case of the Hardy space discussed in the preceding section, we explore whether the underlying Hilbert space possesses bounded point evaluations. To this aim we turn to the polynomial algebra $\mathbb{C}[z]$ and its filtration given by degree

$$\mathbb{C}_n[z] = \{ p \in \mathbb{C}[z] : \deg p \leq n \}, \quad n \in \mathbb{N}.$$

Assume the degree n is finite and the Hankel matrix $(s_{k+j})_{k,j=0}^n$ is positive semidefinite. The formula

$$\left\langle \sum_{j=0}^n p_j x^j, \sum_{j=0}^n q_j x^j \right\rangle = \sum_{k,j=0}^n s_{k+j} \, p_k \overline{q_j}$$

defines a positive-semidefinite inner product on $\mathbb{C}_n[z]$. Clearly,

$$s_{k+j} = \left\langle z^k, z^j \right\rangle, \quad k, j \leq n$$

provides Kolmogorov's factorization of Hankel's kernel. Note that we deal here with finite-dimensional spaces.

For every $w \in \mathbb{C}$, the evaluation functional

$$p \mapsto p(w), \quad p \in \mathbb{C}_n[z],$$

is linear and continuous, therefore one can speak of a reproducing kernel

$$K_n : \mathbb{C} \times \mathbb{C} \longrightarrow \mathbb{C}$$

associated with the Hilbert space quotient $H_n = \mathbb{C}_n[z]/N$. As before, N stands for the subspace of null vectors. We already know that

$$K_n(z, w) = \sum_{j=0}^m p_j(z) \overline{p_j(w)},$$

where $p_0, p_1, \ldots, p_m$ is an orthonormal basis of H_n. Traditionally one chooses p_j to be the associated orthonormal polynomials. Note $m = \dim H_n \leq n$ with $m < n$ in the degenerate case $\det(s_{k+j})_{k,j=0}^n = 0$.

Definition 2.2.1 The *Christoffel–Darboux kernel* (CD kernel) associated with the truncated moment data $s_0, s_1, \ldots, s_n$ is the reproducing kernel $K_n \in \mathbb{C}[z, \overline{w}]$, while the *Christoffel function* is $z \mapsto \Lambda_d(z) = \frac{1}{K_n(z,z)}$.

When a generating measure μ is known, usually one carries it over to the notation: K_n^μ, respectively Λ_n^μ for the reproducing kernel and the Christoffel function.

If $s_0 > 0$ then one can choose $p_0(z)$ in the decomposition of $K_n(z, z)$ to be a nonvanishing constant, hence $K_n(z, z) > 0$ for all $z \in \mathbb{C}$. In this case we have proved in the previous section the intrinsic characterization of the Christoffel function

$$\Lambda_n(z) = \inf\left\{ \|p\|^2 : \ \deg p \le n, \ p(z) = 1 \right\}.$$

In the case that larger moment data are available, the above optimization problem interpretation yields

$$\Lambda_n(z) \ge \Lambda_{n+1}(z).$$

We write

$$\Lambda(z) = \lim_n \Lambda_n(z), \quad z \in \mathbb{C}.$$

Although we will not make use of the following theorem, the reader should be aware of the principal role played by the Christoffel–Darboux (CD) kernel in uniqueness and approximation results of this kind. Notable is the evaluation of the Christoffel function at *nonreal* points in the complex plane, even when dealing with a purely real variable problem. Here is one of the cornerstone results of early spectral analysis and function theory of complex variables.

Theorem 2.2.2 *Let* $(s_{k+j})_{k,j=0}^{\infty}$ *be a positive-definite Hankel matrix with real entries. The moment problem* (2.6) *is determinate, that is, there exists a unique positive measure* μ *with these data, if and only if* $\Lambda(w) = 0$ *for a nonreal* $w \in \mathbb{C}$. *In this case* $\Lambda(\zeta) = 0$ *for all* $\zeta \in \mathbb{C} \setminus \mathbb{R}$.

Returning to the Christoffel function of a truncated moment problem, its values at real points are also remarkable. For finite n and $x_0 \in \mathbb{R}$ (the so-called *truncated moment problem*), $\Lambda_n(x_0)$ coincides with the maximal mass a solution μ can charge the point x_0:

$$\Lambda_n(x_0) = \max\{ \mu(\{x_0\}) : \ s_j = \int x^j \, d\mu(x), \ 0 \le j \le n \}.$$

The proof was known to Akhiezer and Krein around 1938, but it might be older. For a definitive account see Krein (1951). A particular infinite-degree case is recorded in the following proposition.

Proposition 2.2.3 *Let* μ *be a positive measure with compact support on the real line. For every* $x_0 \in \mathbb{R}$, *one has*

$$\Lambda^{\mu}(x_0) = \mu(\{x_0\}). \tag{2.7}$$

Proof We remark that $\Lambda_n^{\mu}(x_0)$ is non-increasing and bounded below, so it has a limit. First using the variational formulation, we have for all x_0, and all $P \in \mathbb{R}_n[x]$, with $P(x_0) = 1$,

$$\int P(x)^2 \, d\mu(x) \ge \mu(\{x_0\}).$$

Using a rescaling (affine invariance), we may consider that the support is contained in the segment $[-1, 1]$ and $x_0 = 0$, in which case, we have for all $k \in \mathbb{N}$, considering $x \mapsto (1 - x^2)^k \in \mathbb{R}_{2k}[x]$,

$$\Lambda^{\mu}_{2k+1}(0) \le \Lambda^{\mu}_{2k}(0)$$
$$\le \int_{-1}^{1} (1 - x^2)^{2k} d\mu(x) \le \int_{\frac{-1}{k^{1/4}}}^{\frac{1}{k^{1/4}}} d\mu(x) + \left(1 - \frac{1}{\sqrt{k}}\right)^{2k} \underset{k \to \infty}{\to} \mu(\{0\}).$$

□

Proposition 2.2.4 *Let d be an integer and $\mathbf{M}_n = (s_{k+j})_{k,j=0}^{n}$ a positive-definite Hankel matrix with real entries. Denote by $\mathbf{v}_n(z) = (1, z, z^2, \ldots, z^n)^T$ the tautological column vector of monomials. Then the associated Christoffel–Darboux kernel is*

$$K_n(z, w) = \mathbf{v}_n(z)^T \mathbf{M}_n^{-1} \mathbf{v}_n(\overline{w}). \tag{2.8}$$

Proof Write

$$K_n(z, w) = \sum_{k,j=0}^{n} a_{kj}\, z^k\, \overline{w}^j .$$

Note that the entries are real and the matrix (a_{kj}) is symmetric. The reproducing property

$$\langle\, z^j \,,\, K(z, w)\, \rangle = w^j, \quad 0 \le j \le n,$$

implies

$$\sum_k \langle\, z^j \,,\, z^k \,\rangle\, a_{kj}\, \overline{w}^j = w^j,$$

hence

$$\sum_k \mathbf{M}_n(j, k)\, a_{kt} = \delta_{jt}.$$

□

More information, with ample bibliographical comments, on the Christoffel–Darboux kernel can be found in Simon (2008).

2.3 Relation with Other Kernels

In this section, for clarity and simplicity of exposition we restrict ourselves to the univariate case and the box $[-1, 1]$ but all concepts easily generalize to the multivariate case in $[-1, 1]^d$ and also on more general compact sets of $\mathbb{R}^d$.

In approximation theory the CD kernel is an important tool which provides *polynomial* approximations to a given function with nice convergence properties. Consider for instance the interval $[-1, 1]$ and the (normalized) Chebyshev polynomials $(T_j)_{j\in\mathbb{N}} \subset \mathbb{R}[x]$ of the first kind, which are orthonormal with respect to the measure $d\mu = \frac{dx}{\pi\sqrt{1-x^2}}$ on $[-1, 1]$, and thus provide an orthonormal basis of $L^2([-1, 1], \mu)$.

An arbitrary $f \in L^2([-1, 1], \mu)$ is expanded in the orthonormal basis as

$$f = \sum_{j=0}^{\infty} \langle f, T_j\rangle T_j .$$

Its orthogonal polynomial projections

$$x \mapsto f_n(x) := \sum_{j=0}^{n} \langle f, T_j\rangle T_j(x) = \sum_{j=0}^{n} \alpha_j T_j(x) \tag{2.9}$$

$$= \int_{-1}^{1} f(y)\, K_n^{\mu}(x, y)\, d\mu(y), \quad \forall x \in [-1, 1], \tag{2.10}$$

for all $n \in \mathbb{N}$, provide polynomial approximations in the sense that

$$\lim_{n\to\infty} \|f - f_n\| = 0,$$

for the norm $\|\cdot\|$ of $L^2([-1, 1], \mu)$. However, the following hold.

- If f is nonnegative then its projections $(f_n)_{n\in\mathbb{N}}$ may not be.
- In addition, even if f is continuous, there is no *uniform* convergence $\lim_{n\to\infty} \sup_{x\in[-1,1]} |f(x) - f_n(x)| = 0$.
- Typical Gibbs oscillations of f_n occur at points x where f is not continuously differentiable.

For instance in Figure 2.1, which shows the CD kernel K_n^{λ} associated with the Lebesgue measure λ on $[-1, 1]$, one clearly sees violations of positivity.

Next, following Weisse et al. (2006), we briefly describe some remedies to the above three issues, initially due to Féjer.

Féjer and Jackson Positive Kernels: For convenience, introduce the (non-polynomial) functions

$$x \mapsto \phi_j(x) := T_j(x)/(\pi\sqrt{1-x^2}), \quad \forall j \in \mathbb{N},$$

and observe that $(\phi_j)_{j\in\mathbb{N}}$ form an orthonormal basis of the Hilbert space $L^2([-1, 1], \nu)$ where $d\nu(x) = \pi\sqrt{1-x^2}dx$. Then an arbitrary $f \in L^2([-1, 1], \nu)$ can be expanded as

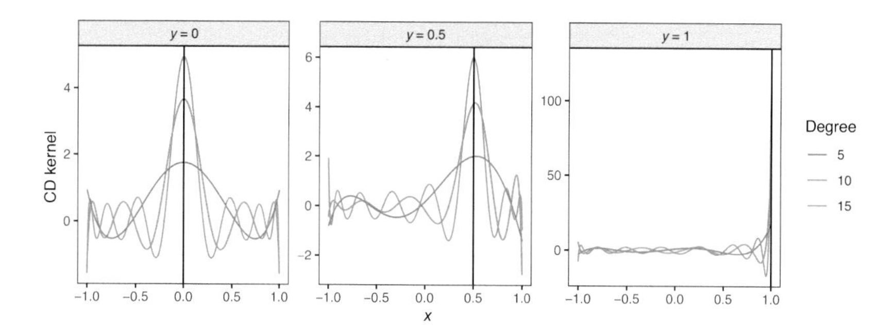

Figure 2.1 $x \mapsto K_n^\lambda(x, y)$, for different values of y and various degrees n (with λ the Lebesgue measure on $[-1, 1]$).

$$f = \sum_{j=0}^{\infty} \langle f, \phi_j \rangle \, \phi_j ,$$

with $\langle f, \phi_j \rangle = \int_{-1}^{1} f(y)\, \phi_j(y)\, \pi \sqrt{1 - y^2}\, dy$. The idea is to consider kernels of the form

$$(x, y) \mapsto K_n(x, y) := g_0\, \phi_0(x)\, \phi_0(y) + 2 \sum_{j=1}^{n-1} g_j\, \phi_j(x)\, \phi_j(y), \tag{2.11}$$

where coefficients $(g_j)_{j=0}^{n-1}$ are chosen appropriately to ensure:

$$\left.\begin{array}{l} \bullet\ K_n(x, y) > 0 \text{ for all } x, y \in [-1, 1], \\ \bullet\ \int_{-1}^{1} K_n(x, y)\, dx = \phi_0(y) \text{ for all } y \in [-1, 1], \text{ i.e. } g_0 = 1, \\ \bullet\ g_1 \to 1 \text{ as } n \to \infty. \end{array}\right\} \tag{2.12}$$

Then one approximates f by the functions

$$x \mapsto f_n(x) := \int_{-1}^{1} K_n(x, y)\, f(y)\, d\nu(y), \quad \forall x \in [-1, 1], \tag{2.13}$$

for all $n \in \mathbb{N}$. Notice that K_n in (2.11) is not a polynomial kernel but is strongly related to a polynomial kernel. In addition, the approximant f_n in (2.13) is not a polynomial but on the other hand $x \mapsto f_n(x) \sqrt{1 - x^2}$ is a polynomial.

A first choice $g_j = 1$ for all $j \in \mathbb{N}$ yields the Dirichlet kernel

$$K_n^D(x, y) := \phi_0(x)\, \phi_0(y) + 2 \sum_{j=1}^{n-1} \phi_j(x)\, \phi_j(y), \quad \forall (x, y) \in [-1, 1]^n,$$

but it does not satisfy the three requirements (2.12). On the other hand, the Féjer kernel

$$K_n^F(x,y) := \frac{1}{n}\sum_{j=1}^{n} K_j^D(x,y), \quad (x,y)\in[-1,1]^2, \tag{2.14}$$

which Césaro-averages out the Dirichlet kernel, satisfies the positivity requirement and its coefficients $(g_j^F)_{j=0}^{n-1}$ satisfy $g_j^F = 1 - j/n$, for all $j = 0,\dots,n-1$. Indeed, the new approximants of f defined by

$$f_n^F(x) := \int_{-1}^{1} K_n^F(x,y)\, f(y)\, d\nu(y), \quad n\in\mathbb{N}, \tag{2.15}$$

are positive whenever f is positive, and with $\varepsilon > 0$ fixed and arbitrary, $f_n \to f$ as $n\to\infty$ *uniformly* on $[-1+\varepsilon, 1-\varepsilon]$. In addition, the Gibbs oscillations are attenuated.

In general, determining *appropriate* coefficients $(g_j)_{j\in\mathbb{N}}$ so that the kernel (2.11) satisfies (2.12) is problem-dependent but a good strategy in many cases is to optimize the rate at which $g_1 \to 1$ as $n\to\infty$. This is what the Jackson kernel

$$K_n^J(x,y) := g_0^J\,\phi_0(x)\phi_0(y) + 2\sum_{j=1}^{n-1} g_j^J\,\phi_j(x)\,\phi_j(y)$$

does, where its coefficients,

$$g_j^J = \frac{(n-j+1)\,\cos(\frac{\pi j}{n+1}) + \sin(\frac{\pi j}{n+1})\,\cot(\frac{\pi}{n+1})}{n+1}, \quad j=0,\dots,n-1,$$

minimize the quantity

$$Q := \int_{-1}^{1}\int_{-1}^{1} (x-y)^2\, K_n(x,y)\, dx\, dy$$

over all kernels (2.11). It turns out that $Q = g_0 - g_1$ and therefore, since $g_0 = 1$, minimizing Q is trying to get g_1 as close to 1 as possible while maintaining positivity of the kernel. Note in passing that

$$Q = \int_{-1}^{1}\int_{-1}^{1} (x-y)^2 \left(1 + \sum_{j=1}^{n-1} g_j\, T_j(x)\, T_j(y)\right) d\mu(x)\, d\mu(y).$$

It turns out that for the Jackson kernel $\sqrt{Q}$ is proportional to $1/n$ for large n, whereas it is only proportional to $1/\sqrt{n}$ for the Féjer kernel. This can be interpreted as yielding an approximation error $\|f - f_n^J\|_\infty$ of the order $1/n$ for continuous functions, when using associated approximants $(f_n^J)_{n\in\mathbb{N}}$ based on the Jackson kernel. For more details the interested reader is referred to Weisse et al. (2006).

The resulting operators (based on positive kernels) that send $f\in C([-1,1])$ to its approximant f_n in (2.13) are of course linear and preserve positivity.

A general framework is the approximation of continuous functions by *positive linear operators*, as described in DeVore (1972) for example.

Machine Learning Kernels: As typical in the machine learning context, a polynomial kernel of degree n is often considered over real variables as follows (see e.g. Schölkopf et al., 2002):

$$\tilde{K}_n : (x, y) \mapsto (1 + x\, y)^n , \quad \forall x, y \in \mathbb{R} .$$

It is straightforward to show that this kernel is positive definite and that the span of $\tilde{K}_n(x, \cdot)$, $x \in \mathbb{R}$, is the space of polynomials of degree up to n. Hence it allows us to endow this space with a Hilbertian structure, that is, an RKHS structure. This view is purely functional, without any dependence on additional data, and can be used in the context of kernel methods for regression or classification tasks as many other nonpolynomial kernels can.

The kernel $\tilde{K}$ is, however, different from the Christoffel–Darboux, Féjer and Jackson kernels. The specificity of the Christoffel–Darboux kernel is that the inner product on polynomials is induced by a measure, an additional piece of data or an additional restriction on the kernel. The kernel $\tilde{K}$ does not fall in this category as it is not induced by a measure. Indeed, the monomials $1, x, \ldots, x^n$ are mutually orthogonal with respect to $\tilde{K}$, while there is no positive measure different from the Dirac mass at zero, making 1 and x^2 orthogonal.

On the one hand, the content of this book is specific to Christoffel–Darboux kernels, as a subclass of polynomial kernels, but on the other hand, the dependency on an additional piece of data given in the form of a measure μ allows for much richer discussion on the relation between a given kernel and the underlying measure. Furthermore, in the context of applications, it allows us to use different properties of the kernel, beyond the reproducing property.

Note that passing to complex variables eliminates the above dichotomy. Specifically, all monomials $1, z, z^2, \ldots$ are square integrable and mutually orthogonal with respect to any positive, rotationally invariant measure on $\mathbb{C}$ and rapidly decaying at infinity.

Beyond polynomials, machine learning applications typically involve more general kernels (Gaussian kernel, Laplacian kernel, ...) and there is a rich connection between learning problems and RKHS (Schölkopf et al., 2002). As we described for the polynomial kernel at the beginning of this section, the underlying RKHS inner product is not a-priori induced by a measure μ and hence a direct connection with CD kernels is not possible. Nonetheless, given a measure μ with compact support X, assuming that the kernel at hand K is continuous on X, it is possible to express K in terms of orthogonal elements of $L^2(X, \mu)$ (Cucker and Smale, 2002). Indeed, Mercer decomposition ensures that there exists a Hilbert basis $(\phi_k)_{k\in\mathbb{N}}$ in $L^2(X,\mu)$ and a nonnegative sequence $(\lambda_k)_{k\in\mathbb{N}}$ such that, for all $x, y \in X$,

$$K(x,y) = \sum_{k=1}^{\infty} \lambda_k \, \phi_k(x)\phi_k(y),$$

where the convergence is absolute (for each x, y) and uniform on $X \times X$. This is one of the foundations of statistical learning and it also makes a direct connection with the CD kernel through orthogonal bases, beyond polynomials. The algebraic structure of the set of polynomials is typically richer than that of Hilbert bases of $L^2(X,\mu)$ and a more precise connection between CD kernels and more general RKHS is still to be formulated.

2.4 Notes and Sources

Section 2.1: Functional spaces with an inner product and explicit reproducing kernel appeared early, in problems arising in mathematical physics. For instance a lucid account of the role of reproducing kernels in potential theory is explicit in Hilbert's collection of articles devoted to integral equations (Hilbert, 1953); see also Hellinger and Toeplitz (1953). Nowadays, the concept of a Hilbert space with a reproducing kernel is as common as a measure space. When working with a Hilbert space of functions, it is natural to regard every linear transformation (orthogonal projection, isometry, involution, self-adjoint operator) in function theory terms, that is, represented by a kernel. This trend continues full force today, especially in conjunction with functional models in operator theory, quantum physics or function theory of a complex variable. Owing to numerous applications spread over more than a century, the literature devoted to the subject is substantial (Aronszajn, 1950; Riesz and Sz.-Nagy, 1990; Alpay, 2003; Paulsen and Raghupathi, 2016).

An authoritative account of Hardy space theory and its key role in many functional models appearing in operator theory is Rosenblum and Rovnyak (1997). Nikolski's inviting text (Nikolski, 2019) offers a different perspective, with relevant ramifications to harmonic analysis, classical functions theory and control theory, all complemented by ample historical notes.

Section 2.2: Determinateness in the moment problem on the line was and remains central since the foundational 1894 memoir by Stieltjes; see Akhiezer (1965) for details. The proof of Theorem 2.2.2 has a rather interesting history. In a few lines, Hermann Weyl has identified a limit circle in the resolvent parametrization of all solutions of a specific vibrating string question on the semi-axis. The discrete analog of this second-order differential equation of a continuum mechanics problem is found in the three-term linear relation satisfied by the orthogonal polynomials associated with a moment data. This analogy led Hellinger (1922) and Marcel Riesz (2013) to identify a limit circle (of radius equal to a multiple of $\sqrt{\Lambda(w)}$) parametrizing different solutions to the original moment problem. A different approach, based on continued fraction expansions and function theory methods led R. Nevanlinna to a similar conclusion and even more refined parametrization. Closely related is Schur's algorithm for expanding and parametrizing bounded analytic functions in the unit disk (Herglotz et al., 1991). Many later developments of contemporary mathematical analysis have roots in these studies. It is beyond the scope of our compilation to develop these ideas. We refer the reader to the monographs Akhiezer (1965) and Schmüdgen (2017) for details.

The indeterminate case, $\Lambda(i) > 0$, is no less interesting. The Lebesgue space $L^2(\mu)$ of an indeterminate positive measure on the line carries bounded point evaluations for every single point of the complex plane. Hilbert spaces of entire functions enter into picture with even more implications, currently under intense exploration. The emerging Krein–de Branges theory is unifying on this ground function theory and spectral analysis. Foundational works are Gorbachuk and Gorbachuk (1997) and de Branges (1968).

In his studies dedicated to the moment problem, M. Riesz discusses a variant of the variational problem defining the Christoffel function, see Troisième Note in Riesz (2013). More precisely, assume that the Hankel kernel $(s_{k+n})_{k,n=0}^{d}$ is positive definite for a finite degree d, so that the hermitian form associated with the Christoffel–Darboux kernel has full rank. Fix a complex number w. Then,

$$\inf\{\langle p, 1\rangle,\ p(w) = 1, \deg p \leq 2d,\ p|_{\mathbb{R}} \geq 0\} = \frac{2}{K_d(w,w) + |K_d(w,\overline{w})|}.$$

This formula is attributed by Riesz to Prawitz. See also Akhiezer (1965) and more ramifications in Schmüdgen (2017).

When aiming to have the monomials $1, z, z^2, \ldots$ mutually orthogonal, the Gaussian measure

$$\exp(-|z|^2)\frac{d\text{Area}(z)}{\pi},$$

defined on $\mathbb{C}$, offers a natural choice. Indeed, with respect to this inner product,

$$\langle z^m, z^\ell\rangle = m!\delta_{m\ell},\quad m, \ell \geq 0.$$

The closure of complex polynomials in the respective norm is a space of entire functions, much studied in quantum physics under the name of the Fock space or Segal–Bargmann space. The reproducing kernel is $K(z, w) = e^{z\overline{w}}$.

Section 2.3: Most of the material is taken from Weisse et al. (2006) where the authors discuss other issues and describe other kernels, some positive (e.g. the Lorentz kernel) and some not (Dirichlet, Lanczos). In particular they mention that positivity of the kernel is essential to guarantee some basic properties of Green functions. The three requirements on the coefficients (g_j) of the kernel (2.11) are used in Korovkin's Theorem to ensure that the approximations $(f_n)_{n\in\mathbb{N}}$ (2.13) based on the resulting kernel, converge uniformly to f on arbitrary intervals $[-1+\varepsilon, 1-\varepsilon]$ as for the Féjer kernel. A general framework common to such positive kernels is the approximation of continuous functions by *positive linear operators* and, for a more detailed account of this theory, the interested reader is referred to DeVore (1972), Donner (1982) and the many references therein.

3

Univariate Christoffel–Darboux Analysis

The main interest in the CD kernel in data analysis, and further applications, is its connection with the support of the underlying measure as illustrated in Chapter 7. The connection between the support, the density of the underlying measure and the CD kernel has attracted research questions in mathematics for more than a century, starting with the work of Gabor Szegő. Results in this direction have been developed throughout the twentieth century, the vast majority of them being asymptotic, in the sense that they relate the underlying measure, its density and its support to the limiting behavior of the Christoffel function.

Most results obtained in this context were limited to the univariate setting, real or complex, where the situation could be characterized very precisely. This chapter presents an overview of such results, starting with the asymptotic distribution of the zeros of orthogonal polynomials then a more systematic study of the asymptotics of the Christoffel function, first on the unit circle in the complex plane as originally formulated by Szegő, and second with extensions on the real line.

This chapter is dedicated to the univariate case, and we have chosen to present some results on the real line, some in the complex plane, depending on the relevance of each setting for the purpose of illustrating the content of the text. We also include a section dedicated to the comparison of both bivariate real and univariate complex settings.

3.1 Zeros of Orthogonal Polynomials

The Christoffel–Darboux kernel was named after two mathematicians in relation to a formula involving orthogonal polynomials. In this context, the Christoffel–Darboux formula allows us to study the distribution of zeros of orthogonal polynomials, a topic developed much further afterwards. We outline some of these results to provide an account of the original questioning around the CD kernel.

3.1.1 The Christoffel–Darboux Formula on the Real Line

Let μ be a positive Borel measure supported on the real line $\mathbb{R}$, rapidly decreasing at infinity so that all its moments are finite. It is also assumed that the support of μ is not finite, so that associated orthonormal polynomials $(P_n)_{n\in\mathbb{N}}$ are well defined. For each $n \in \mathbb{N}$, write

$$P_n(z) = \gamma_n(\mu)z^n + \cdots,$$

where $\gamma_n(\mu) > 0$ is the leading coefficient of P_n, assumed to be positive with no loss of generality. As described in Chapter 2, the associated Christoffel–Darboux kernel of bi-degree (n, n) is given by

$$K_n^{\mu}(z, w) = P_0(z)P_0(w) + P_1(z)P_1(w) + \cdots + P_n(z)P_n(w).$$

In this setting, the *Christoffel–Darboux formula*, obtained for every $x, y \in \mathbb{R}$, $x \neq y$ and every $n \geq 0$, reads:

$$K_n^{\mu}(x, y) = \frac{\gamma_n(\mu)}{\gamma_{n+1}(\mu)} \frac{P_n(x)P_{n+1}(y) - P_{n+1}(x)P_n(y)}{y - x}. \tag{3.1}$$

By passing to the limit on the diagonal, we obtain for all real x,

$$K_n^{\mu}(x, x) = \frac{\gamma_n(\mu)}{\gamma_{n+1}(\mu)}[P'_{n+1}(x)P_n(x) - P'_n(x)P_{n+1}(x)].$$

Recall that the left-hand side is a sum of squares, hence positive. Then a simple recursion allows us to show that all zeros of P_n are real, each with multiplicity 1. Furthermore they are interlaced with the zeros of P_{n+1}. So a natural question that comes to mind is what space is filled up with all such zeros when n increases.

3.1.2 Asymptotics in the Complex Plane

The study of the asymptotic distribution of the zeros of orthogonal polynomials generated a lot of questions referring to CD kernels. We reproduce below one of the classical results in the complex plane. Let μ be a positive measure on $\mathbb{C}$, rapidly decaying at infinity, so that its moments

$$a_{k\ell} = \int z^k \bar{z}^\ell \, d\mu, \quad k, \ell \geq 0,$$

are all well defined. Assume furthermore that the support of μ is infinite so that orthogonal polynomials are well defined. A foundational theorem regarding the distribution of zeros of orthogonal polynomials was given by Widom.

Theorem 3.1.1 (Widom) *The zeros of the orthonormal polynomials* $P_n(z)$ *are contained in the convex hull of the support* $\mathrm{supp}(\mu)$ *of the generating measure* μ. *If* U *denotes the unbounded component of* $\mathbb{C} \setminus \mathrm{supp}(\mu)$, *then for every compact subset* $K \subset U$, *the number of zeros of* P_n *contained in* K *is bounded as n tends to infinity.*

To appreciate the consequences of this theorem, let $\lambda_1(n), \lambda_2(n), \ldots, \lambda_n(n)$ denote the zeros of the polynomial P_n, repeated in the enumeration according to their multiplicity. The *counting measure* supported by these zeros, given by the sum of Dirac delta measures

$$\nu_{P_n} = \frac{1}{n}[\delta_{\lambda_1(n)} + \cdots + \delta_{\lambda_n(n)}],$$

encodes the geometry and distribution of the n zeros. Widom's Theorem implies that any weak-* limit point of the sequence of counting measures is supported by the polynomial convex hull of $\mathrm{supp}(\mu)$, that is, the $\mathrm{supp}(\mu)$ union with the bounded open components of its complement. For instance, if the support of the measure μ is contained in a finite union F of disjoint closed disks, then the zeros of P_n will be "attracted" in the limit by F. Another interesting example is when the support of μ is the unit circle, then the zeros of P_n will be "attracted" by the unit disk.

3.2 Asymptotics on the Complex Unit Circle

3.2.1 Szegő's Extremal Problem

The first results related to the asymptotic study of the Christoffel function were proved by Gabor Szegő at the begining of the twentieth century for measures supported on the unit circle in the complex plane. Let $u(t) \geq 0$ be a Lebesgue integrable weight on $[-\pi, \pi)$ and consider the measure $\nu = \frac{1}{2\pi}u(t)dt$ supported by the unit torus $\mathbb{T}$.

The Christoffel function associated with ν is denoted Λ_n^ν; see Definition 2.2.1. Szegő proved around 1914 that Λ_n^ν satisfies

$$\lim_{n\to\infty} \Lambda_n^\nu(0) = \exp\left(\frac{1}{2\pi}\int_{-\pi}^{\pi} \ln u(t)dt\right).$$

The right-hand side is the *geometric mean* of u. It is well defined under Szegő's condition,

$$\int_{-\pi}^{\pi} \ln u(t)dt > -\infty,$$

and can be set to be equal to 0 otherwise.

The problem of determination of the asymptotics is often termed Szegő's extremal problem, the term "extremal" being related to the variational formulation (2.2) of the Christoffel function. On the unit torus in the complex plane, the problem can equivalently be formulated using monic polynomials (with leading coefficient is 1). Indeed, for any z on the unit circle, one has $z\bar{z} = 1$, hence for any $A_1, \ldots, A_n$ complex, one has

$$|z^n + A_1 z^{n-1} + \cdots + A_n| = |1 + \overline{A_1} z + \cdots + \overline{A_n} z^n|, \quad |z| = 1,$$

and the expression on the right-hand side is a general polynomial of degree less than or equal to n, having value 1 at $z = 0$. Hence the Christoffel function at 0 is equivalently expressed as

$$\Lambda_n^\nu(0) = \min_{A_j \in \mathbb{C}, j=1,\ldots n} \frac{1}{2\pi} \int_{-\pi}^{\pi} |e^{int} + A_1 e^{i(n-1)t} + \cdots + A_n|^2 u(t)dt.$$

The asymptotic result can be generalized to any point w in the unit disk, $|w| < 1$, using a Möbius transform. For the same measure $\nu = \frac{1}{2\pi} u(t)dt$, one has

$$\lim_{n\to\infty} \Lambda_n^\nu(w) = (1 - |w|^2) \exp\left[\frac{1}{2\pi} \int_{-\pi}^{\pi} \Re \frac{e^{it} + w}{e^{it} - w} \ln u(t)dt\right].$$

Note that taking $w = 0$ provides the geometric mean result.

3.2.2 Density Identification on the Unit Circle

Regarding the characterization of the asymptotics of the Christoffel function, the picture is not complete without a description of its limiting behavior on the boundary of the disk. The question of the asymptotics on the unit torus, that is, precisely on the support of ν, required much more effort and a definite answer came out much later. The following result is 80 years younger than Szegő's original result and provides a definitive answer regarding the unit circle in the complex plane.

Theorem 3.2.1 (Maté–Nevai–Totik, 1991) *Let μ be a positive measure on the unit circle $\mathbb{T} = \{e^{it}, -\pi \le t < \pi\}$, with absolutely continuous part with respect to normalized arc length $u = \mu'$. If the measure μ belongs to Szegő's class, that is,*

$$\int_{\mathbb{T}} \log u(t)dt > -\infty,$$

then the Christoffel function Λ_n^ν *satisfies*

$$\lim_n n\,\Lambda_n^\mu(e^{it}) = u(t), \quad a.e.\text{-}dt.$$

The primary example illustrating Theorem 3.2.1 is arc length measure itself, $d\sigma(t) = \frac{dt}{2\pi}$. The orthonormal polynomials in this case are the monomials $1, z, z^2, \ldots$, with Christoffel–Darboux kernel

$$K_n^\sigma(z, w) = \frac{1 - z^{n+1}\,\overline{w}^{n+1}}{1 - z\,\overline{w}}, \quad z \neq w\,.$$

On the diagonal we find $K_n^\sigma(z, z) = n + 1$, for all z such that $|z| = 1$. Thus,

$$\lim_n n\,\Lambda_n^\mu(e^{it}) = \lim_n \frac{n}{n+1} = 1.$$

In conclusion, for positive measures μ on the circle belonging to Szegő's class, one can detect their point masses from the point limits

$$\lim_n \Lambda_n^\mu(e^{it}) = \mu\{e^{it}\}, \quad t \in [-\pi, \pi),$$

while Theorem 3.2.1 identifies the absolutely continuous part of μ, with respect to arc length.

Note that the Szegő class condition ensures that u is positive almost everywhere and can be interpreted as a condition to ensure that the support of μ is indeed the torus and not a strict subset of it. In the context when μ has a density on the torus, Theorem 3.2.1 asserts that, after proper rescaling, the Christoffel function converges to the density almost everywhere.

3.3 Asymptotics of the Christoffel Function on the Real Line

3.3.1 Asymptotics on the Unit Segment

The classical theory of orthogonal polynomials was primarily developed in the complex plane. For our purpose and for potential applications to data analysis, it is natural to focus on the univariate real case. There is a strong connection between complex and real orthogonal polynomials which in the end provides clear asymptotic behavior for measures on the real line. Interestingly, the qualitative description of one-dimensional asymptotics is similar to the multivariate real setting which is of current interest in applications. The following is a consequence of Theorem 3.2.1 and was proved in Máté et al. (1991).

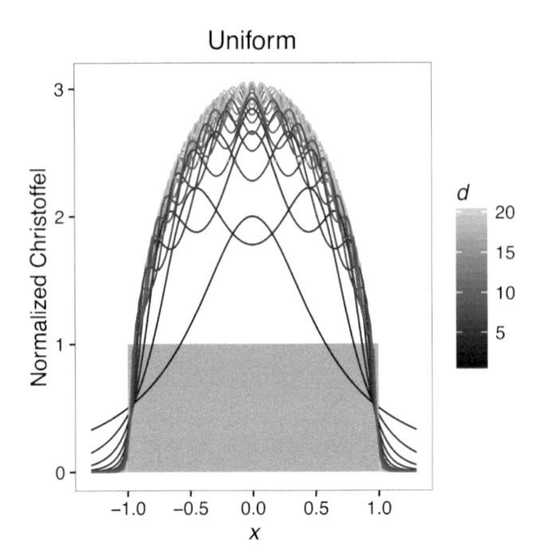

Figure 3.1 The Christoffel function of the Lebesgue measure on $[-1, 1]$ (the constant density is depicted by the gray rectangle). The normalized Christoffel function approaches a semi-ellipse as predicted by Theorem 3.3.1.

Theorem 3.3.1 (Maté–Nevai–Totik, 1991) *Let μ be a positive measure on the unit segment $[-1, 1]$, with absolutely continuous part with respect to the Lebesgue measure $u = \mu'$. If the measure μ belongs to Szegő's class, that is,*

$$\int_{-1}^{1} \frac{\log u(x)}{\sqrt{1-x^2}} dx > -\infty,$$

then the Christoffel function Λ_n^μ satisfies

$$\lim_n n\Lambda_n^\mu(x) = \pi u(x)\sqrt{1-x^2}, \quad a.e.\text{-}dx.$$

Theorem 3.3.1 is illustrated on Figure 3.1, where we choose the constant unit density on the unit segment. Beyond providing a characterization of the asymptotic behavior of the Christoffel function, Theorem 3.3.1 calls for the following remark. The asymptotics is described by a product of two factors:

- a density factor which corresponds to the absolutely continuous part of the measure;
- a support factor which higlights the fact that the support of the measure is $[-1, 1]$.

Note that, in this case, Szegő's condition implies that the support of the measure is indeed the whole segment, not a strict subset of $[-1, 1]$. A normalization argument would lead to similar behavior for measures supported on a different segment. This qualitative behavior was not explicit when considering the univariate complex circle, which is somewhat isotropic and does not induce a support factor. On the other hand, in multivariate real settings, this type of behavior is typical, as will be described in later chapters.

3.3.2 The General Case

A leading thread in the classical theory of orthogonal polynomials is the use of potential theoretic tools to derive asymptotic behavior, root distribution and other qualitative features. These topics have a long history and a wealth of deep results of importance to approximation theory, function theory, statistics and mathematical physics. In general, one has to impose on the original measure some balance between uniform and L^2 norms, usually assured by Bernstein–Markov type inequalities. These measures are called *regular*; see Stahl and Totik (1992) for the definitive monograph on the subject. For instance, an absolutely continuous measure with respect to length on an interval is regular (Erdős–Turán criterion; see Chapter 4 in Stahl and Totik (1992)). In general, potential theory is better handled with complex variables, and consequently it is not surprising that the theory of real orthogonal polynomials on the line is formulated in complex analytic terms.

Concerning the Christoffel function asymptotics, a century of partial results and accumulated essays, in particular Theorems 3.2.1 and 3.3.1, culminates with the following result.

Theorem 3.3.2 (Totik, 2000) *Let μ be a regular measure with compact support E on the real line. Assume that E is regular and $I \subset E$ is an interval on which μ satisfies the Szegő condition* $\log \mu' \in L^1$.

Then, for almost every $x \in I$,

$$\lim_{n\to\infty} n\,\Lambda_n^{\mu}(x) = \frac{\mu'(x)}{\omega_E(x)},$$

where ω_E denotes the equilibrium measure of E.

The set E is called *regular* if the domain $(\mathbb{C}\cup\{\infty\})\setminus E$ is regular with respect to Dirichlet's problem. The proof appeared in Totik (2000). In the special case when the support of the measure μ is an interval, say $E = [-1, 1]$, the weight of the respective equilibrium measure is $\omega_E = \frac{1}{\pi\sqrt{1-x^2}}$, which recovers Theorem 3.3.1 as a special case.

3.4 Asymptotics Outside the Support

Remaining in the regular measure case, for points outside the convex hull of the support of μ, the Christoffel function decays exponentially to zero, with a rate dictated by the Green function $g_\Omega(z, \infty)$ of $\Omega = (\mathbb{C} \cup \{\infty\}) \setminus \mathrm{co}E$, with a pole at infinity:

$$\lim_{n\to\infty} \Lambda_n^\mu(z)^{\frac{1}{n}} = e^{-2g_\Omega(z,\infty)}, \quad z \notin \mathrm{co}\ \mathrm{supp}(\mu).$$

3.4.1 Indeterminate Measures

Returning briefly to moment problems, we note that the case of indeterminate measures on the line is not less remarkable. Let μ be a positive measure on the real line, rapidly decreasing at infinity. Recall that μ is said to be *determinate* if there is no other measure with the same moments, and *indeterminate* otherwise.

Theorem 2.2.2 assures *uniqueness* of the measure μ with prescribed power moments in terms of the vanishing condition $\Lambda^\mu(w) = 0$ for some nonreal w. The indeterminate case corresponds to $\Lambda^\mu(z) \neq 0$ for all $z \in \mathbb{C}$. To be more precise, under this condition there are two different measures μ and ν with the same power moments. The growth of $\Lambda^\mu(z)^{-1}$ for $|z|$ is elucidated by the following cornerstone result in the theory of moments.

Theorem 3.4.1 (M. Riesz, 1923) *Let μ be a positive measure on the real line, rapidly decreasing at infinity. If μ is indeterminate from its power moments, then for every $\epsilon > 0$ there exists a constant C_ϵ with the property*

$$K^\mu(z, z) \leq C_\epsilon\, e^{\epsilon|z|}, \quad z \in \mathbb{C}.$$

In particular, every $w \in \mathbb{C}$ is a bounded point evaluation for the closure H of $\mathbb{C}[z]$ in $L^2(\mu)$. In other terms, H is a Hilbert space of entire functions possessing the reproducing kernel $K^\mu(z, w)$.

So Theorem 3.4.1 reveals a distinguishing feature of the complex Christoffel function compared with its real counterpart, for a given measure (here with a support on the real line considered as a subspace of $\mathbb{C}$). Even if the support is contained in $\mathbb{R}$, the asymptotic behavior of the complex Christoffel function on $\mathbb{C}$ offers precise qualitative information on the measure, not provided by the real Christoffel function.

3.4.2 Simply Connected Domains and Jordan Curves

One of the best understood cases of asymptotic behavior of the Christoffel function is offered by area measure supported by a simply connected domain with smooth boundary, or by arc length measure along a Jordan curve. We reproduce from Gustafsson et al. (2009) a few details concerning the first case.

We start with the unit disk $\mathbb{D} = \{z \in C,\ |z| < 1\}$ supporting area measure. The orthogonal polynomials are

$$P_n(z) = \sqrt{\frac{n+1}{\pi}}\, z^n, \quad n \geq 0, \tag{3.2}$$

with the Christoffel–Darboux kernel, also known as the Bergman kernel,

$$K^{\mathbb{D}}(z, w) = \frac{1}{\pi(1 - z\overline{w})^2}, \quad |z|, |w| < 1,$$

and the inner Christoffel function

$$\Lambda^{\mathbb{D}}(z) = \pi(1 - |z|^2)^2, \quad |z| < 1.$$

Thus $\sqrt{\Lambda^{\mathbb{D}}(z)}$ is proportional to the distance from an inner point z to the boundary. The truncated Christoffel function is rotationally invariant, and it can be expressed in closed form:

$$\Lambda_n^{\mathbb{D}}(z) = \frac{\pi(1 - |z|^2)^2}{(n+1)|z|^{2n+4} - (n+2)|z|^{2n+2} + 1}, \quad z \in \mathbb{C}.$$

We deduce from the above expression the rapid decay of $\Lambda_n^{\mathbb{D}}$ outside the closed disk.

With the aid of potential theory and conformal mapping, such qualitative features of the Christoffel function can be generalized and made more precise on a large class of domains. We reproduce a few illustrative results. Let $G \subset \mathbb{C}$ be a bounded simply connected domain with boundary Γ. Denote by $\Omega = \mathbb{C} \setminus \overline{G}$ the complement of the closure of G. The orthogonal polynomials $P_n(z)$ associated with area measure on G are known as *Bergman orthogonal polynomials*. Let

$$\Phi(z) = \frac{z}{\gamma} + \alpha_0 + \frac{\alpha_1}{z} + \frac{\alpha_2}{z^2} + \cdots$$

be the conformal mapping of Ω onto the exterior of the unit disk, normalized by $\Phi(\infty) = \infty$ and $\gamma > 0$. The constant γ is an important potential theoretic entity, called the *capacity* of Γ. We denote by $\Lambda_n^G(z)$ the associated Christoffel function. For many inverse problems, it is, however, $\sqrt{\Lambda_n^G(z)}$ that is of interest. We provide estimates for this later.

If the curve Γ is real analytic, then the conformal mapping $w = \Phi(z)$ extends across the boundary, with values covering the region $|w| > \rho$, with $\rho < 1$. The key asymptotics go back in this case to a century-old observation.

Theorem 3.4.2 (Carleman, 1932) *Assume the boundary Γ of the simply connected domain G is real analytic, and the external conformal mapping $w = \Phi(z)$ analytically extends up to $|w| > \rho$, where $\rho < 1$. Then Bergman's orthogonal polynomials satisfy:*

$$P_n(z) = \sqrt{\frac{n+1}{\pi}}\Phi'(z)\Phi(z)^n[1 + O(\sqrt{n})\rho^n], \quad z \notin G.$$

From Carleman's Theorem and general principles of potential theory one deduces sharp asymptotics for the Christoffel function:

Theorem 3.4.3 (Gustafsson et al., 2009) *Let Γ be a real analytic Jordan curve surrounding the domain G, so that the external conformal mapping $w = \Phi(z)$ analytically extends up to $|w| > \rho$, where $\rho < 1$. Then there are positive constants C, with the following properties:*

$$0 < \sqrt{\Lambda_n^G(z)} - \sqrt{\Lambda^G(z)} \leq C_1|\Phi(z)|^n \left[\mathrm{dist}(z,\Gamma) + \frac{1}{n}\right], \quad \rho < \Phi(z) \leq 1. \quad (3.3)$$

On the boundary,

$$\lim_n n\sqrt{\Lambda_n^G(\zeta)} = \frac{\sqrt{2\pi}}{|\Phi'(\zeta)|}, \quad \zeta \in \Gamma. \quad (3.4)$$

And outside the domain,

$$C_2 \mathrm{dist}(z,\Gamma)\delta(z) \leq \sqrt{\Lambda_n^G(z)} \leq \frac{C_3}{\sqrt{n}|\Phi(z)|^n}, \quad z \notin \overline{G}, \quad (3.5)$$

where

$$\delta(z) = \frac{|\Phi(z)|^2 - 1}{|\Phi(z)|} \frac{1}{\sqrt{(n+1)|\Phi(z)^{2n}(|\Phi(z)|^2 - 1) + 1}}.$$

For a bounded, simply connected domain G, we also note the bounds

$$\pi\ \mathrm{dist}(z,\Gamma)^2 \leq \Lambda^G(z) \leq 16\pi\ \mathrm{dist}(z,\Gamma)^2, \quad z \in G;$$

the proof does not require any regularity of the boundary.

The central gauge in the above estimates is the absolute value of the external conformal mapping and its level sets. This is nothing more than the exponential of the *Green function* $g_\Omega(z,\infty)$ of the complement Ω, with a pole at infinity:

$$\ln|\Phi(z)| = g_\Omega(z,\infty), \quad z \notin \overline{G}. \quad (3.6)$$

A class of domains which possess a simple Green function are the *lemniscates*

$$G = \{z \in \mathbb{C}, |q(z)| < 1\},$$

where $q(z)$ is a monic polynomial of degree d. Indeed, assuming G is simply connected and smooth,

$$g_\Omega(z,\infty) = \frac{\ln|q(z)|}{d}.$$

A celebrated theorem due to Hilbert asserts that every planar domain can be approximated in Hausdorff distance by a sequence of lemniscates.

3.5 Further Results and Remarks

3.5.1 Gaussian Quadrature

To conclude and illustrate properties and hidden strengths of the CD kernel, we go back to the early discoveries of mid and late nineteenth century, essentially referring to mechanical quadratures.

Theorem 3.5.1 (Gaussian quadrature) *Let μ be a positive, rapidly decreasing measure of infinite support contained in the real line with associated orthonormal polynomials $(P_n)_{n\in\mathbb{N}}$ and CD kernel K_n^μ. Fix a point $t \in \mathbb{R}$ with the property $P_{n-1}(t) \neq 0$ and denote by $\alpha_1, \ldots, \alpha_n$ the zeros of the polynomial $K_n^\mu(t, \cdot)$. Then,*

$$\int h(x)d\mu(x) = \sum_{j=1}^{n} \Lambda_{n-1}^\mu(\alpha_j)h(\alpha_j),$$

for every polynomial h of degree less than or equal to $2n - 2$. If $P_n(t) \neq 0$, then the formula is also valid for polynomials h of degree $2n - 1$.

Hence, remarkably, the Christoffel function Λ_{n-1}^μ evaluated at the points (support) (α_j) of the quadrature, provides the positive weights of the quadrature.

3.5.2 Markov–Stieltjes inequalities

In the same spirit, the celebrated *Markov–Stieltjes inequalities* reveal the central role of the Christoffel function in solving the moment problem on the line.

Theorem 3.5.2 (Markov–Stieltjes inequalities) *Under the conditions of Theorem 3.5.1, the following inequalities hold:*

$$\sum_{j:\alpha_j \leq t} \Lambda_{n-1}^\mu(\alpha_j) \geq \mu((-\infty, t]) \geq \mu((-\infty, t)) \geq \sum_{j:\alpha_j < t} \Lambda_{n-1}^\mu(\alpha_j).$$

Even in the case $P_{n-1}(t) = 0$ the above inequalities are valid, with an appropriate definition of the nodes α_j.

Again and remarkably, the above bounds express in precise terms, solely depending on the Christoffel function, how much mass the measure μ puts on a semi-bounded interval. According to standard terminology, sharp estimates of the *distribution function* of μ are encoded in Markov–Stieltjes inequalities. From here one finds

$$\mu\{t\} \leq \Lambda^{\mu}_{n-1}(t).$$

We already proved that, in the limit, the preceding inequality becomes equality; see Proposition 2.2.3.

3.5.3 Density in L^p

Szegő's Theorem had unexpected consequences. We record first an early, surprising theorem. Let $\mu \geq 0$ be a positive Borel measure on $[-\pi, \pi)$ with Lebesgue decomposition

$$\mu = u(t)\frac{dt}{2\pi} + \mu_{sc} + \mu_d,$$

where $u(t)$ has bounded variation, μ_{sc} denotes the singular continuous part and μ_d denotes the singular discrete part.

Theorem 3.5.3 (Kolmogorov, 1941; Krein, 1945) *The system* $1, z, z^2, \ldots$ *is dense in* $L^p(\mu), p \geq 1$, *if and only if*

$$\int_{-\pi}^{\pi} |\ln u(t)| dt = \infty.$$

The immediate relation of the above result with Szegő's Theorem follows from the observation that the function $\overline{z}$ can be approximated in $L^p(u(t)\frac{dt}{2\pi})$ by complex polynomials if

$$\inf_{a_1,\ldots,A_n} \|z^n + A_1 z^{n-1} + \cdots + A_n\| = \inf_{a_1,\ldots,A_n} \|\overline{z} + A_1 + A_2 z + \cdots + A_n z^{n-1}\| = 0.$$

3.6 Notes and Sources

Section 3.1: The theory of orthogonal polynomials in the complex domain is masterfully presented in the monograph by Stahl and Totik (1992). Potential theory techniques are central in their study of nth root asymptotics of orthogonal polynomials, zero distribution and regularity criteria for measures. Applications to rational approximation of Cauchy transforms of measures are also amply commented there. Widom's Theorem appeared in Widom (1967).

For the reader inclined towards numerical matrix analysis or operator theory, the approach recently advocated by Barry Simon and collaborators might be appealing (Simon, 2008, 2009; Simanek, 2012). This is a direct extension of the classical correspondence between Jacobi matrices (i.e. three-diagonal symmetric matrices), orthogonal polynomials on the line and moment problems (Akhiezer, 1965; Stone, 1990). We expand a few details.

Let μ be a positive measure on $\mathbb{C}$, rapidly decreasing at infinity. Assume that μ has infinite support, so that all orthonormal polynomials $P_n(z)$, $n \geq 0$, are well defined. Denote, as in the previous chapter, H_n to be the span of $P_0, P_1, \ldots, P_n$, that is, $H_n = \mathbb{C}_n[z]$ is the space of complex polynomials of degree at most n. Obviously H_n is a finite-dimensional subspace of $L^2(\mu)$ with orthogonal projection

$$(\pi_n f)(z) = \int K_n^{\mu}(z, w) f(w) d\mu(w), \quad f \in \mathbb{C}[z].$$

Denote by T_z multiplication by the complex variable:

$$(T_z f)(z) = z f(z), \quad f \in \mathbb{C}[z].$$

This linear transform might be unbounded on $L^2(\mu)$. However, with respect to the orthonormal basis $(P_n)_{n=0}^{\infty}$ it is represented by an infinite matrix with a nonzero subdiagonal, a so-called *Hessenberg matrix*. Denote by T_n the compression of T_z to the finite-dimensional subspace H_n:

$$T_n f = \pi_n(z f), \quad f \in H_n, \quad n \geq 0.$$

The matrix associated with T_n is a Hessenberg $(n+1) \times (n+1)$-matrix. The crucial observation, well known in the operator theory community, is

$$\det(\lambda I - T_n) = \frac{1}{\gamma_{n+1}(\mu)} P_{n+1}(\lambda).$$

We sketch an elementary proof. The matrix T_n possesses a cyclic vector, namely the constant function $\mathbf{1}$. Hence its characteristic polynomial $Q(\lambda) = \det(\lambda I - T_n)$ coincides with its minimal polynomial, and in virtue of the Cayley Hamilton Theorem, $Q(T_n) = 0$. Note that the vectors $\mathbf{1}, T_n \mathbf{1} = z, \ldots, T_n^n \mathbf{1} = z^n$ are linearly independent in H_n and

$$\langle Q, z^k \rangle_{2,\mu} = \langle \pi_n Q(T_z) \mathbf{1}, T_n^k \mathbf{1} \rangle = \langle Q(T_n) \mathbf{1}, T_n^k \mathbf{1} \rangle = 0, \quad 0 \leq k \leq n.$$

Hence Q is the monic orthogonal polynomial of degree $n+1$, associated with the measure μ. Thus the distribution of the zeros of the orthogonal polynomials P_n goes hand in hand with the distribution of the eigenvalues of the *finite central truncations* of the Hessenberg matrix T_z. This dictionary has far reaching consequences; see Liesen and Strakoš (2013) for a general guide and Simon (2009) for specific computations related to the Christoffel function.

Freud (1969) is outstanding in relation to the classical aspects of orthogonal polynomials on the line or on the circle. He was the first to recognize the essential role of, and exploit, the Christoffel function in approximation theory. The eulogy by Nevai (1986) of Geza Freud and his "Christoffel function syndrome" is also an invaluable source for the multifaceted role of the Christoffel function in modern analysis. The proofs of Theorems 3.5.1 and 3.5.2 can be found in the first chapter of Freud (1969).

The theory of orthogonal polynomials on the unit circle is parallel, but far from identical, to the theory of orthogonal polynomials on the real line. Szegő (1975) remains fresh and very informative. Today it is complemented by the comprehensive books of Simon (2005a,b). Szegő proved his celebrated limit theorem a century ago for smooth weights u. Szegő's extremal problem and corresponding limit theorem are discussed in detail and generalized in Addenda B of Ahiezer (1965). The more recent text Simon (2011) offers the current state of the art on the subject, from the perspective of Hilbert space theory. Without entering into the proof of Theorem 3.5.3, one key idea is to use Szegő's Theorem to infer, that, if $G(u) > 0$, then e^{-it} cannot be approximated by $1, e^{it}, e^{i2t}, \ldots$ in $L^2(\mu)$. Again, Addenda B in Ahiezer (1965) is very informative and complete on these topics.

Sections 3.2–3.3: Many partial results à la Szegő were recorded before the definitive result was proved in Nevai (1986) and Máté et al. (1987, 1991). The analog for an interval of the real line is also discussed in Máté et al. (1991). In case Szegő's condition is imposed only on a collection of intervals, or a more general set E, the result was settled by Totik (2000). In that case the equilibrium measure of E stands for the reference measure (instead of arc length). An operator theory approach to the Maté–Nevai–Totik Theorem and its generalizations is offered by Simon (2008, 2009).

In the field of approximation theory, the role of the Christoffel–Darboux kernel is paramount. We illustrate this with a simple idea, explicitly used by Lebesgue around 1905 in his study of the convergence of Fourier series. Let $\mu \geq 0$ be a positive measure supported on a compact set $I \subset \mathbb{R}$. For a continuous function $f \in C(I)$, we set

$$S_N(\mu, f, x) = \sum_{k=0}^{N} \langle f, P_k \rangle_\mu P_k(x),$$

where P_k are orthogonal polynomials, or trigonometric polynomials in case $I = [-\pi.\pi]$, and we work on the torus. Then

$$\sup_{\|f\|_{\infty, I} \leq 1} |S_N(\alpha, f, x)|^2 \leq \|f\|_{2,\alpha}^2 K_N^\mu(x, x) \leq \mu(I) K_N^\mu(x, x).$$

As before, $K_N^\mu(x,x) = \sum_{k=0}^N |P_k(x)|^2$ stands for the Christoffel–Darboux kernel. Consequently, for every polynomial Q of degree at most N, one finds via the reproduction property

$$|f(x) - S_N(\mu, f, x)| = |f(x) - Q(x) - S_N(\mu, f - Q, x)|$$
$$\leq \inf_{\deg Q \leq N} \|f - Q\|_{\infty,K}(1 + \mu(I)\sqrt{K_N^\mu(x,x)}).$$

In this way the best uniform approximation of f by polynomials and the growth of $[\Lambda_N^\mu(x)]^{-1} = K_N^\mu(x,x)$ control the convergence of the generalized Fourier expansion.

Section 3.4: The original proof of Theorem 3.4.1 can be found in Riesz (2013). A slight simplification of Riesz's proof is contained in Akhiezer (1965). The sub-exponential growth of the Christoffel–Darboux kernel established by M. Riesz in the indeterminate case was essential in Nevanlinna's parametrization of all solutions to the respective moment problem. Also, from this theorem Riesz deduced some remarkable determinateness criteria for the moment problem on the line; see Akhiezer (1965).

Approximation theory in the complex domain is well described in Gaier (1987). One can find there a thorough discussion of Bergman space and Bergman orthogonal polynomials, a proof of Carleman's Theorem and many other relevant topics. Gustafsson et al. (2009) extends Theorem 3.4.3 to an archipelago, that is, a collection of disjoint simply connected domains. A reconstruction algorithm of such an archipelago from finitely many moments, via the level sets of the truncated Christoffel functions, is discussed in the same work. See also Saff et al. (2015) for a generalization to an archipelago of non-simply connected domains, that is, islands with lakes. A different approach to Theorem 3.4.3 and variants, based on lemniscate approximation, is contained in Totik (2010). The analog results for arc length measures supported by a collection of disjoint Jordan curves appeared much earlier in the groundbreaking study by Widom (1969).

4

Multivariate Christoffel–Darboux Analysis

The concepts and results explored in Chapter 3 have analogs in the multivariate setting. However, in this framework almost all topics (moment problems, determinateness, quadrature formulas, asymptotics of reproducing kernels) encounter major complications. Some modest progress in solving them has accumulated only during the last decades. We offer below a few snapshots of the multivariate aspects of Christoffel–Darboux kernels, with the specific aim of treating the statistical and spectral analysis questions that constitute the main body of the present book.

Denote by $\mathbf{x} = (x_1, \ldots, x_d)$ a d-variate vector. To define polynomials, we adopt the multi-index notation

$$\alpha = (\alpha_1, \alpha_2, \ldots, \alpha_d) \in \mathbb{N}^d,$$

$$\mathbf{x}^\alpha = x_1^{\alpha_1} x_2^{\alpha_2} \ldots x_d^{\alpha_d}$$

and

$$|\alpha| = \alpha_1 + \alpha_2 + \cdots + \alpha_d.$$

In short form, we denote the set of d-variate polynomials by $\mathbb{R}[\mathbf{x}] = \mathbb{R}[x_1, x_2, \ldots, x_d]$. Recall that the dimension of $\mathbb{R}_n[\mathbf{x}]$, the space of d-variate polynomials of degree at most n, is given by $s(n) = \binom{n+d}{d}$.

In this chapter, unless explicitly stated, we assume that μ is a positive Borel measure on $\mathbb{R}^d$, with support S equal to the closure of a bounded open set with a "nice" boundary. "Nice" means either Lipschitz (which can be for instance C^1-smooth, piecewise C^1-smooth without cusps) or real-analytic with singularities. We restrict the assumptions to such "fat" subsets of $\mathbb{R}^n$ to assure their regularity in the sense of pluripotential theory (Pawłucki and Pleśniak, 1986; Bloom, 1997). This regularity assumption will be necessary for some of the asymptotic estimates we record in the second part of this chapter. Owing to the fact that S

possesses interior points, no nontrivial polynomial vanishes on S:

$$(\, p \in \mathbb{R}[\mathbf{x}],\ p(\mathbf{x}) = 0,\ \ \mathbf{x} \in S\,) \quad \Rightarrow \quad (\, p = 0\,)\,.$$

Also, since S is a compact set, all power moments of the measure μ are finite.

4.1 Preliminaries

Due to the restrictive assumptions imposed on the measure μ, the construction of orthonormal polynomials and the associated reproducing kernel mirrors the univariate case treated earlier, with some minor modifications; see Sections 2.2 and 2.1.

4.1.1 The Christoffel–Darboux Kernel

We follow the exposition in Pauwels et al. (2021). For any $n \in \mathbb{N}$, $n \geq 1$, consider $\mathbb{R}_n[\mathbf{x}]$ the space of polynomials of degree at most n. The natural map

$$\mathbb{R}_n[\mathbf{x}] \longrightarrow L^2(\mu), \quad p \mapsto p$$

is injective. Henceforth, we denote by $\|\cdot\|_{2,\mu}$ or simply $\|\cdot\|_2$ the Hilbert space norm of $L^2(\mu)$:

$$\langle p, q\rangle_2 = \int_{\mathbb{R}^d} p(\mathbf{x})q(\mathbf{x})d\mu(\mathbf{x}), \quad p, q \in \mathbb{R}[\mathbf{x}].$$

Indeed, the support S has interior points, hence

$$(p \in \mathbb{R}[\mathbf{x}], \|p\|_{2,\mu} = 0) \Rightarrow (p = 0).$$

For every $\mathbf{z} \in \mathbb{R}^d$, the point evaluation functional

$$\delta_{\mathbf{z}} : p \mapsto p(\mathbf{z})$$

is continuous on the finite-dimensional subspace $\mathbb{R}_n[\mathbf{x}]$. Thus $(\mathbb{R}_n[\mathbf{x}], \|\cdot\|_2)$ is a reproducing kernel Hilbert space.

Definition 4.1.1 The Christoffel–Darboux kernel (CD kernel) of degree n associated with μ is denoted by K_n^μ and is the reproducing kernel of $(\mathbb{R}_n[\mathbf{x}], \langle\cdot,\cdot\rangle_\mu)$.

In other terms, K_n^μ is a polynomial on $\mathbb{R}^d \times \mathbb{R}^d$ with the reproducing property

$$p(\mathbf{z}) = \int_{\mathbb{R}^d} p(\mathbf{y})K_n^\mu(\mathbf{z}, \mathbf{y})d\mu(\mathbf{y}), \ \mathbf{z} \in \mathbb{R}^d, \ \ p \in \mathbb{R}_n[\mathbf{x}].$$

In view of the discussion following Lemma 2.1, setting

$$X_0 = \left\{\mathbf{x} \in \mathbb{R}^d, K_n^\mu(\mathbf{x}, \mathbf{x}) = 0\right\},$$

we have $K_n^\mu(\mathbf{x}, \mathbf{y}) = 0$ for all $\mathbf{x} \in X_0$ and $\mathbf{y} \in \mathbb{R}^d$. We deduce from the reproducing property that

$$p(\mathbf{x}) = \int_{\mathbb{R}^p} p(\mathbf{y}) K_n^\mu(\mathbf{x}, \mathbf{y}) d\mu(\mathbf{y}) = 0$$

for all $p \in \mathbb{R}_n[\mathbf{x}]$, so that $X_0 = \emptyset$.

Following Definition 2.1.3 and identity (2.5), given any basis of $\mathbb{R}_n[\mathbf{x}]$, orthonormal with respect to $\langle\cdot,\cdot\rangle_{2,\mu}$, $(p_i)_{i=1}^{s(n)}$, we have

$$K_n^\mu : (\mathbf{x}, \mathbf{y}) \mapsto \sum_{i=1}^{s(n)} p_i(\mathbf{x}) p_i(\mathbf{y}). \tag{4.1}$$

Notice that orthonormal bases are not unique, either choice producing the same kernel (4.1).

To illustrate the ambiguity in selecting an orthonormal basis of polynomials in the multivariate setting, we start with the ubiquitous Gaussian weight in $\mathbb{R}^2$:

$$w(x, y) = \frac{1}{\pi} e^{-x^2-y^2}, \quad x, y \in \mathbb{R}.$$

Note that on this example we depart from the compact support assumption. This is of course a product of independent one-dimensional weights, whence we can choose the orthonormal basis in $L^2(\mathbb{R}^2, w dx dy)$ the tensor products of Hermite polynomials:

$$H_k(x) H_\ell(y) = (-1)^{k+\ell} e^{x^2+y^2} \left[\frac{\partial}{\partial x}\right]^k \left[\frac{\partial}{\partial y}\right]^\ell e^{-x^2-y^2}, \quad k, \ell \geq 0.$$

One can equally well exploit the rotational symmetry of the measure, and consider, after changing to polar coordinates, the polynomials

$$P_{j,n-2j}(x, y) = L_j^{(n-2j)}(r^2) r^{n-2j} \cos(n-2j)\theta, \quad 0 \leq j \leq n/2,$$

$$Q_{j,n-2j}(x, y) = L_j^{(n-2j)}(r^2) r^{n-2j} \sin(n-2j)\theta, \quad 0 \leq j \leq n/2.$$

Here, the $L_j^{\cdot}$ are Laguerre polynomials. In spite of the stark difference between the chosen bases, the Christoffel–Darboux kernel is the same:

$$\begin{aligned} K_N^w(x, y; u, v) &= \sum_{k+\ell \leq N} H_k(x) H_k(u) H_\ell(y) H_\ell(v) \\ &= \sum_{n=0}^{N} \sum_{j=0}^{n/2} [P_{j,n-2j}(x, y) P_{j,n-2j}(u, v) + Q_{j,n-2j}(x, y) Q_{j,n-2j}(u, v)]. \end{aligned}$$

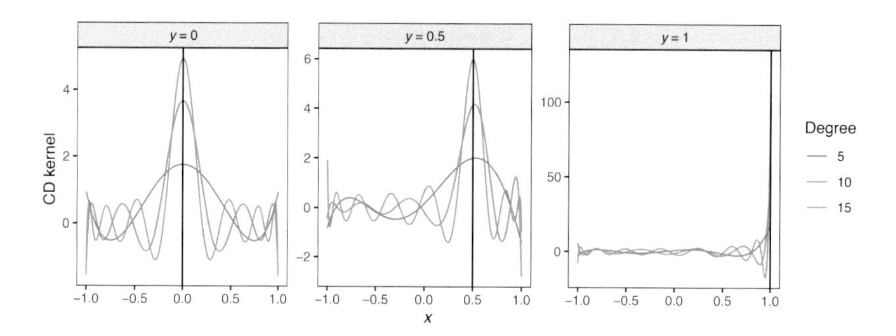

Figure 4.1 Representation of the function $x \mapsto K_n^\mu(x, y)$, for different values of y and different degree n. This figure illustrates the fact that, as the degree grows to infinity, the CD kernel approximates Dirac delta measures.

Explicit Computation from Moments: The following statement mirrors Proposition 2.2.4 in dimension 1 and highlights the accessibility and computation of the Christoffel–Darboux kernel from the truncated moment matrix.

Proposition 4.1.2 *Let $\mathbf{v}_n : \mathbb{R}^d \mapsto \mathbb{R}^{s(n)}$ be a vector whose entries correspond to a basis of $\mathbb{R}_n[\mathbf{x}]$. The moment matrix of μ in this basis is given by*

$$\mathbf{M}_{\mu,n} = \int_{\mathbb{R}^d} \mathbf{v}_n(\mathbf{x})\mathbf{v}_n(\mathbf{x})^T d\mu(\mathbf{x}) \in \mathbb{R}^{s(n)\times s(n)}. \tag{4.2}$$

For all $p\colon \mathbf{x} \mapsto \mathbf{c}_p^T \mathbf{v}_n(\mathbf{x})$ and $q\colon \mathbf{x} \mapsto \mathbf{c}_q^T \mathbf{v}_n(\mathbf{x})$ in $\mathbb{R}_n[\mathbf{x}]$, we have $\langle p, q\rangle_\mu = \mathbf{c}_p^T \mathbf{M}_{\mu,n} \mathbf{c}_q$. Hence $\mathbf{M}_{\mu,n}$ is invertible and, for all $\mathbf{x}, \mathbf{y} \in \mathbb{R}^d$, we infer

$$K_n^\mu : (\mathbf{x}, \mathbf{y}) \mapsto \mathbf{v}_n(\mathbf{x})^T \mathbf{M}_{\mu,n}^{-1} \mathbf{v}_n(\mathbf{y}). \tag{4.3}$$

It is interesting to interpret the polynomial $\mathbf{y} \mapsto K_n^\mu(\mathbf{x}, \mathbf{y})$ (and visualize it in dimension 1 or 2). With $\mathbf{x}$ fixed, consider the signed measure $\nu_\mathbf{x} := K_n^\mu(\mathbf{x}, \mathbf{y})\, \mu(d\mathbf{y})$ with polynomial "density" $\mathbf{y} \mapsto K_n^\mu(\mathbf{x}, \mathbf{y})$, with respect to μ. From the reproducing property of K_n^μ, for every $\alpha \in \mathbb{N}^n$ with $|\alpha| \leq n$,

$$\int \mathbf{y}^\alpha\, \nu_\mathbf{x}(d\mathbf{y}) = \int K_n^\mu(\mathbf{x}, \mathbf{y})\, \mathbf{y}^\alpha\, d\mu(\mathbf{y}) = \mathbf{x}^\alpha = \int \mathbf{y}^\alpha\, \delta_\mathbf{x}(d\mathbf{y}).$$

Hence the signed measure $\nu_\mathbf{x}$ "mimics" the Dirac measure at $\mathbf{x}$ when considering only moments of order at most n.

In Figure 4.1 the function $\mathbf{x} \mapsto K_n^\mu(\mathbf{x}, \mathbf{y})$ is displayed for the Lebesgue measure μ restricted to $[-1, 1]$. Then, as expected, one may indeed see a "peak" at the point $\mathbf{y}$, which becomes sharper and sharper when n increases.

4.1.2 The Christoffel Function

The Christoffel Function and Equivalence of Norms: Recall that the reciprocal of the diagonal of the Christoffel–Darboux kernel is called the Christoffel function, and it is characterized by the following variational property (see the discussion relating to (2.2)), for all $\mathbf{x} \in \mathbb{R}^d$,

$$\begin{aligned}\Lambda_n^\mu(\mathbf{x}) = \frac{1}{K_n^\mu(\mathbf{x},\mathbf{x})} &= \min_{p\in\mathbb{R}_n[\mathbf{x}]} \int_{\mathbb{R}^d} p(\mathbf{z})^2 d\mu(\mathbf{z}) \quad \text{for } p(\mathbf{x}) = 1 \\ &= \min_{p\in\mathbb{R}_n[\mathbf{x}]} \frac{\int_{\mathbb{R}^d} p(\mathbf{z})^2 d\mu(\mathbf{z})}{p^2(\mathbf{x})} \quad \text{for } p(\mathbf{x}) \neq 0. \end{aligned} \tag{4.4}$$

Consequently,

$$K_n^\mu(\mathbf{x},\mathbf{x}) = \max_{p\in\mathbb{R}_n[\mathbf{x}]} \frac{p(\mathbf{x})^2}{\|p\|_{2,\mu}^2}, \quad \mathbf{x} \in \mathbb{R}^d.$$

Since the support S of the measure μ is compact, we find

$$\max_{\mathbf{x}\in S} K_n^\mu(\mathbf{x},\mathbf{x}) = \max_{\mathbf{x}\in S}\max_{p\in\mathbb{R}_n[\mathbf{x}]} \frac{p(\mathbf{x})^2}{\|p\|_{2,\mu}^2} = \max_{p\in\mathbb{R}_n[\mathbf{x}]}\max_{\mathbf{x}\in S} \frac{p(\mathbf{x})^2}{\|p\|_{2,\mu}^2} = \max_{p\in\mathbb{R}_n[\mathbf{x}]} \frac{\|p\|_S^2}{\|p\|_{2,\mu}^2},$$

where $\|p\|_S$ denotes the infinity norm on S. Whence

$$\|p\|_S^2 \leq \|p\|_{2,\mu}^2 \max_{\mathbf{x}\in S} K_n^\mu(\mathbf{x},\mathbf{x}), \quad p \in \mathbb{R}_n[\mathbf{x}]. \tag{4.5}$$

Owing to finite dimensionality the equality in (4.5) is attained.

Computation: One may obtain the Christoffel function Λ_μ^n explicitly in closed form for all $\mathbf{x}$ by inversion of the moment matrix $\mathbf{M}_{\mu,n}$. Indeed, by (4.3),

$$(\Lambda_n^\mu(\mathbf{x}))^{-1} = K_n^\mu(\mathbf{x},\mathbf{x}) = \mathbf{v}_n(\mathbf{x})^T \mathbf{M}_{\mu,n}^{-1} \mathbf{v}_n(\mathbf{x}), \quad \forall \mathbf{x} \in \mathbb{R}^d. \tag{4.6}$$

As this may be computationally costly, an alternative is to obtain $\Lambda_n^\mu(\mathbf{x})$ numerically at a specific point $\mathbf{x} \in \mathbb{R}^d$, only when needed, by solving (4.4). It turns out that the variational formulation (4.4) also reads

$$(\Lambda_n^\mu(\mathbf{x}))^{-1} = K_n^\mu(\mathbf{x},\mathbf{x}) = \min_{\mathbf{p}\in\mathbb{R}^{s(n)}} \{ \mathbf{p}^T \mathbf{M}_{\mu,n}\, \mathbf{p} : \ \mathbf{p}^T \mathbf{v}_n(\mathbf{x}) = 1 \}, \tag{4.7}$$

which is a *convex* quadratic optimization problem (because $\mathbf{M}_{\mu,n} \succ 0$) that can be solved efficiently for relatively large dimension of $\mathbf{M}_{\mu,n}$. If one thus avoids the costly inversion of $\mathbf{M}_{\mu,n}$, one obtains only the numerical value at $\mathbf{x}$. Its optimal solution is the vector of coefficients $\mathbf{p}^* \in \mathbb{R}^{s(n)}$ of the polynomial

$$\mathbf{z} \mapsto p^*(\mathbf{z}) = \Lambda_n^\mu(\mathbf{x})\, K_n^\mu(\mathbf{z},\mathbf{x}) = \frac{K_n^\mu(\mathbf{z},\mathbf{x})}{K_n^\mu(\mathbf{x},\mathbf{x})}. \tag{4.8}$$

Asymptotics for the Christoffel–Darboux kernel: We saw in the previous chapter that the asymptotic behavior of the CD kernel has been of central interest for more than a century, for multiple reasons. The importance of the same quest in several variables cannot be underestimated, although much less is known. From the statistician's point of view, such asymptotics are important due to the fact that the CD kernel encodes precise information about the support of the underlying measure and its Lebesgue decomposition into point masses, absolutely continuous part and singular part.

For instance, it is obvious from (4.1) that

$$\int_{\mathbb{R}^d} K_n^{\mu}(\mathbf{x}, \mathbf{x}) d\mu(\mathbf{x}) = s(n). \tag{4.9}$$

Since the kernel is positive definite, the typical values on the support of μ of the Christoffel–Darboux kernel are of order $s(n)$, which is equivalent to n^d for a fixed dimension d. This provides a rough idea of the correct order of magnitude, but a lot more can be said.

4.2 Explicit Asymptotics for Special Geometries

Extending univariate asymptotic results to measures on $\mathbb{R}^d$ has been a topic of interest for several decades. One natural way to attack this problem is to consider special support geometries, such as the unit ball, the cube, simplex, all carrying densities with special symmetries. In such contexts, the relation between the Christoffel–Darboux kernel and orthogonal polynomials allows us to leverage explicit computation of orthogonal bases on special sets. We refer the reader to Dunkl and Xu (2014) for a detailed account of this material. Below we confine ourselves to sketching a few relevant results.

4.2.1 The Euclidean Ball

Some specific measures supported on the unit Euclidean ball have been of great interest because the structure of associated orthogonal polynomials (e.g. spherical harmonics) is more transparent. For instance, the central symmetry offers a natural link to the univariate setting. We refer to Bos (1994), Bos et al. (1998) and Xu (1996, 1999) for significant advances. The following result provides an intuition of the phenomena in place.

Lemma 4.2.1 (Bos et al., 1998) *Let μ be the probability measure on the unit Euclidean ball with density*

$$\mathbf{x} \mapsto \frac{2}{\omega_d} \frac{1}{\sqrt{1 + \|\mathbf{x}\|_2^2}},$$

where ω_d is the area of the d-dimensional unit sphere in $\mathbb{R}^{d+1}$. Then,

$$\lim_{n\to\infty} \frac{K_n^\mu(\mathbf{x}, \mathbf{x})}{s(n)} = \begin{cases} 1 & \text{if } \|\mathbf{x}\|_2 < 1, \\ 2 & \text{if } \|\mathbf{x}\|_2 = 1. \end{cases}$$

The convergence is uniform on compact subsets of the interior of the ball.

The above phenomenon calls for two observations:

- In the interior of the ball the convergence rate is exactly $s(n)$, and a uniform limit (in a certain sense) exists.
- The asymptotics is linked to a special weight function, and a qualitative jump at the boundary is displayed.

For more general measures, typical results regarding asymptotics for the Christoffel–Darboux kernel involve the product of a specific weight function and a density term. This is illustrated in the following theorem.

Theorem 4.2.2 *Let μ_0 be the probability measure with density w_0 defined in Lemma 4.2.1. Let μ be absolutely continuous on the ball with density $\mathbf{x} \mapsto w(\mathbf{x})$ such that w/w_0 is symmetric, Lipschitz and positive. Then,*

$$\lim_{n\to\infty} \frac{K_n^\mu(\mathbf{x}, \mathbf{x})}{s(n)} = \frac{w_0(\mathbf{x})}{w(\mathbf{x})}$$

uniformly on compact subsets of the interior of the ball.

Under the conditions of Theorem 4.2.2, the limit of the reciprocal Christoffel function is notable:

$$\lim_{n\to\infty} s(n)\Lambda_n^\mu(\mathbf{x}) = Cw(\mathbf{x})\sqrt{1 + \|\mathbf{x}\|_2^2}$$

for a positive constant C. We clearly see that the limit involves a product of two factors:

- a density term which relates to the Lebesgue measure;
- an additional weight which relates to the geometry of the support. This weight would correspond to the asymptotics for the restriction of the Lebesgue measure to the unit ball.

We stress that the exact formula for the Christoffel–Darboux kernel corresponding to the Lebesgue measure on the unit ball has been revealed by Xu. According to Theorem 4.2.2, for Lebesgue measure μ restricted to the unit Euclidean ball one finds

$$\lim_{n\to\infty} \frac{K_n^\mu(0,0)}{s(n)} = \frac{2}{\omega_d}. \tag{4.10}$$

4.2.2 The Simplex

Let $\Delta_d = \left\{\mathbf{x} \in \mathbb{R}^d,\ x_i \geq 0,\ i = 1, \ldots, d,\ \sum_{i=1}^d x_i \leq 1\right\}$ be the standard d-dimensional simplex in $\mathbb{R}^d$.

Theorem 4.2.3 (Xu, 1999) *Let μ be the restriction of the Lebesgue measure to Δ_d. Then, uniformly on compact subsets in the interior of Δ_d, we have*

$$\lim_{n\to\infty} s(n)\Lambda_n^\mu(\mathbf{x}) = C\sqrt{\left(1 - \sum_{i=1}^d x_i\right)\prod_{i=1}^n x_i},$$

where C is a normalizing constant.

This result suggests that similar asymptotics as for the Euclidean ball may be obtained with a different weight related to the geometry of the simplex.

4.2.3 The Cube

Assume that μ is supported on the box with a product structure

$$d\mu(\mathbf{x}) = d\mu_1(x_1)\ldots d\mu_d(x_d).$$

As noted in Xu (1995), it is possible to construct orthogonal polynomials for μ given the orthogonal polynomials for each factor μ_j. A result in this direction is stated below.

Theorem 4.2.4 (Xu, 1995) *Let μ be supported on $[-1,1]^d$ with density $\mathbf{x} \mapsto \prod_{j=1}^d \frac{1}{\pi\sqrt{1-x_j^2}}$, then for all $\mathbf{x} \in [-1,1]^d$, we have*

$$\lim_{n\to\infty} s(n)\Lambda_n^\mu(\mathbf{x}) = 1.$$

The theorem reveals that the geometric weight related to the cube is the product of the weights found on the unit segment $[-1,1]$, as seen in the previous chapter.

4.3 Quantitative Asymptotics and the Bernstein–Markov Property

In this section we assume that the measure μ is supported on a compact set S. We provide quantitative bounds of the Christoffel function, both in the interior points of S and in the exterior of S. An exponential transition between the interior and exterior behavior of the support will emerge. To this end we recall the Bernstein–Markov property (of a measure) as the main technical tool needed in comparing the L^∞-norm with L^2-norm.

4.3.1 Asymptotics Outside the Domain

In their study of CD kernels, Kroó and Lubinsky introduced a needle polynomial which takes value 1 at the origin and is exponentially small in the unit Euclidean ball with the exception of a small neighborhood of the origin (Kroó and Lubinsky, 2013a). This polynomial can be used to provide explicit bounds on the Christoffel–Darboux kernel outside the support of μ.

Lemma 4.3.1 (Lasserre and Pauwels, 2019) *Assume μ is a positive Borel measure supported on the compact set $S \subset \mathbb{R}^d$. Let $\mathbf{x} \notin S$ and δ be such that* $\mathrm{dist}(\mathbf{x}, S) \geq \delta$*. Then, for any $n \in \mathbb{N}$, $n > 0$, we have*

$$\frac{K_n^\mu(\mathbf{x}, \mathbf{x})}{s(n)} \geq 2^{\frac{\delta n}{\delta + \mathrm{diam}(S)} - 3} n^{-d} \left(\frac{d}{e}\right)^d \exp\left(-\frac{d^2}{n}\right).$$

Note that in the above lemma no additional assumption on the geometry of the set S is made, for instance existence of interior points or smoothness of the boundary. An important feature for our envisaged applications are the explicit constants in the estimate above. From this result, we clearly infer that the dependency in n is exponential, the rate depending essentially on the distance to the domain. A more precise lower bound for the Christoffel function involves potential theoretic objects, whose numerical accessibility depends on the geometry of the set S.

4.3.2 Asymptotics Inside the Domain

The variational characterization in (4.4) allows us to infer the following: if the measure μ dominates μ_0 in the sense that $\mu_0(A) \leq \mu(A)$ for any measurable set A, then

$$K_n^\mu(\mathbf{x}, \mathbf{x}) \leq K_n^{\mu_0}(\mathbf{x}, \mathbf{x}), \quad \mathbf{x} \in \mathbb{R}^d. \tag{4.11}$$

This observation can be combined with the explicit asymptotics for the unit Euclidean ball (4.10) in order obtain the following result.

Lemma 4.3.2 (Lasserre and Pauwels, 2019) *Let μ be a positive Borel measure supported by S, the closure of a bounded domain U with nice boundary. Assume that $\mu|_U$ has a density with respect to the Lebesgue measure λ restricted to U, bounded from below by $c > 0$. Let $\delta > 0$ and $\mathbf{x} \in U$ such that* $\mathrm{dist}(\mathbf{x}, \partial U) \geq \delta$. *Then, for all $n \in \mathbb{N}$, $n > 0$,*

$$\frac{K_n^\mu(\mathbf{x}, \mathbf{x})}{s(n)} \leq 2\frac{\lambda(S)}{c\delta^d \omega_d}(1+d)^3,$$

where ω_d is the area of the d-dimensional unit sphere in $\mathbb{R}^{d+1}$ of μ.

Note that in the above lemma, the upper bound does not depend on n, so the magnitude of the Christoffel–Darboux kernel inside the support is a polynomial in n at most.

4.3.3 The Bernstein–Markov Property

At least for specific measures, the results mentioned in the previous sections highlight an exponential transition between the interior and the exterior rate of convergence of the associated CD kernel. However, these results do not shed any light regarding what happens at the boundary of the domain. Recall the one-dimensional setting described by Theorem 3.4.3. Examples of explicit computation on simple supports (e.g. simplex or cube) carrying Lebesgue measure with an integrable weight, or as in Lemma 4.2.1, suggest that the behavior on the boundary is related to the dimensional structure of the corresponding face. In order to obtain further qualitative description for Christoffel–Darboux asymptotics, a standard assumption is to ensure that the asymptotic behavior on the boundary of the domain still obeys the exponential dichotomy.

Definition 4.3.3 We say that a compactly supported measure μ satisfies the Bernstein–Markov property if there exists a sequence of positive numbers $(M_n)_{n\in\mathbb{N}}$ such that, for all $n \in \mathbb{N}$ and $p \in \mathbb{R}_n[\mathbf{x}]$, we have

$$\|p\|_S \leq M_n \cdot \|p\|_{2,\mu}$$

and $\lim_{n\to\infty} \frac{\log(M_n)}{n} = 0$.

It is convenient sometimes to formulate the Bernstein–Markov property as follows: for every $\epsilon > 0$ there exists a constant C_ϵ such that

$$\|p\|_S \leq C_\epsilon (1+\epsilon)^{\deg p} \|p\|_{2,\mu}, \quad p \in \mathbb{R}[\mathbf{x}].$$

Further discussion on this property is given in Section 4.4.

In other terms,

$$K_n^{\mu}(\mathbf{x},\mathbf{x}) \leq C_\epsilon(1+\epsilon)^n, \quad n \in \mathbb{N}$$

Hence the Bernstein–Markov property turns out to be equivalent to

$$\limsup_{n\to\infty} \max_{\mathbf{x}\in S} \frac{\log\left(K_n^{\mu}(\mathbf{x},\mathbf{x})\right)}{n} = 0.$$

In light of the remarks of the previous section, this condition ensures that the rate of growth of the kernel is qualitatively similar on the boundary and in the interior of S and different from the exponential growth outside the support. Quantitative versions of the Bernstein–Markov property can be formulated for special geometric properties of the support using results in Section 4.2. For example, if the boundary of S is an embedded C^1 hypersurface with Lipschitz normal vector (seen as an element of the ambient space; see Walther (1999)), then a combination of (4.11) and explicit asymptotics on the Euclidean ball allow us to provide quantitative bounds for M_n in Definition 4.3.3.

4.4 Qualitative Asymptotics

In this section we reproduce a few general asymptotic estimates for the Christoffel–Darboux kernel. The results we state below are less numerically explicit in a prescribed degree, but on the other hand they are precise in the limit. The one-dimensional context is an ideal comparison basis in this respect.

4.4.1 Uniform Convergence on Compact Sets

The following result of Kroó and Lubinsky (2013a) is an extension of the particular computations obtained for special domains.

Theorem 4.4.1 (Kroó and Lubinsky, 2013a) *Let μ_0 be supported on set S such that, uniformly on compact subsets of* int(S),

$$\lim_{n\to\infty} s(n)\,\Lambda_n^{\mu_0}(\mathbf{x}) = W_0(\mathbf{x}),$$

where W_0 is continuous and positive on int(S). *Assume that μ has continuous and positive density D, with respect to μ_0 on* int(S). *Then, uniformly on compact subsets of* int(S),

$$\lim_{n\to\infty} s(n)\,\Lambda_n^{\mu}(\mathbf{x}) = W_0(\mathbf{x})D(\mathbf{x}).$$

This can be combined with results described in Section 4.2, for example, to describe more general asymptotics for measures supported on special sets.

4.4.2 Qualitative Limiting Behaviour

Exponential divergence: A more detailed account of the following function, together with examples, is provided in the Notes and Sources section. We limit ourselves to stating the definition in this section.

Definition 4.4.2 (Siciak extremal function) For any $\mathbf{x} \in \mathbb{R}^d$, let

$$V_S(\mathbf{x}) = \sup \left\{ \frac{\log |p(\mathbf{x})|}{\deg p}, \ \|p\|_S \leq 1, \ \deg p > 0 \right\}.$$

The definition of Siciak's function extends without change to $\mathbb{C}^d$. A compact subset $S \subset \mathbb{R}^d$ is called *regular* if Siciak's function is continuous in the whole space. Our initial assumption on S to be the closure of a domain with nice boundary assures its regularity (Pawłucki and Pleśniak, 1986). The following is a reformulation of the same result presented in the Notes and Sources section to the special setting of this section.

Theorem 4.4.3 (Bloom and Shiffman, 2007) *Assume the pair (S, μ) satisfies Bernstein–Markov property in Definition 4.3.3. Then,*

$$\lim_{n \to \infty} \frac{1}{2n} \log K_n^\mu(\mathbf{x}, \mathbf{x}) = V_S(\mathbf{x}) \tag{4.12}$$

uniformly on compact subsets of $\mathbb{R}^d$.

In view of the results described in Section 4.2, V_S is positive in the exterior of S. Furthermore, from Definition 4.3.3, V_S vanishes on S. The information carried by the preceding theorem essentially lies in the exterior of S, where we note

$$\lim_n [\Lambda_n^\mu(\mathbf{z})]^{\frac{1}{2n}} = e^{-V_S(\mathbf{z})} < 1 \tag{4.13}$$

locally uniformly on $\mathbb{R}^d \setminus S$.

Weak-$*$ limits: Recall that a sequence of (probability) measures μ_n supported on (compact) S converges in the weak-$*$ topology to the measure μ if, for any continuous function ϕ on S,

$$\int_S \phi(\mathbf{x}) d\mu_i(\mathbf{x}) \underset{i \to \infty}{\to} \int_S \phi(\mathbf{x}) d\mu(\mathbf{x}).$$

To give an idea of weak-$*$ convergence, consider the sequence of measures $\mu_n = \sin(nt)dt$ on the interval $[0, \pi]$. According to the Riemann–Lebesgue Lemma, for every continuous function ϕ on $[0, \pi]$,

$$\lim_{n\to\infty} \int_0^{\pi} \phi(t)\sin(nt)dt = 0.$$

Hence weak-$*$ $\lim_{n\to\infty} \mu_n = 0$.

Theorem 4.4.4 (Berman et al., 2011) *Assume the pair (S, μ) possesses the Bernstein–Markov property. Then there exists a probability measure μ_S supported on S such that*

$$\text{weak-}*\ \lim_{n\to\infty} \frac{\mu}{s(n)\Lambda_n^{\mu}} = \mu_S,$$

that is, $\displaystyle\lim_{n\to\infty} \int_S \frac{\phi}{s(n)\,\Lambda_n^{\mu}}\,d\mu = \int_S \phi\,d\mu_S$*, for all continuous functions* ϕ.

The limit μ_S is called the *equilibrium measure* and it is a central object of study in potential theory. An interesting feature of the equilibrium measure is that it can be approximated by discrete measures that solve a certain equidistribution/variational problem; for more details see the Notes and Sources section at the end of this chapter.

4.4.3 Complex Versus Real Variables

Following the conclusions of the one-variable case, it is natural and necessary to treat measures supported by $\mathbb{R}^d$ as operating on complex polynomials, with complex point evaluations (recall Marcel Riesz's fundamental results) and so on. The Christoffel–Darboux kernel is constructed *mutatis mutandis* by considering $\mathbf{z} = (z_1, \ldots, z_d)$ a vector of d complex variables, replacing absolute values by modulus, symmetric bilinear forms functions by hermitian functions and working on the space $\mathbb{C}_n[\mathbf{z}]$ instead of $\mathbb{R}_n[\mathbf{x}]$. In this way the powerful tools of function theory of several complex variables enters into the scene, with deep impact on purely real statements. We will provide in the Notes and Sources section a few details in this direction, belonging to a rich and very dynamic field of modern mathematical analysis known as pluripotential theory.

We touch on a single illustrative situation. Seeing $\mathbb{R}^d$ as a subset of $\mathbb{C}^d$, or $\mathbb{C}^d$ as equal to $\mathbb{R}^{2d}$, produces quite different CD kernels. We consider the unit disk in $\mathbb{C} = \mathbb{R}^2$.

The real picture is quite general. We start by reproducing Xu's computations for the Christoffel functions of certain rotationally invariant weights in the unit ball of $\mathbb{R}^d$. Let $\theta \geq 0$ be a parameter, and consider the measure

$$\mu_\theta = \omega_\theta(1 - \|\mathbf{x}\|^2)^{\theta-\frac{1}{2}}\chi_{\|x\|\leq 1}d\mathbf{x},$$

where $\mathbf{x} = (x_1, x_2, \ldots, x_d) \in \mathbb{R}^d$. The constant ω_θ is chosen so that the measure μ_θ has total mass 1.

The orthogonal polynomials $(P_\alpha)_{\alpha \in \mathbb{N}^d}$ associated with this measure can be expressed in terms of ultra-spherical polynomials of one variable; see Xu (1996). The asymptotics of the respective Christoffel–Darboux kernel is

$$\lim_{n\to\infty} \frac{\sum_{|\alpha|\le n} |P_\alpha(\mathbf{x})|^2}{\binom{n+d}{d}} = \frac{\omega_0}{\omega_\theta}(1 - \|\mathbf{x}\|^2)^{-\theta}, \quad \mathbf{x} \in \mathbb{R}^d, \ \|\mathbf{x}\| < 1.$$

In case $\|\mathbf{x}\| = 1$ one finds the above limit to be infinity for $\theta > 0$ and $\frac{1}{2}$ for $\theta = 0$. For details and comments see Xu (1996).

Let us consider the particular case $d = 2$ and $\theta = 1/2$. The measure is then simply the normalized area measure $\frac{dA}{\pi}$ of the unit disk $\mathbb{D} \subset \mathbb{C}$. Taking advantage of the complex coordinate $z = x_1 + ix_2$, one can speak of the associated complex orthogonal polynomials and their Christoffel function. In the previous chapter we called them Bergman orthogonal polynomials (Section 3.4.2):

$$Q_n(z) = \sqrt{n+1}\, z^n, \quad n \ge 0.$$

Note the slight difference due to the normalized measure $\frac{dA}{\pi}$ versus dA. The limit of the complex Christoffel function is therefore

$$^{\mathbb{C}}\Lambda^{\mathbb{D}}(z) = \lim_n \frac{1}{\sum_{k=0}^n (k+1)|z|^{2k}} = (1 - |z|^2)^2 = (1 - \|\mathbf{x}\|^2)^2, \quad \|\mathbf{x}\| < 1,$$

and it is quite different from the real one:

$$\begin{aligned} {}^{\mathbb{R}}\Lambda_n^{\mathbb{D}}(\mathbf{x}) &= \frac{1}{\sum_{|\alpha|\le n} |P_\alpha(\mathbf{x})|^2} \sim \frac{\omega_0}{\omega_{1/2}} \frac{2}{(n+2)(n+1)} \sqrt{1 - \|\mathbf{x}\|^2} \\ &= \frac{1}{(n+2)(n+1)} \sqrt{1 - \|\mathbf{x}\|^2}, \quad \|\mathbf{x}\| < 1, \end{aligned}$$

so that $\lim_{n\to\infty} \frac{n^2}{2}\, {}^{\mathbb{R}}\Lambda_n^{\mathbb{D}}(\mathbf{x}) = \sqrt{1 - \|\mathbf{x}\|^2}$, whenever $\|\mathbf{x}\| < 1$.

4.5 Notes and Sources

Sections 4.1–4.2: Orthogonal polynomials in several variables appeared early, for instance in relation to special functions or distinguished bases in commutative algebra (Appell, 1890; Gröbner, 1948). The memoir by Koornwinder (1975) contains a rich collection of orthogonal polynomials attached to simple geometric shapes. See also Ricci (1978). Suetin (1999) deals exclusively with orthogonal polynomials in two real variables. The reference monograph for the modern reader is Dunkl and Xu (2014).

As a matter of fact Kroó and Lubinsky prove in the same articles a universality in the bulk result, allowing varying points in the argument of the Christoffel function (Kroó and Lubinsky, 2013a,b). The main results were generalized by Kroó to convex and starlike domains (Kroó, 2015). Similar formulae to those due to Kroó and Lubinsky were obtained for specific weights by Bos and collaborators (Bos, 1989, 1994; Bos et al., 1998). Yuan Xu provided early closed form asymptotics for the Christoffel function on a collection of special weights supported by a ball, cube or simplex (Xu, 1995, 1996, 1999). The inner behavior of the real 2D Christoffel function in a planar domain with corners in its boundary is discussed in Prymak and Usoltseva (2019).

Sections 4.3–4.4: A guide to further reading: *Pluripotential theory* is a multivariate generalization of logarithmic potential theory, with pluriharmonic functions representing the real part of analytic functions of several complex variables. The differences between the two theories are sensible. The monograph by Klimek (1991) is an authoritative reference, although there have been many developments since then. In this subsection all positive measures are defined on $\mathbb{C}^d$, with fast decay at infinity. We test these measures on multivariate polynomials with complex coefficients.

Roughly speaking, the Christoffel function attached to a positive measure μ quantifies how big the modulus $|p|$ of a polynomial is at a prescribed point, under the square norm normalization $\|p\|_{2,\mu} \le 1$. In many instances, including one-variable settings, it is convenient to separate the above extremal problem from the measure μ, and consider first a purely geometric, uniform norm variational problem. We offer a few indications in this direction.

Siciak's extremal function. Let $E \subset \mathbb{C}^d$ be a compact set, fix a point $\mathbf{w} \in \mathbb{C}^d$, exterior to E, and seek the largest value of $|p(\mathbf{w})|$ for a polynomial $p \in \mathbb{C}_n[\mathbf{z}]$ of degree at most n, normalized by $\|p\|_E = \|p\|_{\infty,E} = \sup_{\mathbf{z}\in E} |p(\mathbf{z})| \le 1$. The following expression, known as the *Siciak extremal function*, encodes this maximal value:

$$V_E(w) = \sup\left\{\frac{\log|p(w)|}{\deg p},\ \|p\|_E \le 1,\ \deg p > 0\right\}. \tag{4.14}$$

In other words,

$$|p(\mathbf{w})| \le \|p\|_E\, e^{V_E(\mathbf{w})\deg p}, \quad p \in \mathbb{C}[\mathbf{z}].$$

The case $d = 1$ brings us back to harmonic functions, as the upper-semi-continuous envelope V_E^* of V_E coincides with the Green function of the complement,

$$V_E^*(\mathbf{w}) = g_{\mathbb{C}\setminus E}(\mathbf{w}, \infty), \quad \mathbf{w} \notin E;$$

compare to (3.6). In several variables the function $\mathbf{w} \mapsto \ln|p(\mathbf{w})|$ is pluri-subharmonic, that is, it is subharmonic along complex lines. The foundational work of Siciak (1962), complemented by the contributions of Baran (1988, 1992), are recommended for the early accounts of the Siciak extremal problem. Regular sets E carry by definition a Siciak function V_E which is continuous on $\mathbb{C}^d$. Various regularity conditions are known; see Klimek (1991).

Siciak's extremal function is central to several deep results in approximation theory, and in particular it is instrumental in computing the asymptotics of the Christoffel function associated with an important class of measures supported on E. The beauty and strength of this approach lies in the fact that Siciak's function can be computed on simple geometric shapes.

Examples of extremal functions. We start with the interval $E = [-1, 1] \subset \mathbb{C}$. For a *real coefficient* polynomial $p \in \mathbb{R}[z]$ of degree $n \geq 1$, it is known that, for any point $w \in \mathbb{C}$, $|w| \geq 1$, the inequality

$$|p(w)| \leq |T_n(w)|, \quad \|p\|_{[-1,1]} \leq 1$$

holds. The above $T_n(\cos t) = \cos(nt)$ is the Chebyshev polynomial of the first kind. For w real this is a well-known extremal characterization of Chebyshev polynomials. For w complex, the inequality was established by Erdős in 1947. As a matter of fact the above inequality remains valid for w real and complex polynomials. All in all, these observations lead to a closed form of Siciak extremal function for the interval

$$V_{[-1,1]}(z) = \sup_n \frac{\log|T_n(z)|}{n} = \log|z + \sqrt{z^2 - 1}|, \quad z \in \mathbb{C} \setminus [-1, 1]. \tag{4.15}$$

The branch of the square root is chosen so that $|z + \sqrt{z^2 - 1}| \geq 1$. The level sets of the Green function $\log|z + \sqrt{z^2 - 1}|$ are confocal ellipses with foci ± 1.

Next, consider $E = \overline{\mathbb{D}} \subset \mathbb{C}$, the closed unit disk. One finds from the maximum principle for subharmonic functions that

$$|p(w)| \leq \|p\|_{\mathbb{D}} |w|^n, \quad p \in \mathbb{C}[z], \ \deg p = n, \ |w| > 1.$$

Therefore,

$$V_{\overline{\mathbb{D}}}(w) = \log|w|, \quad |w| > 1.$$

More generally, if $\eta(\mathbf{x})$ is a norm in $\mathbb{R}^d$, and

$$E = B_\eta(1) = \{\mathbf{x} \in \mathbb{R}^d, \eta(\mathbf{x}) \leq 1\}$$

is the closed unit ball with respect to it, then it is known that

$$V_{B_\eta(1)}(\mathbf{x}) = \log(\eta(\mathbf{x}) + \sqrt{\eta(\mathbf{x})^2 - 1}), \quad \eta(\mathbf{x}) > 1.$$

Note that $B_\eta(1)$ can be any convex and balanced set which contains the origin in its interior. Similarly, for a norm $\kappa(\mathbf{z})$ on $\mathbb{C}^d$ and the ball

$$E = B_\kappa(1) = \{\mathbf{z} \in \mathbb{C}^d, \ \kappa(\mathbf{z}) \leq 1\},$$

one computes

$$V_{B_\kappa(1)}(\mathbf{z}) = \log \kappa(\mathbf{z}), \quad \kappa(\mathbf{z}) > 1.$$

Equilibrium measure. Given a compact subset $E \subset \mathbb{C}^d$ on can speak of its *equilibrium measure* μ_E, in the sense of pluripotential theory. This measure minimizes an energy functional, very much as the classical equilibrium measure in one complex variable minimizes the logarithmic potential energy. A great deal of geometric and analytic information is carried by the equilibrium measure.

We recall the standard one-dimensional setting of $E = [-1, 1] \subset \mathbb{C}$. Then $\mu_{[-1,1]} = \frac{dx}{\pi\sqrt{1-x^2}}$. Or, if $E = \overline{\mathbb{D}} \subset \mathbb{C}$, then $\mu_{\overline{\mathbb{D}}} = \frac{d\theta}{2\pi}$, where $\theta = \arg z$. In higher dimension, if S is a compact subset of $\mathbb{R}^d$, then the measure μ_S is absolutely continuous on the interior of S with respect to the Lebesgue volume measure in $\mathbb{R}^d$ (Bedford and Taylor, 1986). In general no closed form for the equilibrium measure is known, with the exception of a few special geometric shapes. For instance, for compact convex subsets S of $\mathbb{R}^d$ with interior points, an exact formula for μ_S appears in Burns et al. (2010).

For a fixed degree n, one can select a linear basis of polynomial functions restricted to E, say $\mathbf{v_n} = (\mathbf{v_1}, \ldots, \mathbf{v_{N(n)}})$. An optimal way to spread a discrete set $\{\mathbf{u}_1, \ldots, \mathbf{u}_{N(n)}\}$ on E is to maximize the Vandermonde determinant:

$$\max_{\mathbf{u}_1,\ldots,\mathbf{u}_{N(n)} \in E} \left|\det\begin{pmatrix} \mathbf{v}_n(\mathbf{u}_1) & \mathbf{v}_n(\mathbf{u}_2) & \ldots & \mathbf{v}_n(\mathbf{u}_{N(n)}) \end{pmatrix}\right|.$$

The optimal configuration $\mathbf{a}_1^n, \mathbf{a}_2^n, \ldots, \mathbf{a}_{N(n)}^n$ bears the name of *Fekete points* and it plays a predominant role in constructive approximation theory. For our specific purposes, the following recent result is notable.

Theorem 4.5.1 (Berman et al., 2011) *Let $E \subset \mathbb{C}^d$ be a regular compact set with equilibrium measure μ_E and configurations of Fekete points $\mathbf{a}_1^n, \mathbf{a}_2^n, \ldots, \mathbf{a}_{N(n)}^n$, $n \geq 1$. Assume that Siciak's function V_E is continuous everywhere on $\mathbb{C}^d$. Then, for every continuous function ϕ on E,*

$$\lim_{n\to\infty} \frac{\phi(\mathbf{a}_1^n) + \phi(\mathbf{a}_2^n) + \cdots + \phi(\mathbf{a}_{N(n)}^n)}{N(n)} = \int_E \phi \, d\mu_E.$$

In standard terminology, the counting measures of Fekete points converge in the weak-$*$ topology to the equilibrium measure. A compact set $E \subset \mathbb{C}^d$ is called *regular* if Siciak's extremal function V_E is continuous everywhere on $\mathbb{C}^d$. For instance, all closed unit balls with respect to an arbitrary norm are regular.

Bernstein–Markov property. Let $E \subset \mathbb{C}^d$ be a compact set and let μ be a positive Borel measure supported by E. The definition of the *Bernstein–Markov property* (see Definition 4.3.3) is generally stated for complex polynomials; the pair (E, μ) satisfies this property if there is a sequence of positive constants M_n, $n \geq 0$, satisfying $\limsup_n M_n^{1/n} = 1$ and

$$\|p\|_E \leq M_n \cdot \|p\|_{2,\mu}, \quad p \in \mathbb{C}[\mathbf{z}], \ \deg p \leq n. \tag{4.16}$$

The terminology is rooted in Serguei Bernstein's classical one-complex-variable inequality

$$\|q'\|_{\mathbb{D}} \leq (\deg q)\, \|q\|_{\mathbb{D}}, \quad q \in \mathbb{C}[\mathbf{z}].$$

We state the following simple criterion.

Proposition 4.5.2 *Let μ be a positive measure on $\mathbb{C}^d$, with a compact and regular support $E = \operatorname{supp}(\mu)$. The pair (E, μ) satisfies the Bernstein–Markov property if there exists $\delta > 0$ and $\alpha > 0$ satisfying:*

$$\mu(B(\mathbf{a}, r)) \geq r^{\alpha}, \quad \mathbf{a} \in E, \ r < \delta.$$

We remark that the equilibrium measure μ_E of every regular compact subset $E \subset \mathbb{C}^d$ produces a pair (E, μ_E) with the Bernstein–Markov property.

Christoffel function asymptotics. At this stage we can relate the asymptotics of the Christoffel function to the Siciak extremal function. We have already mentioned the results below in the case of subsets of real Euclidean space. Their natural framework is in complex space.

Theorem 4.5.3 (Bloom and Shiffman, 2007) *Assume the pair (E, μ) satisfies the Bernstein–Markov property and E is a regular compact set. Then*

$$\lim_n \frac{1}{2n} \log K_n^{\mu}(\mathbf{z}, \mathbf{z}) = V_E(\mathbf{z}) \tag{4.17}$$

uniformly on compact subsets of $\mathbb{C}^d$.

We recall that $K_n^{\mu}(\mathbf{z}, \mathbf{w}) = \sum_{j=0}^{N(n)} P_j(\mathbf{z})\overline{P_j(\mathbf{w})}$, where $P_1, \ldots, P_{N(n)}$ is an orthonormal sequence of the subspace of $L^2(\mu)$ generated by all complex polynomials of degree at most n. In other words,

$$\lim_{n \to \infty} [\, \Lambda_n^{\mu}(\mathbf{z})\,]^{\frac{1}{2n}} = e^{-V_E(\mathbf{z})} \tag{4.18}$$

locally uniformly on $\mathbb{C}^d$.

A stronger convergence result for the Christoffel function is contained in the following theorem.

Theorem 4.5.4 (Berman et al., 2011) *Assume the pair (E, μ) satisfies the Bernstein–Markov property and E is a regular compact set. Then*

$$\lim_{n \to \infty} \frac{d\mu}{N(n)\, \Lambda_n^{\mu}} = \mu_E,$$

as a weak-$*$ limit.

It is worth mentioning that the above result is actually much more generally stated on abstract manifolds, allowing us to consider measures supported on algebraic sets for example.

A lucid presentation of pluripotential theory with an additional weight (or external field) is Bloom and Levenberg (2003). For the Bernstein–Markov property in higher dimensions we refer to the survey Bloom et al. (2015). Theorem 4.5.3 has appeared in Bloom and Shiffman (2007). The revolutionary works of Berman and collaborators were motivated by complex geometry and statistical physics (Berman et al., 2011). More refined aspects of Markov–Bernstein inequalities can be found in Baran et al. (2013) and Daras (2014).

Numerical methods for computing or approximating the extremal function, the distribution of Fekete points, equilibrium measure and associated orthogonal polynomials on a compact subset of $\mathbb{R}^d$ are developed in Piazzon (2019b).

5
Singular Supports

In this chapter we are concerned with measures supported by 'thin' subsets of Euclidean space. These are measures that are singular with respect to Lebesgue volume measure, and the main tools (orthogonal polynomials, CD kernel, asymptotics) have to be adapted and restricted to the new framework. The only meaningful case is for supports S contained in an algebraic set (that is, a zero set of polynomial equations in $\mathbb{C}^d$ or in $\mathbb{R}^d$). Fortunately, there is ample theoretical work (to be outlined in the Notes and Sources section) for this refinement in Christoffel–Darboux analysis.

The motivation will become transparent in Chapter 7 where, briefly, we will treat and analyze clouds of points (the set S) lying in some algebraic set V of $\mathbb{R}^n$ (for instance think of data points on some subset S of the unit sphere $V := \mathbb{S}^{n-1}$ or on the torus). Often, in practical applications, the set $S \subset V$ of interest (data points) is obtained with some uncertainty (e.g. coming from error measurements). In some situations the uncertainty refers to the precise location *on* V while in some other situations, noise may lead to measurements of data points close to such a set $S \subset V$ but not exactly on V. We argue that there are intrinsic connections between both situations using a continuity argument. We also believe that understanding the more general noisy setting requires understanding the, sometimes ideal, noiseless setting.

5.1 Preliminary Material

While the RKHS and CD kernel setting is still appropriate, its precise description needs some care, and, similarly, some results of previous chapters need to be adapted or require some additional assumptions. For instance, if

$S \subset \mathbb{R}^d$ is contained in a real algebraic subvariety V of the Euclidean space $\mathbb{R}^d$, then

$$\langle p, q \rangle_\mu = \int_S p(\mathbf{x})\, q(\mathbf{x})\, d\mu(\mathbf{x}), \quad p, q \in \mathbb{R}[\mathbf{x}]$$

is not a valid scalar product on $L^2(\mu)$ anymore. Indeed the set

$$I(\mu) := \left\{ p \in \mathbb{R}[\mathbf{x}] \colon \int_S p^2\, d\mu = 0 \right\}$$

is a nontrivial ideal of $\mathbb{R}[\mathbf{x}]$ which contains all polynomials that are annihilated by the measure μ on S.

For illustration purposes let μ be the arc length measure on the circle $S := \{\mathbf{x} = (x, y) \in \mathbb{R}^2\ x^2 + y^2 = 1\} \subset \mathbb{R}^2$. Then,

$$\int_S x^3\, d\mu = \int_S (x - xy^2)\, d\mu.$$

Thus, it is not clear how to define orthogonal polynomials with respect to μ without reordering the monomials $x^k y^\ell$ and excluding the redundant ones $x^{k+2} y^\ell \sim x^k y^\ell - x^k y^{\ell+2}$. This operation can be done invariantly, at the cost of accepting some algebraic terminology. In particular, the associated space of polynomials on S of degree at most n has dimension strictly less than $\binom{d+n}{n}$, and to define a valid scalar product on $L^2(\mu)$ one has to quotient $\mathbb{R}_n[\mathbf{x}]$ by the ideal $I(\mu) \subset \mathbb{R}[\mathbf{x}]$ of polynomials vanishing on V.

To this end, let us have a closer look at the ideal $I(\mu)$. First we prove the converse, namely that

$$\int |p|^2 d\mu = 0$$

implies that the polynomial p vanishes on the support of μ. Let $a \in \operatorname{supp}(\mu)$. Assume by contradiction that $p(a) \neq 0$. We can assume by rescaling that there exists $\delta > 0$ such that $|p(x)| \geq 1$ for $|x - a| \leq \delta$. Then

$$\int_{|x-a| \leq \delta} d\mu(x) \leq \int_{|x-a| \leq \delta} |p|^2 d\mu \leq \int |p|^2 d\mu = 0,$$

a contradiction. Thus, we have proved that $I(\mu)$ is a real ideal, that is, if $p^{2n} + \sigma \in I(\mu)$, for some integer $n \geq 1$ and a sum of squares σ, then $f \in I(\mu)$. An ideal $I \subset \mathbb{R}[\mathbf{x}]$ is called a *real* ideal if $p_1^2 + p_2^2 + \cdots + p_m^2 \in I$ implies each $p_j \in I,\ 1 \leq j \leq m$. Note that every real ideal is radical. The *Zariski closure* of a set $S \subset \mathbb{R}^d$ is the common zero set of all polynomials vanishing on S. It is a real algebraic variety with possible singular points, and obviously extends to the complex Zariski closure, which lies in $\mathbb{C}^d$.

But there is more to highlight, in the spirit of the classical Nullstellensatz. The duality between ideals and their geometric support (i.e. common zeros) can go very wrong over the real field. For instance, in two variables $(x, y) \in \mathbb{R}^2$, the origin is the zero set of each element $x^{2n} + y^{2m}, \; n, m \geq 1$. This variety has codimension 2, although it is given by a single equation, and two polynomials sharing it as a zero set do not divide each other.

An array of important results correct such deviations from the complex algebraic geometry intuition. We mention only a couple of theorems, relevant for the subsequent more applied chapters.

Theorem 5.1.1 (Dubois–Risler) *Let $J \subset \mathbb{R}[\mathbf{x}]$ be a real ideal. A polynomial p which vanishes on the real zero set of J also vanishes on the complex zero set of J, and hence there exists a positive integer n, such that $p^n \in J$.*

For principal ideals we state the following useful criterion.

Theorem 5.1.2 (Dubois and Efroymson, 1970) *A nonzero polynomial $p \in \mathbb{R}[\mathbf{x}]$ generates a real ideal if and only if it is a square-free product of irreducible polynomials $p = q_1 q_2 \dots q_m$ and each q_j assumes both positive and negative values in $\mathbb{R}^d$.*

The original proof is in Dubois and Efroymson (1970). Later developments and similar results can be found in Lam (1984), Bochnak et al. (1998) and Prestel and Delzell (2001).

An example and a warning. Consider the measure

$$p \mapsto \int_{-1}^{0} p\left(t, \sqrt{t(t^2 - 1)}\right) dt, \quad p \in \mathbb{R}[x, y],$$

where the square root has positive values. The Zariski closure of the support of this measure is described by the equation

$$V = \{(x, y) \in \mathbb{R}^2, \; y^2 = x(x^2 - 1)\},$$

with principal ideal generated by the irreducible polynomial $y^2 - x(x^2 - 1)$. According to the above mentioned theorem, this ideal is real, and contrary to common sense, the variety V (well known under the name of elliptic curve) has *two connected components* with respect to the topology of $\mathbb{R}^2$, although the measure consists of integration along a *connected arc*.

5.2 The CD Kernel on a Real Variety

It is well known that the moment matrix $\mathbf{M}_{\mu,n}$ contains all information needed to construct (with some additional adjustments) orthonormal polynomials, the Christoffel–Darboux kernel and the Christoffel function.

The central thesis of the whole book is the relevance of these structured data to more refined questions relating to inverse problems. Specifically we state the leading paradigm as follows:

- *The geometry of the supporting variety* can be deduced from simple matrix analysis manipulations of the moment matrix, related to a sophisticated concept of algebraic geometry, the *Hilbert function* associated with a variety.
- Asymptotic evaluations of the associated CD kernel decode the *nature of the generating measure.*

Consider a measure μ whose support S is contained in its Zariski closure, a real algebraic variety $V \subset \mathbb{R}^d$. Let $I(\mu)$ be the corresponding real ideal.

Recall Definition 4.2 of the moment matrix $\mathbf{M}_{\mu,n}$ associated with μ. Let $0 \neq p \in \mathbb{R}_n[\mathbf{x}]$ be an element of $I(\mu)$ such that p vanishes on V. Then, as $S \subset V$,

$$\langle \mathbf{p}, \mathbf{M}_{\mu,n}\, \mathbf{p} \rangle \;=\; \int_S p^2 \, d\mu \;=\; 0,$$

which shows that $\mathbf{M}_{\mu,n}$ is singular. Therefore the characterization (4.3) of the CD kernel K_n^μ in Proposition 4.1.2 is not valid anymore because $\mathbf{M}_{\mu,n}$ is not invertible.

5.2.1 Construction of the Christoffel–Darboux Kernel

The vector subspace $\mathbb{R}_n[\mathbf{x}] + I(\mu) \subset L^2(\mu)$ is infinite dimensional, preventing a natural definition of orthogonal polynomials. But as a matter of fact, the consecutive quotients in the filtration given by these subspaces are finite dimensional. This follows from the observation that

$$\frac{\mathbb{R}_n[\mathbf{x}] + I(\mu)}{I(\mu)} \simeq \frac{\mathbb{R}_n[\mathbf{x}]}{\mathbb{R}_n[\mathbf{x}] \cap I(\mu)} =: L_n^2(\mu)$$

is a finite-dimensional subspace of $L^2(\mu)$ which, equipped with the (genuine) scalar product

$$\langle p, q \rangle_\mu \;:=\; \int_S p\, q \, d\mu, \qquad p, q \in L_n^2(\mu),$$

is a Hilbert space (with norm $\|\cdot\|_\mu$).

Next, the pointwise evaluation map $p \mapsto \delta_{\mathbf{x}}(p) := p(\mathbf{x})$, $p \in L^2(\mu)$, is continuous with respect to $\|\cdot\|_\mu$, and therefore, from Chapter 2, $L_n^2(\mu)$ is an RKHS. To characterize its Christoffel–Darboux kernel K_n^μ, let $\mathbb{P}_n = (p_1^n, p_2^n, \ldots, p_{m_n}^n)$ be a row vector of polynomials in $\mathbb{R}_n[\mathbf{x}]$ which defines an orthonormal basis of the orthogonal complement $(\mathbb{R}_n[\mathbf{x}] + I(\mu)) \ominus (\mathbb{R}_{n-1}[\mathbf{x}] + I(\mu))$. Then

$$K_n^\mu(\mathbf{x}, \mathbf{y}) = \sum_{k=0}^{n} \mathbb{P}_k(\mathbf{x})\mathbb{P}_k(\mathbf{y})^T \tag{5.1}$$

with the reproducing property

$$\int_S K_n^\mu(\mathbf{x}, \mathbf{y})\, p(\mathbf{y})\, d\mu(\mathbf{y}) = p(\mathbf{x}), \quad \forall p \in L_n^2(\mu).$$

5.2.2 The Christoffel Function

The variational formulation of the Christoffel function in (4.4) now reads

$$\mathbf{z} \mapsto \Lambda_n^\mu(\mathbf{z}) = \inf_{p \in L_n^2(\mu)} \left\{ \int_S p(\mathbf{x})^2\, d\mu(\mathbf{x}) : \; p(\mathbf{z}) = 1 \right\}, \tag{5.2}$$

and therefore $\Lambda_n^\mu(\mathbf{z}) = 0$ for all $\mathbf{z} \notin V$, for large enough n.

Indeed, in the case of the circle $\mathbb{T}$ with equation $x^2 + y^2 = 1$ in $\mathbb{R}^2$ and normalized arc length measure $\sigma = \frac{d\theta}{2\pi}$ supported on it, affine functions $\alpha z + \overline{\alpha z} + a$, with $z = x + iy$ and parameters $\alpha \in \mathbb{C}$, $a \in \mathbb{R}$, we find that

$$\int_{\mathbb{T}} |\alpha z + \overline{\alpha z} + a|^2 d\sigma = 2|\alpha|^2 + a^2$$

combined with the constraint

$$\alpha w + \overline{\alpha w} + a = 1$$

yield

$$\Lambda_1^\sigma(w) > 0$$

for *every* point $w \in \mathbb{C}$.

In the end we will consider values of the Christoffel function only for large n, such pathologies being avoided. However, by definition of the Zariski closure V of S, a polynomial vanishing on $\mathrm{supp}(\mu)$ also vanishes on V and so

$$\left\{ \mathbf{z} \in \mathbb{R}^n : \Lambda_{\mu,n}(\mathbf{z}) = 0 \right\} \cap V = \emptyset. \tag{5.3}$$

Therefore $\Lambda_n^\mu(\mathbf{z}) > 0$ whenever $\mathbf{z} \in V$.

We provide a relevant example, against immediate intuition. Namely, consider *Cartan's umbrella*

$$Z = \{(x, y, z) \in \mathbb{R}^3, \; z(x^2 + y^2) = x^3\}.$$

It is an algebraic variety given by an irreducible polynomial. Z is connected in the metric topology of $\mathbb{R}^3$, with the peculiarity of carrying a “stick” (the z-axis) not immediately seen from the measure ν:

$$q \mapsto \int_{-\pi}^{\pi}\int_{1}^{2} q(r\cos t, r\sin t, r\cos(3t))r dr dt, \quad q \in \mathbb{R}[x,y,z].$$

In other words, the Zariski closure of the support of this innocent area type integration measure contains the full z-axis (of smaller dimension), in addition to the two-dimensional leaf on which the Euclidean closed support lives. In particular, for every $n \geq 1$ and every $z \neq 0$, $\Lambda_{\nu,n}(0,0,z) > 0$, although $\Lambda_{\nu,n}(x,y,z) = 0$ for small values of $(x,y) \neq (0,0)$.

5.2.3 Computation from Moments

We first need the following technical lemma:

Lemma 5.2.1 *Let $t \in \mathbb{N}$, $\mathbf{M} \in \mathbb{R}^{t\times t}$ be symmetric semidefinite and $\mathbf{u} \in \mathbb{R}^t$. Let $\mathbf{M}^\dagger$ denotes the Moore–Penrose pseudo-inverse of $\mathbf{M}$: Then,*

$$\inf_{\mathbf{x}\in\mathbb{R}^t} \left\{\mathbf{x}^T\mathbf{M}\mathbf{x} \colon\ \mathbf{x}^T\mathbf{u} = 1\right\} = \begin{cases} \frac{1}{\mathbf{u}^T\mathbf{M}^\dagger\mathbf{u}} & \textit{if} \quad \mathrm{proj}_{\ker(\mathbf{M})}(\mathbf{u}) = 0, \\ 0 & \textit{otherwise}. \end{cases}$$

Let $\mathbf{z} \in V$. Then Λ_n^μ in (5.2) also reads

$$\begin{aligned} \Lambda_n^\mu(\mathbf{z}) &= \inf_{p\in\mathbb{R}_n[\mathbf{x}]} \left\{ \int_S p^2\, d\mu \colon\ p(\mathbf{z}) = 1\right\} \\ &= \inf_{\mathbf{p}\in\mathbb{R}^{s(n)}} \{\mathbf{p}^T\mathbf{M}_{\mu,n}\mathbf{p} \colon\ \mathbf{p}^T\mathbf{v}_n(\mathbf{z}) = 1\}. \end{aligned} \tag{5.4}$$

As $\mathbf{M}_{\mu,n}$ is not invertible, we may invoke Lemma 5.2.1 to obtain

$$\Lambda_n^\mu(\mathbf{z}) = (\mathbf{v}_n(\mathbf{z})^T\mathbf{M}_{\mu,n}^\dagger\,\mathbf{v}_n(\mathbf{z}))^{-1}, \quad \forall \mathbf{z},\ \Lambda_n^\mu(\mathbf{z}) > 0, \tag{5.5}$$

and, in addition,

$$\Lambda_n^\mu(\mathbf{z})K_n^\mu(\mathbf{z},\mathbf{z}) = 1, \quad \forall \mathbf{z},\ \Lambda_n^\mu(\mathbf{z}) > 0. \tag{5.6}$$

Note finally that, for all $\mathbf{z} \in V$, we have $\Lambda_n^\mu(\mathbf{z}) > 0$.

Remark Notice that (5.5) provides us with an analytical formula for Λ_n^μ on V via the Moore–Penrose pseudo-inverse $\mathbf{M}_{\mu,n}^\dagger$. But we can also obtain the numerical value $\Lambda_n^\mu(\mathbf{z})$ at a particular point $\mathbf{z} \in V$ by solving the convex quadratic optimization problem (5.4).

So when $\mathbf{z} \in V$, (5.5) and (5.6) provide the nonsingular analogs of (4.6). An important difference with the nonsingular case is when $\mathbf{z} \notin V$. Indeed, following the variational formula (5.2), $\Lambda_n^\mu(\mathbf{z}) = 0$ whereas, by (5.1), $K_n^\mu(\mathbf{z}, \mathbf{z}) > 0$.

5.2.4 The Hilbert Function and Kernel of $\mathbf{M}_{\mu,n}$

It turns out that the kernel of the moment matrix $\mathbf{M}_{\mu,n}$ of μ provides important information on the geometry of the support S of μ and on the real radical $I(\mu)$. For this we need to introduce the *Hilbert function* associated with a variety, an important concept of algebraic geometry.

Definition 5.2.2 Let $J \subset \mathbb{R}[\mathbf{x}]$ be an ideal. The Hilbert function of the ideal J is by definition

$$\mathbf{HF}(n) = \dim \frac{\mathbb{R}_n[\mathbf{x}]}{\mathbb{R}_n[\mathbf{x}] \cap J}.$$

For large values of n, the Hilbert function is a polynomial with rational coefficients known as the *Hilbert polynomial*. The degree of this polynomial function equals the dimension of the variety associated with J, both regarded over the complex field. For instance, for an ideal of finite codimension in $\mathbb{R}[\mathbf{x}]$, the Hilbert polynomial is a constant, with the attached variety consisting of finitely many points.

Working over the real field is again counterintuitive, as the following simple example shows. Consider the principal ideal $(x^2 + y^2) \subset \mathbb{R}[x, y]$. The zero variety reduces to a single point, the origin of coordinates. However, the associated Hilbert function

$$n \mapsto \dim \frac{\mathbb{R}_n[x, y]}{\mathbb{R}_n[x, y] \cap (x^2 + y^2)} = 2n + 1$$

is not constant, even for large values of n. Fortunately, we focus on *real* ideals, avoiding again the pathologies.

Proposition 5.2.3 *For all $n \in \mathbb{N}$,* $\operatorname{rank}(\mathbf{M}_{\mu,n}) = \mathbf{HF}(n)$*, where* $\mathbf{HF}$ *denotes the Hilbert function of $I(\mu)$ and gives the dimension of the space of polynomials of degree up to n restricted to V (i.e. $L_n^2(\mu)$). For n large enough,* $\operatorname{rank}(\mathbf{M}_{\mu,n})$ *is a polynomial in n whose degree is the dimension of V, and* $\ker(\mathbf{M}_{\mu,n})$ *provides a basis that generates the real radical ideal $I(\mu)$.*

It is notable that, as n increases, the asymptotic behavior of a (simply checked) algebraic property of the moment matrix $\mathbf{M}_{\mu,n}$, namely its rank, determines in finitely many steps the dimension of the underlying variety V which contains the support of μ.

5.2.5 The Bivariate Real Christoffel Function on the Unit Circle

In most considerations presented in Chapter 3, a single complex variable $z = x + iy$ entered into discussion. When considering the Christoffel function on the unit circle in Section 3.2, one could work equally well with real polynomial algebra $\mathbb{R}[x, y]$ and treat the circle $|z| = 1$ as a real algebraic variety in $\mathbb{R}^2$ given by equation $x^2 + y^2 - 1 = 0$. For the special case of the unit circle the two versions of Christoffel function are related by a simple identity.

Fix a positive measure μ defined on the real variety $\mathbb{T} = \{(x, y) \in \mathbb{R}^2,\ x^2 + y^2 - 1 = 0\}$. The algebra of real polynomials restricted to $\mathbb{T}$ is represented by the quotient

$$\mathbb{R}[\mathbb{T}] = \frac{\mathbb{R}[x, y]}{(x^2 + y^2 - 1)}.$$

The ideal generated by $(x^2 + y^2 - 1)$ is real radical: if $p(x, y) \in \mathbb{R}[x, y]$ vanishes on $\mathbb{T}$, then $p(x, y) = (x^2 + y^2 - 1)q(x, y)$, where $q \in \mathbb{R}[x, y]$; this fact has been discussed in Section 5.1.

The filtration by degree on the quotient algebra is

$$\mathbb{R}_n[\mathbb{T}] = (\mathbb{R}_n[x, y]+(x^2+y^2-1)/(x^2+y^2-1) = \mathbb{R}_n[x, y]/((x^2+y^2-1)\cap\mathbb{R}_n[x, y]).$$

Thus the *real Christoffel function* relative to the measure μ and variety $\mathbb{T}$ is by definition

$$\Lambda^{\mu}_{\mathbb{R},n}(x_0, y_0) = \inf\{\|p\|^2_{\mu},\ \ p \in \mathbb{R}_n[x, y] + (x^2 + y^2 - 1),\ p(x_0, y_0) = 1\}.$$

We recall and adapt the notation for the complex Christoffel function we have already encountered:

$$\Lambda^{\mu}_{\mathbb{C},n}(x_0, y_0) = \inf\{\|q\|^2_{\mu},\ \ q \in \mathbb{C}_n[x + iy],\ q(x_0 + iy_0) = 1\}.$$

Note that $\Lambda^{\mu}_{\mathbb{R},n}(x_0, y_0) = 0$ for every point $(x_0, y_0) \notin \mathbb{T}$, while $\Lambda^{\mu}_{\mathbb{C},n}$ does not vanish at any point.

Proposition 5.2.4 *The relative real Christoffel function and the complex Christoffel function satisfy for any positive measure μ supported on the torus*

$$\Lambda^{\mu}_{\mathbb{R},n}(x_0, y_0) = \Lambda^{\mu}_{\mathbb{C},2n}(x_0, y_0),\ \ n \in \mathbb{N},\ (x_0, y_0) \in \mathbb{T}. \tag{5.7}$$

On the other hand,

$$0 = \Lambda^{\mu}_{\mathbb{R},n}(x_0, y_0) < \Lambda^{\mu}_{\mathbb{C},2n}(x_0, y_0),\ \ n \in \mathbb{N},\ (x_0, y_0) \notin \mathbb{T}.$$

Proof Start by noting that in the variational definition of $\Lambda^{\mu}_{\mathbb{R},n}$ one can use complex-coefficient polynomials. Indeed, every element $p(x, y) \in \mathbb{C}[x, y]$ decomposes as $p = p_1 + ip_2$ with $p_1, p_2 \in \mathbb{R}[x, y]$, and

$$|p|^2 = |p_1|^2 + |p_2|^2.$$

One step further, one can rewrite without changing the degree $p \in \mathbb{C}[x, y]$ as $P \in \mathbb{C}[z, \overline{z}]$:

$$p(x, y) = P(x + iy, x - iy).$$

Assume $\deg P = n$. By passing to the quotient algebra $\mathbb{C}[\mathbb{T}] = \mathbb{C}[z, \overline{z}]/(z\overline{z} - 1)$, we can assume

$$P(z, \overline{z}) = a_0 + a_1 z + \cdots + a_n z^n + b_1 \overline{z} + b_2 \overline{z}^2 + \cdots + b_n \overline{z}^n,$$

where $a_0, a_1, \ldots, a_n, b_1, \ldots, b_n \in \mathbb{C}$. But,

$$\begin{aligned}|P(z, \overline{z})| &= |\overline{z}^n (a_0 z^n + a_1 z^{n+1} + \cdots + a_n z^{2n} + b_1 z^{n-1} + b_2 z^{n-2} + \cdots + b_n| \\ &= |a_0 z^n + a_1 z^{n+1} + \cdots + a_n z^{2n} + b_1 z^{n-1} + b_2 z^{n-2} + \cdots + b_n|, \quad |z| = 1.\end{aligned}$$

Fix a point $z_0 = x_0 + iy_0 \in \mathbb{T}$. The optimal polynomial $P \in \mathbb{C}_n[z, \overline{z}]$ which achieves $\min \|P\|_\mu^2$ and satisfies $P(x_0 + iy_0) = 1$ yields a complex polynomial $Q \in \mathbb{C}_{2n}[z]$

$$Q(z) = \frac{P(z, \overline{z})\, \overline{z_0}^n}{\overline{z}^n}$$

with the same $L^2(\mu)$ norm and satisfying $Q(z_0) = 1$.

The identities can be reversed, proving the proposition. □

The above observation and the Maté–Nevai–Totik Theorem (3.2.1) imply the following:

Corollary 5.2.5 *Let $\mu = u(t)\frac{dt}{2\pi} + \mu_{sc} + \mu_d$ be the Lebesgue decomposition of a positive measure on the unit torus. Then*

$$\lim_n n\Lambda^\mu_{\mathbb{R},n}(\cos t, \sin t) = \frac{u(t)}{2}, \quad dt\text{-}a.e. \text{ on } \mathbb{T}.$$

The next section presents a generalization of this result.

5.3 Asymptotics

In this section we assume that μ has a well-behaved density with respect to a reference measure λ ($\mu \ll \lambda$) and, under some conditions, we provide an asymptotic relation between the Christoffel function and the density associated with the underlying measure μ.

Assumption 5.3.1 Let Z be a compact subset of $\mathbb{R}^d$ and assume that there exists a reference Borel probability measure λ whose support is Z and a polynomial function $N\colon \mathbb{R}_+ \mapsto \mathbb{R}_+^*$ such that

$$\lim_{n\to\infty} \sup_{\mathbf{z}\in Z} |N(n)\Lambda_n^\lambda(\mathbf{z}) - 1| = 0.$$

Remark The constant 1 is arbitrary and could be replaced by a continuous and strictly positive function of $\mathbf{z}$.

Example 5.3.2 (Integration along an algebraic variety) The typical example for a ground measure λ is the integration against area measure of the regular points of a real algebaric variety. Without entering into cumbersome details, the general picture is as follows. A real algebraic set is the union of finitely many irreducible components: for example, the two coordinate axes are the union of two straight lines. An irreducible algebraic set W has a dense subset of regular points, glued by the singular locus, which in its turn is stratified by smooth parts. For instance, the curve $W\colon x^3 = y^2$ has two smooth branches and a singular point $Y = \{(0,0)\}$, the origin. Assume the irreducible real algebraic subset $W \subset \mathbb{R}^d$ has a singular locus $Y \subset W$, so that $W \setminus Y$ is a smooth submanifold of $\mathbb{R}^d$. Then the volume measure in $\mathbb{R}^d$ induces by restriction an "area measure" along $W \setminus Y$. We denote it σ_W. Continuous functions in the full space, in particular polynomials, are locally integrable with respect to σ_W.

For instance, in the case of the curve W of equation $x^3 = y^2$ in $\mathbb{R}^2$, the measure σ_W is simply the arc length on the regular part $W \setminus \{(0,0)\}$. That is, for a continuous function f of compact support in $\mathbb{R}^2$,

$$\int_W f\, d\sigma_W = \int_{\mathbb{R}\setminus\{(0,0)\}} f(t^2,t^3)t\sqrt{4+9t^2}\,dt = \int_{-\infty}^{\infty} f(t^2,t^3)t\sqrt{4+9t^2}\,dt.$$

Notice in this simple example the different behavior of the density function

$$r \mapsto \int_{\|x-a\|<r} d\sigma_W(x)$$

at regular, respectively singular, points $a \in W$.

In case W is a smooth algebraic variety, the measure σ_W is the familiar "surface area" induced by the embedding $W \subset \mathbb{R}^d$.

Example 5.3.3 (The sphere) The principal example that fits Assumption 5.3.1 is the $(d-1)$-dimensional sphere $\mathbb{S}^{d-1}$ of $\mathbb{R}^d$. The dimension $N(n)$ of the vector space of polynomials over $\mathbb{S}^{d-1}$ is given by:

$$\binom{d+n-1}{d-1} + \binom{d+n-2}{d-1} = \left(1 + \frac{2n}{d-1}\right)\binom{n+d-2}{d-2} =: N(n),$$

which grows with n like $\frac{2n^{d-1}}{d-1}$ for a fixed value of d. As a function of d it is exactly the Hilbert polynomial associated with the real algebraic set $\mathbb{S}^{d-1}$. Here we may choose for λ the rotation-invariant probability measure on $\mathbb{S}^{d-1}$ (as normalized area measure). In this case $\Lambda_n^\lambda(\mathbf{z}) = \frac{1}{N(n)}$ for all $\mathbf{z} \in \mathbb{S}^{d-1}$ and all n by rotational invariance of both the sphere and the Christoffel function.

The case of the sphere is important because it helps us construct many more situations which satisfy Assumption 5.3.1:

- the product of spheres with products of area measures – the bi-torus in $\mathbb{R}^4$ with the corresponding area measure;
- affine transformations of such sets with the pushforward of the reference measure with respect to the affine map, for instance the ellipsoid;
- rational embeddings of the sphere in a higher-dimensional space;

to mention only a few natural choices of admissible operations.

Given a reference measure λ as in Assumption 5.3.1, and another measure $\mu \sim \lambda$ (i.e. $\lambda \ll \mu$ and $\mu \ll \lambda$), one can describe a precise relation with the underlying density of μ.

Theorem 5.3.4 *Let Z and λ satisfy Assumption 5.3.1. Let μ be a Borel probability measure on $\mathbb{R}^d$, absolutely continuous with respect to λ, with density $f : Z \to \mathbb{R}_+^*$ which is continuous and positive. Then,*

$$\lim_{n\to\infty} \sup_{\mathbf{x}\in Z} |N(n)\Lambda_n^\mu(\mathbf{x}) - f(\mathbf{x})| = 0.$$

Finally, we are able to obtain explicit quantitative bounds and a convergence rate, which to the best of our knowledge is the first estimate of this type for the Christoffel function.

Corollary 5.3.5 *Let $f : \mathbb{R}^d \to \mathbb{R}_+$ be Lipschitz on $\mathbb{S}^{d-1}$, with $0 < c \leq f \leq C < +\infty$ on $\mathbb{S}^{d-1}$, and assume that μ has density f with respect to the rotational invariant measure on $\mathbb{S}^{d-1}$. Then, for every $\alpha \in (1/2, 1)$,*

$$\sup_{\mathbf{x}\in\mathbb{S}^{d-1}} |N(n)\Lambda_n^\mu(\mathbf{x}) - f(\mathbf{x})| = O(n^{\alpha-1}).$$

5.4 Notes and Sources

Most of the material of this chapter is from Pauwels et al. (2021). Real algebra and real algebraic geometry are well-established disciplines. We refer readers to the monograph by Bochnak et al. (1998) for an authoritative guide. Below we comment only on some aspects of (pluri)potential theory and relevant asymptotic expansions on complex spaces.

Pluripotential theory on complex manifolds, or even on complex analytic spaces with singularities, is well advanced, although challenges abound and not all open questions have been settled. A clear dichotomy separates the investigations on Stein spaces and compact complex spaces. The first class carries sufficiently many holomorphic functions so that a Stein space can be embedded into affine space $\mathbb{C}^d$; hence speaking about polynomials and their growth on prescribed sets makes perfect sense. The second class contains in particular projective manifolds; they possess enough meromorphic functions to separate points and directions, while polynomial functions are replaced by sections of tensor powers of line bundles. The basic concepts related to the Siciak extremal problem, Bernstein–Markov and Bernstein–Walsh inequalities and equilibrium measure are at home in both settings, with deep impact on problems of approximation theory, statistical mechanics, algebraic geometry and function theory. We outline only a few references which, in time, may prove to be beneficial for applications we envisage in the present book.

The pioneering work of Sadullaev stands out. In a thorough report (Sadullaev, 1981), he discusses in detail the Dirichlet problem on a Stein manifold, with respect to the Monge–Ampere equation, the existence of equilibrium measure, characteristics of pluriharmonic capacity and more, all complementing breakthrough advances due to Bedford and Taylor. The companion situation of an analytic subspace of $\mathbb{C}^d$, with possible singularities, is treated in Sadullaev (1982), from the point of view of Bernstein-type inequalities for polynomial functions. One of the main results of this article states that, given a compact subset $K \subset X$ of a connected analytic space $X \subset \mathbb{C}^d$, Siciak's extremal function V_K is locally bounded along X if and only if X is algebraic. The following counterexample of the same article is very relevant:

Let $X = \{(z, w) \in \mathbb{C}^2,\ w = \exp(1/z)\}$ and consider the compact subset $K = \{(z, w) \in X,\ |z| = 1\}$. Then,

$$V_K(z, w) = \begin{cases} \infty & |z| < 1, \\ \log|z| & |z| \geq 1, \end{cases}$$

$(z, w) \in X$. Sadullaev (1985) is also a very informative survey. A different path towards the conclusion that only along algebraic varieties can one have a well-defined Siciak function, and much more, is contained in Demailly (1985).

The study of polynomial growth on nonalgebraic varieties, in particular graphs of transcendental functions, attracted a lot of attention. We reproduce a striking result from Coman and Poletsky (2010).

Let $X = \{(e^{\zeta}, e^{\alpha\zeta}), \zeta \in \mathbb{C}\}$, where $\alpha \in (0, 1)$ is an irrational number. As usual, denote by $\mathbb{D}$ the unit disk. Define

$$E_n(X) = \sup\{\|P\|_{\infty,\mathbb{D}^2},\ P \in \mathbb{C}_n[z, w],\ \sup_{\zeta\in\mathbb{D}} |P((e^{\zeta}, e^{\alpha\zeta})| \leq 1\},$$

and $e_n(\alpha) = \log E_n(X)$. Let p_s/q_s be the convergents of order s to α in its continued fraction expansion. If $q_s \leq n < q_{s+1}$, then

$$\max\left\{\frac{n^2 \log n}{2} - n^2, \left[\frac{n}{q_s}\right] \log q_{s+1} - n\right\} \leq e_n(\alpha) \leq \frac{n^2 \log n}{2} + 9n^2 + \frac{n}{q_s} \log q_{s+1}.$$

Thus a Markov–Walsh-type inequality along the analytic curve $X \subset \mathbb{C}^2$ is directly linked to the Diophantine approximation of the irrational slope α. More fascinating results along these lines can be found in Brudnyi (2008) and Bos et al. (2010).

The equilibrium measure of some specific shapes in $\mathbb{R}^d$ or $\mathbb{C}^d$ is easily derivable from the invariance under a large group of transformations. For instance, the pluripotential equilibrium measure on the sphere $S^{d-1} \subset \mathbb{R}^d$ is rotationally invariant and hence absolutely continuous with respect to surface area measure. And similarly for the torus $\mathbb{T}^d \subset \mathbb{C}^d$. The multivariate orthogonal polynomials with respect to these measures are obviously indispensable in any approximation theory question. They turn out to be spherical harmonics (for the sphere) and the Fourier modes on the torus. Moreover, these systems of orthogonal polynomials coincide with the eigenfunctions of a properly defined Laplace–Beltrami operator. This fundamental observation is analyzed and pushed to more general supports in a recent article by Piazzon (2019a). An array of useful orthogonal polynomials and kernels formulas for the ball, simplex and sphere can be found there.

The bi-torus, that is, the cartesian product of two circles, can be seen as an algebraic subset of $\mathbb{R}^3$ via the defining equation

$$(x_1^2 + x_2^2 + x_3^2 + R^2 - r^2)^2 = 4R^2(x_1^2 + x_2^2).$$

But we can also consider a second realization of the bi-torus $\mathbb{T}^2 \subset \mathbb{C}^2$. A lucid pluripotential analysis of the former (as a compact subset of a complex algebraic variety) was carried out in Piazzon (2018). For the second realization there is much more to report. Specifically, as the unit circle $\mathbb{T}$ and the unit disk $\mathbb{D}$ carry essential portions of harmonic analysis and function theory of a complex variable in one variable, the bi-torus $\mathbb{T}^2$ and the bi-disk $\mathbb{D}^2$ play a similar role in two dimensions. Dimension 2 is also special for a generalized von Neumann inequality due to Ando,

$$\|p(T_1, T_2)\| \leq \|p\|_{\infty,\mathbb{T}^2}, \quad p \in \mathbb{C}[z_1, z_2],$$

and T_1, T_2 are commuting contractive linear operators acting on a Hilbert space. Such an infinite matrix bound hides a lot of familiar concepts circulating in our text: RKHS, orthogonal polynomials, corresponding Christoffel–Darboux kernel estimates, numerical schemes, stationary processes, and so on. The reader can glimpse these topics in Foias and Frazho (1990) and can also consult Geronimo and Woerdeman (2004, 2007) for some specific kernel computations.

Finally, pluripotential theory on compact complex manifolds, especially its lasting impact on current problems of statistical mechanics and separately algebraic geometry, deserves a separate book. The discoveries by Berman (2009) and Berman et al. (2011) (some mentioned in a preceding chapter) are only two acclaimed examples from an extensive area of modern mathematical analysis. See also Ross and Nyström (2019) and Bleher et al. (2020). Demailly (2013) offers a general view of the applications of pluripotential theory to algebraic geometry; this can be complemented by the recent account of Dinew (2019) of the theory on compact hermitian manifolds.

PART TWO

STATISTICS AND APPLICATIONS TO DATA ANALYSIS

6
Empirical Christoffel–Darboux Analysis

In this chapter we introduce the statistical setting allowing us to manipulate the Christoffel function associated with a discrete measure supported on a random sample. This endeavor is of interest in applications as it permits us to infer properties of an unknown measure from the knowledge of only a sample.

6.1 The Empirical Christoffel Function

6.1.1 Empirical Measure

We consider the statistical context where μ is a probability measure on $\mathbb{R}^d$ which represents intrinsic randomness in an uncharacterized natural phenomenon, and we assume for simplicity that μ has a compact support. In a statistical context, μ is called the population measure; it is fixed, and its associated Christoffel function can be called the *population* Christoffel function. The statistician does not have access to μ, for example it is not possible to compute moments of μ or any expectation. On the other hand, we have access to statistical observations. We adopt the following notation and hypothesis throughout this chapter.

A sequence of $\mathbb{R}^d$ valued random variables $(X_i)_{i\in\mathbb{N}}$, which are independent and identically distributed according to μ, is given. This means that the measure describing the randomness of the sequence $(X_i)_{i\in\mathbb{N}}$ is the product replicate of μ. Another way to describe this is: for any $N \in \mathbb{N}$ and measurable subsets $A_1, \ldots, A_N$ in $\mathbb{R}^p$, the probability of the following event is

$$\mathbb{P}\left[(X_1 \in A_1) \,\&\, (X_2 \in A_2) \,\&\, \ldots \,\&\, (X_N \in A_N)\right] = \prod_{i=1}^{N} \mu(A_i).$$

For any $N \in \mathbb{N}$, we let μ_N be the emiprical measure associated with $X_1, \ldots, X_N$,

$$\mu_N = \frac{1}{N} \sum_{i=1}^{N} \delta_{X_i},$$

where $\delta_{\mathbf{x}}$ denotes the Dirac measure supported on $\mathbf{x} \in \mathbb{R}^d$. Note that μ_N is itself random since it is supported on a random sample. For our purposes, we will essentially rely on the strong law of large numbers (see e.g. Durrett, 2019, Theorem 2.4.1). More specifically, for any continuous f,

$$\lim_{N \to \infty} \int f d\mu_N = \lim_{N \to \infty} \frac{1}{N} \sum_{i=1}^{N} f(X_I) = \int f d\mu, \tag{6.1}$$

almost surely. Since we are describing convergence of random quantities, we need to clarify the meaning of almost-sure convergence . The expression "almost sure" refers to the randomness of the sequence $(X_i)_{i \in \mathbb{N}}$; although the quantity in (6.1) is random, it converges almost surely to a deterministic limit. This convergence is in particular true for monomials, which in turn will be an essential step towards proving the stability of empirical Christoffel functions.

6.1.2 The Empirical Christoffel Function

As in previous chapters, with the measure μ_N is associated a Christoffel function, parametrized by its degree $n \in \mathbb{N}$:

$$\Lambda_n^{\mu_N} : \mathbf{z} \mapsto \inf_{p \in \mathbb{R}_n[\mathbf{x}],\, p(\mathbf{z})=1} \int p^2 \, d\mu_N, \quad n \in \mathbb{N}. \tag{6.2}$$

This is what we call the *empirical* Christoffel function. This function has to be distinguished and contrasted with Λ_n^{μ} described in previous chapters, which stands for the population Christoffel function in this chapter. In view of Lemma 5.2.1, denote by $\mathbf{v}_n$ a vector of $s(n)$ polynomials forming a basis of $\mathbb{R}_n[\mathbf{x}]$ and consider the design matrix $D \in \mathbb{R}^{N \times s(n)}$, such that each row is given by $\mathbf{v}_n(X_i)$, $i = 1, \ldots, N$. A simple algebraic expression for the moment matrix is

$$\mathbf{M}_{\mu_N,n} = \frac{1}{N} D^T D. \tag{6.3}$$

This relation will allow us to use concentration of random matrices to provide statistical sensitivity analysis and asymptotics. Now the emprical Christoffel function $\Lambda_n^{\mu_N}$ can be computed as follows:

$$\Lambda_n^{\mu_N}(\mathbf{z}) := \begin{cases} 0 & \text{if } \exists p \in \mathbb{R}_n[\mathbf{x}],\, p(\mathbf{z}) \neq 0 \text{ and } p(X_i) = 0,\, i = 1, \ldots, N, \\ \dfrac{1}{\mathbf{v}_n(\mathbf{z})^T \mathbf{M}_{\mu_N,n}^{\dagger} \mathbf{v}_n(\mathbf{z})} & \text{otherwise.} \end{cases} \tag{6.4}$$

As seen in previous chapters, the population Christoffel function encodes a great deal of information on the geometry of the support of the underlying measure. As for the empirical Christoffel function, the geometry of the support is quite trivial; however, if $\Lambda_n^{\mu_N}$ is close to Λ_n^{μ} in a certain sense, then these discrete data can still be used to infer properties of μ.

6.1.3 A Remark on Computation

When the the moment matrix $\mathbf{M}_{\mu_N,n}$ is nonsingular and an additional data point $\mathbf{u} \in \mathbb{R}^d$ is to be considered, the Christoffel function $\Lambda_n^{\mu_{N+1}}$ associated with the new empirical measure $\mu_{N+1} = \frac{1}{N+1}\sum_{i=1}^{N+1} \delta_{\mathbf{x}_i}$, with $\mathbf{x}_{N+1} = u$, is obtained from $\Lambda_n^{\mu_N}$ by a simple rank-1 update of $\mathbf{M}_{\mu_N,n}^{-1}$. Indeed, by the Sherman–Morrison–Woodbury formula,

$$\begin{aligned}((N+1)\,\mathbf{M}_{\mu_{N+1},n})^{-1} &= (N\,\mathbf{M}_{\mu_N,n} + \mathbf{v}_n(\mathbf{u})\mathbf{v}_n(\mathbf{u})^T)^{-1}\\ &= \frac{1}{N}\mathbf{M}_{\mu_N,n}^{-1} - \frac{1}{N^2}\frac{\mathbf{M}_{\mu_N,n}^{-1}\mathbf{v}_n(\mathbf{u})\mathbf{v}_n(\mathbf{u})^T\mathbf{M}_{\mu_N,n}^{-1}}{(1+\frac{1}{N}\mathbf{v}_n(\mathbf{u})^T\mathbf{M}_{\mu_N,n}^{-1}\mathbf{v}_n(\mathbf{u}))},\end{aligned}$$

and therefore

$$\frac{1}{N+1}\Lambda_n^{\mu_{N+1}}(\xi) = \frac{1}{N}\Lambda_n^{\mu_N}(\xi) - \frac{\frac{1}{N^2}K_n^{\mu_N}(\xi,\mathbf{u})^2}{(1+\frac{1}{N}\Lambda_n^{\mu_N}(\mathbf{u}))}, \quad \forall \xi \in \mathbb{R}^d.$$

In particular, when evaluated at the point $\mathbf{u}$,

$$\Lambda_n^{\mu_{N+1}}(\mathbf{u}) = \frac{\frac{N+1}{N}\Lambda_n^{\mu_N}(\mathbf{u})}{1+\frac{1}{N}\Lambda_n^{\mu_N}(\mathbf{u})},$$

which shows how the Christoffel function varies with the addition of a new point $\mathbf{u}$ to an existing sample.

Hence once an inverse $\mathbf{M}_{\mu_N,n}$ is available, if one adds m observations, the resulting Christoffel function $\Lambda_n^{\mu_{N+m}}$ is obtained from $\Lambda_n^{\mu_N}$ by m successive rank-1 updates, which avoids a costly inversion. Clearly this is an attractive feature of the Christoffel function. More details on the stability of this operation (known in the orthogonal polynomials literature as *Uvarov's transform*) appear in Section 9.1.

6.1.4 Asymptotic Behavior

Large Degree: In this subsection, $\mathbf{x}_1, \ldots, \mathbf{x}_N$ are fixed vectors in $\mathbb{R}^p$, not random, but arbitrary. Recalling the construction in Chapters 4 and 5, the empirical Christoffel function is associated with a measure supported on a set of N points in $\mathbb{R}^p$. This set can be interpreted as an algebraic manifold of dimension 0. Proposition 5.2.3 ensures that the rank $\mathbf{HF}(n)$ of $\mathbf{M}_{\mu_N,n}$ will stabilize to a fixed value as $n \to \infty$. This value is the dimension of the space of polynomials (of any degree) restricted to the set of N points of interest. Note that this space is finite dimensional; according to (6.3), its dimension has to be smaller than N.

Furthermore, for any $i = 1, \ldots, N$, the polynomial $p_i : \mathbf{x} \mapsto \prod_{j \neq i} \|\mathbf{x} - \mathbf{x}_j\|^2$ can be used in (6.2) to show that if $n \geq 2N - 2$, $\Lambda_n^{\mu_N}(\mathbf{x}_i) = 1/N$ for all $i = 1, \ldots, n$. Actually, for all $n \geq 2N$, we have

$$\Lambda_n^{\mu_N} : \mathbf{z} \mapsto \begin{cases} 0 & \mathbf{z} \neq \mathbf{x}_i,\ i = 1, \ldots, N, \\ \frac{1}{N} & \text{otherwise.} \end{cases} \tag{6.5}$$

This highlights the fact that the asymptotic behavior for fixed sample size N and large degree n is trivial and reflects only the fact that the support is finite.

Large Sample: In the next subsection, we fix the degree bound n, consider μ_N associated with the random sequence $(X_i)_{i \in \mathbb{N}}$ and let N to ∞. The law of large numbers ensures that almost surely

$$\lim_{N \to \infty} \mathbf{M}_{\mu_N,n} = \mathbf{M}_{\mu,n}. \tag{6.6}$$

Considering formula (6.4), one can grasp the intuition that $\Lambda_n^{mu_N}$ and Λ_n^{μ} should also be close in a certain sense since the moment matrices are close. So, for a fixed degree bound, in the limit of a large sample size, the empirical Christoffel function should carry similar information to the population Christoffel function.

Finite Sample Analysis for the Christoffel Function: As described in Chapter 4, the population Christoffel function captures information of the support for large degree bound n. However, for a fixed sample size N, we saw that the empirical Christoffel function has a trivial behaviour for $n \geq 2N$. On the other hand if n is fixed and the sample size goes to infinity, then the empirical Christoffel function should get close to the population Christoffel function. This means that, in order to study the asymptotics of the empirical Christoffel function, and retain relevant information in relation with its population counterpart, one needs to let the degree bound n grow. On the other hand, n should not grow too fast, as N grows, in order to avoid trivial behaviors. In the following sections we provide a quantitative criterion that makes this heuristic observation more precise.

6.2 A Stability Result and a Law of Large Numbers

The following lemma is adapted from Vu et al. (2019) and we reproduce its proof for completeness.

Lemma 6.2.1 *Let $n, N \in \mathbb{N}$, $\mathbf{x}_1, \ldots, \mathbf{x}_N$ be fixed in the support of μ in $\mathbb{R}^d$, $\mathbf{v}_n$ a vector of $\mathbf{HF}(n)$ polynomials in $\mathbb{R}_n[\mathbf{x}]$ forming an orthonormal basis in $L_n^2(\mu)$, and $\mathbf{M}_{\mu_N,n}$ be the empirical moment matrix in this basis (note that the size of the basis could be smaller than $s(n)$). Then we have for all $\mathbf{x} \in \mathbb{R}^d$,*

$$|\Lambda_n^{\mu}(\mathbf{x}) - \Lambda_n^{\mu_N}(\mathbf{x})| \leq \Lambda_n^{\mu}(\mathbf{x}) \cdot \|\mathbf{M}_{\mu_N,n} - I\|_{\mathrm{op}}.$$

Proof If $\Lambda_n^{\mu}(\mathbf{x}) = 0$, then the result holds trivially. If $\Lambda_n^{\mu_N}(\mathbf{x}) = 0$, then there is a nonzero polynomial in $L_n^2(\mu)$ vanishing on $\mathbf{x}_1, \ldots, \mathbf{x}_N$, of degree at most n, and hence $\mathbf{M}_{\mu_N,n}$ does not have full rank and $\|\mathbf{M}_{\mu_N,n} - I\|_{\mathrm{op}} \geq 1$, which proves the result. Otherwise, let us assume that both $\Lambda_n^{\mu}(\mathbf{x})$ and $\Lambda_n^{\mu_N}(\mathbf{x})$ are nonzero; we can then use (6.4) since we assumed that the points are in the support of μ, and in this case minimizing in (6.2) over $\mathbb{R}_n[\mathbf{x}]$ or over the linear span of polynomials in $\mathbf{v}_n$ provides the same result given that any polynomial of degree up to n is a sum of a polynomial vanishing on the support of μ and a polynomial in this linear span. Notice that, in the basis given by $\mathbf{v}_n$, we have $\mathbf{M}_{\mu,n} = I$ and $\Lambda_n^{\mu}(\mathbf{x}) = \mathbf{v}_n(\mathbf{x})^T\mathbf{v}_n(\mathbf{x})$. Since $\Lambda_n^{\mu}(\mathbf{x}) > 0$, we can also use (5.5). Putting things together, we have

$$\begin{aligned}|\Lambda_n^{\mu}(\mathbf{x}) - \Lambda_n^{\mu_N}(\mathbf{x})| &= \left|\frac{1}{\mathbf{v}_n(\mathbf{x})^T\mathbf{v}_n(\mathbf{x})} - \frac{1}{\mathbf{v}_n(\mathbf{x})^T\mathbf{M}_{\mu_N,n}^{\dagger}\mathbf{v}_n(\mathbf{x})}\right| \\ &= \Lambda_n^{\mu}(\mathbf{x})\Lambda_n^{\mu_N}(\mathbf{x})\left|\mathbf{v}_n(\mathbf{x})^T(I - \mathbf{M}_{\mu_N,n}^{\dagger})\mathbf{v}_n(\mathbf{x})\right|.\end{aligned}$$

According to Lemma 5.2.1, $\mathbf{v}_n(\mathbf{x}) \in \mathrm{Im}(\mathbf{M}_{\mu_N,n})$, and therefore

$$\mathbf{v}_n(\mathbf{x})^T\mathbf{v}_n(\mathbf{x}) = (\mathbf{M}_{\mu_N,n}^{\frac{\dagger}{2}}\mathbf{v}_n(\mathbf{x}))^T\mathbf{M}_{\mu_N,n}\,\mathbf{M}_{\mu_N,n}^{\frac{\dagger}{2}}\,\mathbf{v}_n(\mathbf{x}),$$

where we have used matrix square root. Consequently,

$$\begin{aligned}|\Lambda_n^{\mu}(\mathbf{x}) - \Lambda_n^{\mu_N}(\mathbf{x})| &= \Lambda_n^{\mu}(\mathbf{x})\Lambda_n^{\mu_N}(\mathbf{x})\left|(\mathbf{M}_{\mu_N,n}^{\frac{\dagger}{2}}\mathbf{v}_n(\mathbf{x}))^T(\mathbf{M}_{\mu_N,n} - I)\mathbf{M}_{\mu_N,n}^{\frac{\dagger}{2}}\mathbf{v}_n(\mathbf{x})\right| \\ &\leq \Lambda_n^{\mu}(\mathbf{x})\,\Lambda_n^{\mu_N}(\mathbf{x})\,\|\mathbf{M}_{\mu_N,n}^{\frac{\dagger}{2}}\mathbf{v}_n(\mathbf{x})\|^2\,\|(\mathbf{M}_{\mu_N,n} - I)\|_{\mathrm{op}} \\ &= \Lambda_n^{\mu}(\mathbf{x})\,\Lambda_n^{\mu_N}(\mathbf{x})\,\mathbf{v}_n(\mathbf{x})^T\mathbf{M}_{\mu_N,n}^{\dagger}\mathbf{v}_n(\mathbf{x})\,\|(\mathbf{M}_{\mu_N,n} - I)\|_{\mathrm{op}} \\ &= \Lambda_n^{\mu}(\mathbf{x})\,\|(\mathbf{M}_{\mu_N,n} - I)\|_{\mathrm{op}}.\end{aligned}$$

□

Let us provide a simpler statement in the absolutely continuous case where the moment matrix is invertible and $\mathbf{HF}(n) = s(n)$.

Corollary 6.2.2 *Assume that μ is absolutely continuous with respect to Lebesgue measure. Let $n, N \in \mathbb{N}$, $\mathbf{x}_1, \ldots, \mathbf{x}_N$ be fixed in $\mathbb{R}^d$, $\mathbf{v}_n$ a vector of $s(n)$ polynomials in $\mathbb{R}_n[\mathbf{x}]$ forming an orthonormal basis of $L^2_n(\mu)$, and let $\mathbf{M}_{\mu_N,n}$ be the empirical moment matrix in this basis. Then for all $\mathbf{x} \in \mathbb{R}^d$,*

$$|\Lambda_n^{\mu}(\mathbf{x}) - \Lambda_n^{\mu_N}(\mathbf{x})| \leq \Lambda_n^{\mu}(\mathbf{x}) \, \|\mathbf{M}_{\mu_N,n} - I\|_{\text{op}}.$$

This stability result allows us to prove a strong law of large numbers for the Christoffel function.

Theorem 6.2.3 (Lasserre and Pauwels, 2019) *Let μ and μ_N be as in Section 6.1. Then for all $n \in \mathbb{N}$,*

$$\lim_{N \to \infty} \|\Lambda_n^{\mu} - \Lambda_n^{\mu_N}\|_\infty = 0 \quad \textit{almost surely.}$$

Proof Note that $X_i \in \operatorname{supp}(\mu)$ for all $i \in \mathbb{N}$ with probability 1. Furthermore, for all $\mathbf{x}$, $\Lambda_n^{\mu}(\mathbf{x}) \leq 1$. Consider, as in Lemma 6.2.1, $\mathbf{v}_n$ a vector of $\mathbf{HF}(n)$ polynomials in $\mathbb{R}_n[\mathbf{x}]$, forming an orthonormal basis in $L^2_n(\mu)$. In view of Lemma 6.2.1, for any $N \in \mathbb{N}$,

$$\|\Lambda_n^{\mu} - \Lambda_n^{\mu_N}\|_\infty \leq \|\mathbf{M}_{\mu_N,n} - I\|_{\text{op}},$$

with probability 1. By the strong law of large numbers, the right-hand side goes to zero with probability 1, which proves the claim. □

The preceding result provides a formal statement regarding the fact that $\Lambda_n^{\mu_N}$ is approaching Λ_n^{μ}. This is, however, not sufficient for many statistical applications as we have only a qualitative asymptotic convergence but no rate.

6.3 Finite Sample Convergence and Bounds

6.3.1 Finite Sample Bounds from Concentration of Random Matrices

The content of this section is reproduced from Vu et al. (2019). Choose $\mathbf{v}_n$ a vector of $\mathbf{HF}(n)$ polynomials in $\mathbb{R}_n[\mathbf{x}]$ forming an orthonormal basis in $L^2_n(\mu)$

and set $D \in \mathbb{R}^{N \times \mathbf{HF}(n)}$ to be the design matrix with rows given by $\mathbf{v}_n(X_i)$, $i = 1, \ldots, N$; we have

$$\mathbf{M}_{\mu_N,n} = \frac{1}{N} D^T D.$$

Note that D is a random matrix, so $\mathbf{M}_{\mu_N,n}$ is also a random matrix. Note also that the expectation of $\mathbf{M}_{\mu_N,n}$ with respect to the draw of the random sample is the identity. Finally, noticing that $\|\mathbf{v}_n(\cdot)\|^2 = K_n^\mu(\cdot,\cdot)$, we obtain with probability 1,

$$\max_{i=1,\ldots,N} \|\mathbf{v}_n(X_i)\|^2 = \max_{i=1,\ldots,N} K_n^\mu(X_i, X_i) \leq \max_{\mathbf{x} \in \text{supp}(\mu)} K_n^\mu(\mathbf{x},\mathbf{x}) := M_{\mu,n}. \quad (6.7)$$

Note that $M_{\mu,n}$ is the quantity appearing in the Bernstein–Markov inequality 4.3.3. The following result appearing in Vu et al. (2019) is based on concentration for random matrices of the form $D^T D$; see, for example, Vershynin (2010).

Theorem 6.3.1 *In the setting of Section 6.1, for all $\alpha \in (0, 1)$, all $n \in \mathbb{N}$, all $N \in \mathbb{N}$, with probability at least $1 - \alpha$, for all $\mathbf{x} \in \mathbb{R}^d$,*

$$|\Lambda_n^\mu(\mathbf{x}) - \Lambda_n^{\mu_N}(\mathbf{x})| \leq \Lambda_n^\mu(\mathbf{x}) \max\left(\sqrt{\frac{16 M_{\mu,n}}{3N} \log\left(\frac{s(n)}{\alpha}\right)}, \frac{16 M_{\mu,n}}{3N} \log\left(\frac{s(n)}{\alpha}\right)\right),$$

where the scalar $M_{\mu,n}$ is given in (6.7).

By the preceding result, observe that, in order for $\Lambda_n^{\mu_N}$ to be close to $\Lambda_n^\mu(\mathbf{x})$, one should choose n such that the scalar $M_{\mu,n}$ is smaller than N. This makes an interesting connection between statistical estimation and approximation theory. We state the following corollary as an application of the Borel–Cantelli Lemma (see e.g. Durrett, 2019, Theorem 2.3.1).

Corollary 6.3.2 *In the setting of Theorem 6.3.1, assume that $n(N)$ is chosen such that $N^{1-\delta} \geq M_{\mu,n(N)}$ and $N \geq s(n(N))$, for all $N \in \mathbb{N}$ and for some $\delta > 0$. Then*

$$\|\Lambda_{n(N)}^\mu - \Lambda_{n(N)}^{\mu_N}\|_\infty \underset{N\to\infty}{\to} 0 \quad \textit{almost surely.}$$

Proof For any $N \in \mathbb{N}$ and any $\epsilon \in (0, 1)$, choosing

$$\alpha_N = \frac{s(n(N))}{\exp\left(\frac{3N\epsilon^2}{16 M_{\mu,n(N)}}\right)},$$

Theorem 6.3.1 implies

$$\mathbb{P}\left[\|\Lambda^{\mu}_{n(N)} - \Lambda^{\mu_N}_{n(N)}\|_\infty > \epsilon\right] \leq \alpha_N \leq \frac{N}{\exp\left(\frac{3N^\delta \epsilon^2}{16}\right)}.$$

The right-hand side is summable, which proves almost sure convergence thanks to the Borel–Cantelli Lemma (Durrett, 2019, Theorem 2.3.1). □

6.3.2 Finite Sample Convergence of the Rank

We adopt the setting of Chapter 5 with population measures restricted to be absolutely continuous with respect to the area measure of a given real algebraic manifold.

Assumption 6.3.3 μ is a positive Borel measure on $\mathbb{R}^d$ with finite moments and V is the Zariski closure of $\mathrm{supp}(\mu)$ endowed with the area measure σ_V. They satisfy the following constraints:

(a) V is an irreducible algebraic set,
(b) μ is absolutely continuous with respect to σ_V.

Under this assumption one infers the following finite-sample stabilization result. The statement formalizes the intuition that the set of polynomials on $\mathrm{supp}(\mu)$ and the set of polynomials on a finite sample are both isomorphic to the set of polynomials on V, almost surely with respect to the random draw of the sample, as long as the sample size is at least $\mathbf{HF}(n)$.

Theorem 6.3.4 *For all $n \geq 1$ and all $N \geq \mathbf{HF}(n)$, it holds almost surely that*

(a) $\mathrm{rank}(\mathbf{M}_{\mu_n,n}) = \mathrm{rank}(\mathbf{M}_{\mu,n}) = \mathbf{HF}(n)$,
(b) $\left\{p \in \mathbb{R}_n[\mathbf{x}];\ \sum_{i=1}^N (p(\mathbf{x}_i))^2 = 0\right\} = I(\mu) \cap \mathbb{R}_n[\mathbf{x}]$.

The proof of this result relies on an extension to the complex-variables setting, where the analytic Nullstellensatz provides a canonical representation of analytic functions vanishing on a prescribed analytic submanifold. Further on, the hypotheses of the theorem allow us to return to the real space setting invoking some classical results of Serre (1956) informally known as GAGA.

We insist on the fact that Assumption 6.3.3 is necessary to obtain the rank stability result. Examples of measures not satisfying this assumption are given in Figure 6.1. In the first case the algebraic set is not irreducible; it is a cross. For a fixed N, there is a small chance that all our sample fall on one branch of the cross so that the sample does not allow us to see the second branch of the cross. In the second case, we have a mixture between uniform distribution on

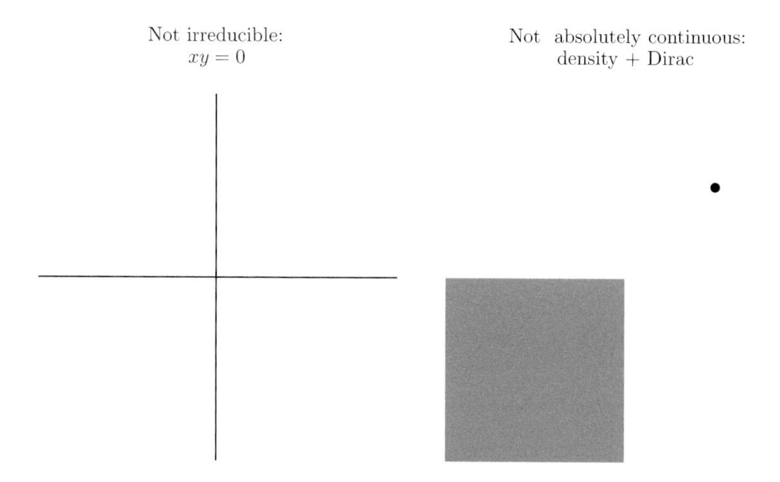

Figure 6.1 Illustrations of two examples for which the hypotheses of Theorem 6.3.4 fail. On the one hand we have an algebraic set that is not irreducible, on the other hand we do not have absolute continuity.

a square and a Dirac mass. Again, for a fixed n, there is a small chance that all samples fall on the Dirac part, completely missing the square.

Let us mention an interesting corollary which relates to Chapter 4. In the Euclidean setting, the area measure is simply Lebesgue measure; furthermore, under absolute continuity assumptions, $\mathbf{HF}(n)$ is simply $s(n)$.

Corollary 6.3.5 *In the statistical setting of Section 6.1, assume that the population measure is absolutely continuous with respect to Lebesgue measure. Then for any $n \in \mathbb{N}$ and $N \geq s(n)$, $\mathbf{M}_{\mu_N,n}$ is invertible.*

6.4 Notes and Sources

The use of the empirical Christoffel function in a data analysis context was initially proposed in Lasserre and Pauwels (2016) and the first theoretical treatment of statistical aspects is in Lasserre and Pauwels (2019). The main results of this chapter are from Pauwels et al. (2021) and Vu et al. (2019).

The statistical literature on support inference is extremely vast and the interested reader is refered to Vu et al. (2019) for an account of the questions at stake and relevant contributions. First results on this subject can be found in Rényi and Sulanke (1963) and Geffroy (1964), which motivated the analysis of convex hull based estimators for convex domains (Chevalier, 1976) or unions of balls for nonconvex sets (Devroye and Wise, 1980). More advanced estimators were developed later, for example the excess mass estimator (Polonik, 1995), density estimators (Cuevas and Fraiman, 1997; Tsybakov, 1997; Molchanov, 1998; Cuevas et al., 2006a) or the R-convex hull (Rodríguez Casal, 2007). A minimax theory is developed in Mammen and Tsybakov (1995).

More broadly, the field of geometric and topological inference is also extremely vast and active. Graph Laplacian based methods were proposed in Belkin and Niyogi (2008) and Hein et al. (2005), and intrinsic dimension estimation was revisited in Levina and Bickel (2004) and Hein and Audibert (2005). In a manifold learning context the questions of finite-sample efficiency were treated in Genovese et al. (2012a,b), Kim et al. (2015) and Aamari and Levrard (2019), and a statistical test was proposed (Fefferman et al., 2016).

Getting access to topological properties of a data distribution through computational topology is at the heart of the field of topological data analysis (Niyogi et al., 2008; Edelsbrunner and Harer, 2008; Ghrist, 2008; Carlsson, 2009). This was cast in a statistical framework in Chazal et al. (2011, 2014) and Bubenik (2015), and in a machine learning framework by Niyogi et al. (2008, 2011).

In an algebraic context, the work of Breiding et al. (2018) focused on computational aspects related to the statistical results presented in this chapter.

7
Applications and Occurrences in Data Analysis

Given a probability distribution μ on $\mathbb{R}^d$, we denote its mean by $\mathbf{m}(\mu) \in \mathbb{R}^d$ and positive definite covariance matrix $C(\mu) \in \mathbb{R}^{d \times d}$, such that

$$\mathbf{m}(\mu) = \int \mathbf{z} d\mu(\mathbf{z}),$$
$$C(\mu) = \int (\mathbf{z} - \mathbf{m}(\mu))(\mathbf{z} - \mathbf{m}(\mu))^{\perp} d\mu(\mathbf{z}).$$

The function $\Delta(\cdot, \mu) : \mathbb{R}^d \to \mathbb{R}$,

$$\mathbf{z} \mapsto \Delta(\mathbf{z}, \mu) := \sqrt{(\mathbf{z} - \mathbf{m}(\mu))^{\perp} C(\mu)^{-1} (\mathbf{z} - \mathbf{m}(\mu))}, \quad \mathbf{z} \in \mathbb{R}^d,$$

is called the *Mahalanobis distance* associated with μ.

Recall the notation $\mathbf{v}_1(\mathbf{z}) = (1, z_1, \ldots, z_d)$, and letting $\mathbf{M}_{\mu,1}$ be the corresponding moment matrix (with moments up to degree 2), we can use a Schur complement argument (see Lasserre and Pauwels, 2016) to obtain

$$K_1^{\mu}(\mathbf{z}, \mathbf{z}) = 1 + \Delta(\mathbf{z}, \mu)^2. \tag{7.1}$$

Hence, up to some additive constant, $K_1^{\mu}(\mathbf{z}, \mathbf{z})$ coincide with the Mahalanobis distance $\Delta(\mathbf{z}, \mu)^2$, which is widely used in data analysis contexts. Hence, for $n > 1$, the Christoffel–Darboux kernel $K_n^{\mu}(\mathbf{z}, \mathbf{z})$ *can be considered as a natural generalization of the Mahalanobis distance*. Such connections between well-known statistical objects and CD kernels abound in the literature, particularly in a parametric regression context. We first provide an overview of these connections and then describe further applications of the results obtained in Chapter 6.

7.1 Parameteric Regression

Besides orthogonal polynomials and potential theory, the Christoffel function entered through the main door in statistics, more specifically in parametric regression with questions related to uncertainty quantification.

7.1.1 Polynomial Regression, Gaussian Model and Least Squares

Let $\mathbf{K} \subset \mathbb{R}^d$ be compact, $n \in \mathbb{N}$ and assume that we have access to $N \geq s(n)$ points $\{\mathbf{x}_i\}_{i=1}^N \subset \mathbf{K}$. Assume furthermore that there is a polynomial $P^* \in \mathbb{R}_n[\mathbf{x}]$ and real random variables $Y_1, \ldots, Y_N$, such that for each $i = 1, \ldots, N$, we have

$$Y_i = P^*(\mathbf{x}_i) + \epsilon_i,$$

where $\epsilon_1, \ldots, \epsilon_N$ are independent and identically distributed unit Gaussian random variables with zero mean and unit variance. Denote by $Y \in \mathbb{R}^n$ the corresponding random vector. Consider any basis $P_1, \ldots, P_{s(n)}$ of $\mathbb{R}_d[\mathbf{x}]$ and $\mathbf{v}_n : \mathbb{R}^d \mapsto \mathbb{R}^{s(n)}$ the function with coordinates given by these polynomials and the design matrix

$$X = \left(P_i(\mathbf{x}_j)\right)_{i=1,\ldots,s(n),\ j=1\ldots N}.$$

Letting $\mu_N = \sum_{i=1}^N \delta_{\mathbf{x}_i}$ be the empirical measure supported on our sample points, we have

$$\mathbf{M}_{\mu_N,n} = \frac{1}{N} X^T X.$$

In the Gaussian model, the maximum likelihood estimate for P^* is the same as the least squares estimate

$$\hat{P} = \arg\min_{P \in \mathbb{R}_n[\mathbf{x}]} \sum_{i=1}^N (P(\mathbf{x}_i) - Y_i)^2.$$

Assuming invertibility, it is given by $\hat{P} \colon \mathbf{x} \mapsto \mathbf{v}_n(\mathbf{x})^T \hat{\theta}$, where

$$\hat{\theta} = (X^T X)^{-1} X^T Y = (X^T X)^{-1} X^T (X\theta^* + \epsilon),$$

θ^* contains the coordinates of P^* and ϵ is a Gaussian random vector with zero mean and identity covariance matrix. In this case $\hat{\theta}$ is itself a Gaussian random vector with mean θ^* and covariance matrix $(X^T X)^{-1} = (\mathbf{M}_{\mu_N,n})^{-1}$. It is interesting to note that the covariance matrix is deterministic and does not depend on Y or ϵ, only X. Hence, for any measure μ with invertible moment matrix, $(\mathbf{M}_{\mu,n})^{-1}$ can be understood as the covariance matrix of the least squares estimator, modulo a factor N.

7.1.2 Leverage Scores

For $\mathbf{z} \in K$ we find

$$\begin{aligned}\hat{P}(\mathbf{z}) &= \mathbf{v}_n(\mathbf{z})^T \hat{\theta} \\ &= \mathbf{v}_n(\mathbf{z})^T (X^T X)^{-1} X^T Y \\ &= \mathbf{v}_n(\mathbf{z})^T \theta^* + \mathbf{v}_n(\mathbf{z})^T (X^T X)^{-1} X^T \epsilon \\ &= P^*(\mathbf{z}) + \mathbf{v}_n(\mathbf{z})^T (X^T X)^{-1} X^T \epsilon.\end{aligned}$$

The second term is random with zero mean, and variance

$$\mathbf{v}_n(\mathbf{z})^T (X^T X)^{-1} \mathbf{v}_n(\mathbf{z}) = \frac{1}{N} K_n^{\mu_N}(\mathbf{z}, \mathbf{z}).$$

Hence the empirical Christoffel–Darboux kernel naturally arises in a statistical context as the variance of the estimated value at a given point $\mathbf{z}$, where the estimation is carried by least squares estimation.

When $n = 1$, we recover the linear regression problem in which case $X \in \mathbb{R}^{N\times(d+1)}$ is the design matrix (with a constant column added for the bias term). In this case, the kernel evaluated at the ith design point has the form

$$K_1^{\mu_N}(\mathbf{x}_i, \mathbf{x}_i) = \mathbf{v}_1(\mathbf{x}_i)^T (X^T X)^{-1} \mathbf{v}_n(\mathbf{x}_i) = [X(X^T X)^{-1} X^T]_{ii}.$$

The quantity on the right-hand side is known as the *leverage score* associated with the ith design point. The interpretation remains valid with larger-degree bounds $n > 1$ in the context of parametric regression. This is a classical notion in the context of regression which was used mostly for uncertainty quantification, perturbation analysis and diagnosis. This notion found a new application in the context of randomized linear algebra applied to parametric and nonparametric regression for large-scale problems.

Note that the Gaussian assumption is here only to make a connection between least squares and maximum likelihood, and the result would still be valid under the assumption that ϵ has zero mean and identity covariance matrix, if one used the least squares estimator.

7.2 Optimal Design of Experiments

Following the notation introduced in Section 7.1, we briefly reproduce after Kiefer and Wolfowitz some classical observations (Kiefer and Wolfowitz, 1959, 1960; Kiefer, 1961; Kiefer and Wolfowitz, 1965).

7.2.1 A Result from Kiefer and Wolfowitz

This section describes a famous result of Kiefer and Wolfowitz (1960) related to optimal design of experiments. Recall that $\mathbf{K}$ is a compact subset of $\mathbb{R}^d$ with nonempty interior. Under the Gaussian model described in the previous section one could imagine that the statistician could pick in advance the design points $\mathbf{x}_1, \ldots, \mathbf{x}_N$ before observing Y. In order to make the situation more favorable, the statistician could decide to choose the design points such that the covariance matrix of $\hat{\theta}$ is small. One reasonable criterion to achieve this goal is to maximize the determinant of the covariance, or moment, matrix. This is the D-optimal design problem and is modeled as an optimization problem over probability measures on K:

$$\max_{\mu \in \mathscr{M}(\mathbf{K})_+,\ \mu(\mathbf{K})=1} \det(\mathbf{M}_{\mu,n}). \tag{7.2}$$

On the other hand, the statistician could look for design points such that the maximal variance of estimated value over $\mathbf{K}$ is small. This is the G-optimal design problem, which is modeled by

$$\min_{\mu \in \mathscr{M}(\mathbf{K})_+,\ \mu(\mathbf{K})=1} \max_{\mathbf{z} \in \mathbf{K}} K_n^{\mu}(\mathbf{z}, \mathbf{z}), \tag{7.3}$$

where we used the relation between variance of estimated value at $\mathbf{z}$ and the Christoffel–Darboux kernel described in the previous section. The main result expounded in Kiefer and Wolfowitz (1960) ensures that, while the extremal solutions may not be unique, rather belonging to an affine space, optimal measures for problems (7.2) and (7.3) are actually the same. The proof relies on the well-known concavity of the function $\ln \det A$ defined on invertible, self-adjoint matrices A. This makes a connection between two different types of optimal design approaches in statistics based on the Christoffel function.

In general, finding the optimal measure ξ is not trivial, even for very simple settings, such as a compact interval on the real axis and $f_1, \ldots, f_n$ the monomials up to degree $n - 1$. The articles Hoel (1961/62) and Hoel and Levine (1964) analyze in detail this later case, where it is not surprising to see Chebyshev polynomials as the main characters. The following section describes an alternative approach in several dimensions for optimal design on basic semialgebraic sets.

7.2.2 Computational Optimal Design

We first retrieve the result of Kiefer and Wolfowitz (1960) via standard arguments of modern convex optimization. Recall that $s(n) = \binom{d+n}{d}$. To solve (7.2), let $\mathcal{M}(\mathbf{K})_n$ be the convex (moment) cone of vectors $\mathbf{y} = (y_\alpha)_{\alpha \in \mathbb{N}^d_{2n}} \in \mathbb{R}^{s(2n)}$ that have a finite representing Borel measure on $\mathbf{K}$ (assumed to have nonempty interior). As $\mathbf{K}$ is compact, the dual cone of $\mathcal{M}(\mathbf{K})_n$ is the convex cone $\mathcal{P}(\mathbf{K})_n$ of polynomials of degree at most $2n$ that are nonnegative on $\mathbf{K}$. Then (7.2) has the equivalent formulation

$$\rho = \sup_{\mathbf{y} \in \mathcal{M}(\mathbf{K})_n} \{\log \det(\mathbf{M}_n(\mathbf{y})) : \; y_0 = 1\}, \tag{7.4}$$

where $\mathbf{M}_n(\mathbf{y}) = \mathbf{M}_{\mu,n}$ is the moment matrix associated with a representing measure μ of $\mathbf{y} \in \mathcal{M}(\mathbf{K})_n$.

Theorem 7.2.1 *Problem* (7.4) *(hence Problem* (7.2)*) has an optimal solution* $\mathbf{y}^* \in \mathcal{M}(\mathbf{K})_n$ *with an associated representing* $\mu^* \in \mathscr{M}(\mathbf{K})_+$ *supported on at least* $\binom{d+n}{d}$ *and at most* $\binom{d+2n}{d}$ *points in the set* $\{\mathbf{x} \in \mathbf{K} : \; K_n^{\mu^*}(\mathbf{x}, \mathbf{x}) = s(n)\}$.

Moreover, as $\int K_n^{\mu}(\mathbf{x}, \mathbf{x})\, d\mu(\mathbf{x}) = s(n)$ *for every probability measure* μ *on* $\mathbf{K}$ *with invertible moment matrix* $\mathbf{M}_{\mu,n}$*, then it follows that* μ^* *also solves* (7.3).

Proof The objective function $\mathbf{y} \mapsto \log \det(\mathbf{M}_n(\mathbf{y}))$ of (7.4) is strictly concave and upper semicontinuous on $\mathcal{M}(\mathbf{K})_n$. As $y_0 = 1$ the feasible set is compact since all moments (up to order $2n$) of probability measures on $\mathbf{K}$ are uniformly bounded. Hence (7.4) has an optimal solution $\mathbf{y}^* \in \mathcal{M}(\mathbf{K})_n$ and $\log \det(\mathbf{M}_n(\cdot))$ is differentiable at $\mathbf{y}^*$. Moreover, as $\mathbf{K}$ has nonempty interior, (7.4) has a strictly feasible solution (take $\mathbf{y} \in \mathcal{M}(\mathbf{K})_n$ the vector of moments up to degree $2n$ of Lebesgue measure on $\mathbf{K}$) and so Slater's condition holds. Therefore by a standard result in convex optimization, $\mathbf{y}^*$ satisfies the Karush–Kuhn–Tucker (KKT) optimality conditions, which read

$$\frac{\partial \log \det \mathbf{M}_n(\mathbf{y}^*)}{\partial y_\alpha} + \lambda^* \delta_{\alpha=0} = p^*_\alpha, \; \forall \alpha \in \mathbb{N}^d_{2n}\,; \; \langle p^*, \mathbf{y}^* \rangle = 0,$$

for some scalar λ^* and $p^* \in \mathcal{P}(K)_n$, and where the second statement encodes the complementarity condition. Developing this yields

$$\lambda^* \delta_{\alpha=0} - \langle \mathbf{M}_n(\mathbf{y}^*)^{-1}, \mathbf{B}_\alpha \rangle = p^*_\alpha, \; \forall \alpha \in \mathbb{N}^d_{2n} \tag{7.5}$$

(where $\mathbf{v}_n(\mathbf{x})\mathbf{v}_n(\mathbf{x})^T = \sum_{\alpha \in \mathbb{N}^d_{2n}} \mathbf{B}_\alpha \mathbf{x}^\alpha$ and $\sum_{\alpha \in \mathbb{N}^d_{2n}} \mathbf{B}_\alpha\, y^*_\alpha = \mathbf{M}_n(\mathbf{y}^*)$). Multiplying (7.5) by y^*_α and summing, one finds

$$\lambda^* - \langle \mathbf{M}_n(\mathbf{y}^*)^{-1}, \mathbf{M}_n(\mathbf{y}^*) \rangle = \langle p^*, \mathbf{y}^* \rangle = 0,$$

and therefore $\lambda^* = s(n)$. Next, multiplying (7.5) by $\mathbf{x}^\alpha$ and summing yields

$$s(n) - \langle \mathbf{M}_n(\mathbf{y}^*)^{-1}, \mathbf{v}_n(\mathbf{x})\mathbf{v}_n(\mathbf{x})^T \rangle = \sum_{\alpha \in \mathbb{N}^d_{2n}} p^*_\alpha \, \mathbf{x}^\alpha = p^*(\mathbf{x}), \quad \forall \mathbf{x}.$$

As $\mathbf{y}^* \in \mathcal{M}(\mathbf{K})_n$, it has a representing measure $\nu^* \in \mathscr{M}(\mathbf{K})_+$ and so $\mathbf{M}_n(\mathbf{y}^*) = \mathbf{M}_{\nu^*,n}$, implying

$$\mathbf{x} \mapsto s(n) - K_n^{\nu^*}(\mathbf{x},\mathbf{x}) = p^*(\mathbf{x}) \geq 0, \quad \forall \mathbf{x} \in \mathbf{K},$$

$$\int_{\mathbf{K}} \underbrace{(s(n) - K_n^{\nu^*}(\mathbf{x},\mathbf{x}))}_{\geq 0} \, d\nu^*(\mathbf{x}) = \langle p^*, \mathbf{y}^* \rangle = 0.$$

Consequently, $K_n^{\nu^*}(\mathbf{x},\mathbf{x}) = s(n)$ for ν^*-almost all (a.a.) $\mathbf{x} \in K$. In view of Tchakaloff's Theorem (Bayer and Teichmann, 2006), there is an atomic probability measure $\mu^* \in \mathscr{M}(\mathbf{K})_+$ supported on at most $s(2n)$ points in $\mathrm{supp}(\nu^*)$. Next, if μ^* was supported on $\ell < s(n)$ points then $\mathbf{M}_{\mu^*,n}$ would have rank less than ℓ, hence would be singular, in contradiction with $\mathbf{M}_n(\mathbf{y}^*) \succ 0$. Finally, as ν^* and μ^* share the same moments up to degree $2n$, $K_n^{\nu^*}(\mathbf{x},\mathbf{x}) = K_n^{\mu^*}(\mathbf{x},\mathbf{x})$ for all $\mathbf{x}$. □

Observe that, remarkably, the optimal design consists of points which *all* lie on the distinguished level set $\{\mathbf{x} : K_n^{\mu^*}(\mathbf{x},\mathbf{x}) = s(n)\}$ of the Christoffel function associated with μ^*.

A Duality Viewpoint in Computational Geometry: Let $\mathcal{S}_n^+$ be the space of real symmetric matrices of size $s(n)$, that are positive semidefinite, and for every $\mathbf{Q} \in \mathcal{S}_n^+$, define $p_\mathbf{Q} \in \mathbb{R}_{2n}[\mathbf{x}]$ by

$$\mathbf{x} \mapsto p_\mathbf{Q}(\mathbf{x}) := \mathbf{v}_n(\mathbf{x})^T \, \mathbf{Q} \, \mathbf{v}_n(\mathbf{x}), \quad \forall \mathbf{x} \in \mathbb{R}^d,$$

that is, $\mathbf{Q}$ is a Gram matrix of the polynomial $p_\mathbf{Q}$.

Consider the optimization problem

$$\rho^* = \inf_{\mathbf{Q} \in \mathcal{S}_n^+} \{-\log\det \mathbf{Q} : s(n) - p_\mathbf{Q} \in \mathcal{M}(\mathbf{K})_n^*\}. \tag{7.6}$$

Lemma 7.2.2 (7.6) *is a dual of* (7.4)*, that is, weak duality holds. In addition, strong duality holds, that is,* $\rho = \rho^*$ *and if* $\mathbf{y}^* \in \mathcal{M}(\mathbf{K})$ *is an optimal solution of* (7.4) *then* $\mathbf{Q}^* := \mathbf{M}_n(\mathbf{y}^*)^{-1}$ *is an optimal solution of* (7.6)*, and* $p_{\mathbf{Q}^*}(\mathbf{x}) = K_n^{\mu^*}(\mathbf{x},\mathbf{x})$ *where* $\mu^* \in \mathscr{M}(\mathbf{K})_+$ *is a representing measure of* $\mathbf{y}^*$.

Proof The Fenchel transform f^* of a concave function $f : \mathcal{S}_n^+ \to \mathbb{R} \cup \{-\infty\}$ is given by

$$\mathbf{M} \mapsto f^*(\mathbf{M}) := \inf_{\mathbf{Q} \in \mathcal{S}_n^+} \mathrm{trace}(\mathbf{M} \cdot \mathbf{Q}) - f(\mathbf{Q}),$$

and in particular the Fenchel inequality states that

$$f^*(\mathbf{M}) + f(\mathbf{Q}) \leq \text{trace}(\mathbf{M} \cdot \mathbf{Q}), \quad \forall\, \mathbf{M}, \mathbf{Q} \in \mathcal{S}_n^+.$$

Therefore $(\log\det)^*(\mathbf{M}) = s(n) - \log\det(\mathbf{M}^{-1})$ for all $\mathbf{M} \in \mathcal{S}_n^+$, and therefore

$$\log\det(\mathbf{Q}) + s(n) + \log\det(\mathbf{M}) \leq \text{trace}(\mathbf{M} \cdot \mathbf{Q}), \quad \forall \mathbf{M}, \mathbf{Q} \in \mathcal{S}_n^+.$$

Let $\mathbf{y} \in \mathcal{M}(\mathbf{K})_n$ (resp. $\mathbf{Q} \in \mathcal{S}_n^+$) be an arbitrary feasible solution of (7.4) (resp. (7.6)). Observe that, since $\mathbf{y} \in \mathcal{M}(\mathbf{K})_n$, it has a representing measure μ on $\mathbf{K}$, and so

$$\begin{aligned} \langle p_{\mathbf{Q}}, \mathbf{y} \rangle &= \int \mathbf{v}_n(\mathbf{x})^T \mathbf{Q} \mathbf{v}_n(\mathbf{x})\, d\mu(\mathbf{x}) = \text{trace}\left(\mathbf{Q} \cdot \int \mathbf{v}_n(\mathbf{x})\, \mathbf{v}_n(\mathbf{x})^T\, d\mu\right) \\ &= \text{trace}\,(\mathbf{Q} \cdot \mathbf{M}_n(\mathbf{y})). \end{aligned}$$

Moreover, $\langle s(n) - p_{\mathbf{Q}}, \mathbf{y} \rangle \geq 0$ as $\mathbf{y} \in \mathcal{M}(\mathbf{K})_n$ and $s(n) - p_{\mathbf{Q}} \in \mathcal{M}(\mathbf{K})_n^*$. Therefore,

$$\begin{aligned} 0 \leq \langle s(n) - p_{\mathbf{Q}}, \mathbf{y} \rangle &= s(n) - \langle p_{\mathbf{Q}}, \mathbf{y} \rangle \\ &= s(n) - \text{trace}(\mathbf{Q} \cdot \mathbf{M}_n(\mathbf{y})) \\ &\leq -\log\det(\mathbf{M}_n(\mathbf{y})) - \log\det(\mathbf{Q}), \end{aligned}$$

which yields the desired weak duality result $\log\det \mathbf{M}_n(\mathbf{y}) \leq -\log\det \mathbf{Q}$, and so $\rho \leq \rho^*$. Finally, let $\mathbf{Q}^* := \mathbf{M}_n(\mathbf{y}^*)^{-1}$ and observe that

$$s(n) - p_{\mathbf{Q}^*}(\mathbf{x}) = s(n) - \mathbf{v}_n(\mathbf{x})^T \mathbf{M}_n(\mathbf{y}^*)^{-1} \mathbf{v}_n(\mathbf{x}) = s(n) - K_n^{\mu^*}(\mathbf{x}, \mathbf{x})$$

for all $\mathbf{x} \in \mathbb{R}^d$, and we have seen that $s(n) - K_n^{\mu^*}$ is nonnegative on $\mathbf{K}$, that is, $s(n) - p_{\mathbf{Q}^*} \in \mathcal{M}(\mathbf{K})_n^*$ $(= \mathcal{P}(\mathbf{K})_n)$; hence $\mathbf{Q}^*$ is a feasible solution of (7.6) with value $-\log\det(\mathbf{Q}^*) = \log\det(\mathbf{M}_n(\mathbf{y}^*)) = \rho \leq \rho^*$, which proves the strong duality result. □

Interpretation: The dual formulation (7.6) of the D-optimal design problem (7.2) has a nice interpretation in computational geometry. Indeed solving the D-optimal design problem is equivalent to searching for a sum of squares (SOS) polynomial p^* of degree at most $2n$ such that $s(n) - p^*$ is nonnegative on K, and its Gram matrix $\mathbf{Q}$ minimizes $\log\det \mathbf{Q}^{-1}$ among all such polynomials. If $n = 1$ then p^* is a quadratic polynomial and the set $\mathcal{E} := \{\mathbf{x} \colon p^*(\mathbf{x}) \leq s(n)\}$ is the unique ellipsoid that contains $\mathbf{K}$ and has minimum volume (indeed $\det \mathbf{Q}$ is proportional to $\text{vol}(\mathcal{E})$). The set $\mathcal{E}$ is the so-called *Löwner–John ellipsoid* in computational geometry. However, when $n > 1$ it is not clear how $\log\det \mathbf{Q}$ relates to the Lebesgue volume of the set $\mathcal{E} = \{\mathbf{x} : p^*(\mathbf{x}) \leq s(n)\}$. Nevertheless,

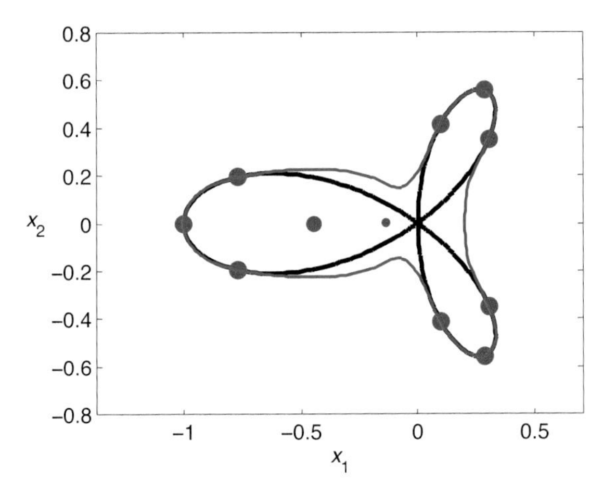

Figure 7.1 Optimal design on the 2D folium; in blue the level set $\{\mathbf{x}\colon K_3^{\mu^*}(\mathbf{x},\mathbf{x}) = s(3)\}$ with contact points on K in red.

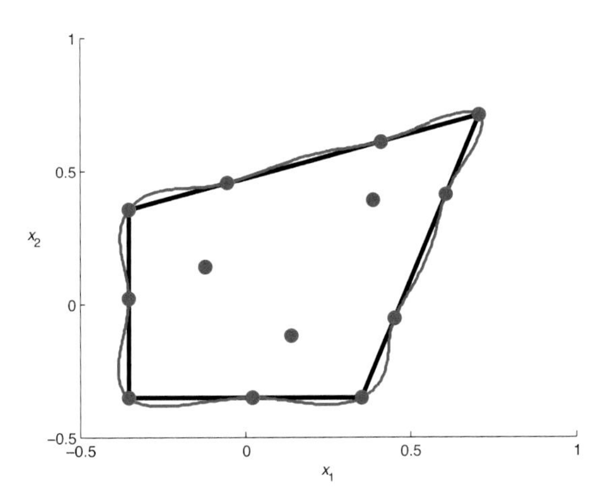

Figure 7.2 Optimal design on the 2D Wynn's polygon; in blue the level set $\{\mathbf{x}\colon K_3^{\mu^*}(\mathbf{x},\mathbf{x}) = s(3)\}$ with contact points on K in red.

as $\mathbf{K} \subset \mathcal{E}$ and the level set $\{\mathbf{x}\colon p^*(\mathbf{x}) = s(n)\}$ intersects $\mathbf{K}$ at at least $s(n)$ points, this suggests that $\mathcal{E}$ is indeed a small-volume set that contains $\mathbf{K}$. This claim is illustrated in Figures 7.1 and 7.2 where the blue curve is the level set $\{\mathbf{x}\colon s(n) = p^*(\mathbf{x})\}$ and $p^* \in \mathbb{R}_6[\mathbf{x}]$.

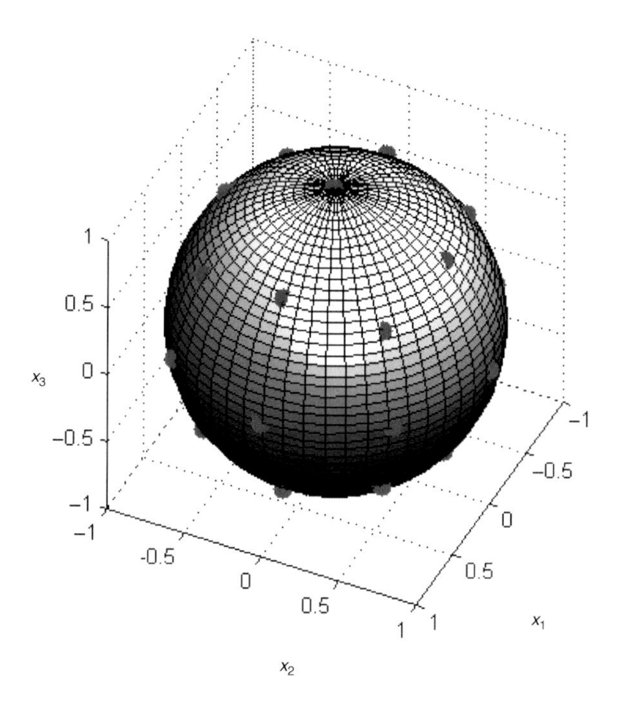

Figure 7.3 Optimal design on the 3D sphere with $n = 3$ and with contact points on K in red.

A Two-step Numerical Scheme: In full generality solving (7.4) is quite difficult even with discretization methods after one has succeeded in constructing a fine grid of the design space $\mathbf{K} \subset \mathbb{R}^n$. However, when $\mathbf{K} \subset \mathbb{R}^n$ is a compact basic semialgebraic set, we describe a two-step mesh-free numerical scheme to compute the atomic measure μ^* (or D-optimal design associated with $\mathbf{K}$) in Theorem 7.2.1. The goal of Step 1 is to compute all moments $\mathbf{y}^* = (y^*_\alpha) \in \mathbb{R}^{s(2n)}$ of μ^* up to degree n (even). The goal of Step 2 is to extract the support of the an atomic measure on $\mathbf{K}$ whose moments up to degree $2n$ agree with $\mathbf{y}^*$.

So let $g_j \in \mathbb{R}[\mathbf{x}]$, $j = 1, \ldots, m$, and let

$$\mathbf{K} := \{\mathbf{x} \in \mathbb{R}^n : \; g_j(\mathbf{x}) \geq 0, \; j = 1, \ldots, m\}$$

be a compact basic semialgebraic set. Let $t_j := \lceil \deg(g_j)/2 \rceil$, $j = 0, 1, \ldots, m$, and $v := \max_{j=1,\ldots,m} t_j$. For convenience we may and will assume that $K \subset [-1, 1]^n$ (possibly after rescaling) and $g_1 = d - \|\mathbf{x}\|^2$. Finally let $g_0(\mathbf{x}) := 1$ for all $\mathbf{x}$ and, with $r \geq \max[n, v]$, consider the optimization problem:

$$\sup_{\mathbf{y}\in\mathbb{R}^{s(r)}} \{\log\det \mathbf{M}_n(\mathbf{y}) : \; y_0 = 1; \; \mathbf{M}_{r-t_j}(g_j\,\mathbf{y}) \succeq 0, \quad j = 0,\ldots,m\}. \tag{7.7}$$

Problem (7.7) is a convex optimization problem which has an optimal solution $\mathbf{y}^r \in \mathbb{R}^{s(r)}$ because its feasible set is compact and the objective function is upper-semicontinuous and concave. Hence it can be solved efficiently by ad hoc methods (e.g. by using the software package CVX (Grant and Boyd, 2014)). The rationale behind (7.7) is quite simple. Indeed (7.7) is a convex relaxation of (7.4) where we have replaced the intractable constraint $\mathbf{y} \in \mathcal{M}(\mathbf{K})_n$ with the simpler and tractable (necessary) constraints $\mathbf{M}_{r-t_j}(g_j\,\mathbf{y}) \succeq 0$ for all $j = 0, 1, \ldots, m$.

A theoretical justification of this convex relaxation is provided by its nice asymptotic guarantee as r increases. Indeed by Putinar's Positivstellensatz (Putinar, 1993), letting $\mathcal{M}(\mathbf{K})$ be the set of all sequences $\mathbf{y} = (y_\alpha)_{\alpha\in\mathbb{N}^d}$ that have a representing measure $\mu \in \mathscr{M}(\mathbf{K})_+$,

$$\mathbf{y} \in \mathcal{M}(\mathbf{K}) \;\Leftrightarrow\; \mathbf{M}_r(g_j\,\mathbf{y}) \succeq 0, \quad j = 0,\ldots,m, \quad \forall r \in \mathbb{N}.$$

This in turn implies that $\mathbf{y}^* \in \mathcal{M}(\mathbf{K})_n$ if and only if there exists $\mathbf{y} = (y_\alpha)_{\alpha\in\mathbb{N}^d}$ such that $y_\alpha = y^*_\alpha$ for all $\alpha \in \mathbb{N}^d_{2n}$ and $\mathbf{M}_r(g_j\,\mathbf{y}) \succeq 0$ for all $j = 0,\ldots,m$ and all $r \in \mathbb{N}$.

So our procedure consists of the following two steps.

Step 1: Fix $r \geq n$ and solve (7.7) to obtain $\mathbf{y}^r \in \mathbb{R}^{s(r)}$ and let $\mathbf{y}^* := (y^r_\alpha)_{\alpha\in\mathbb{N}^d_{2n}}$. In general $\mathbf{y}^r$ is not the vector of moments of a probability measure on K but, in view of what precedes, in minimizing $\log\det \mathbf{M}_n(\mathbf{y})$ in (7.7) we expect $\mathbf{y}^*$ to be the moments up to degree $2n$ of a measure μ^* as in Theorem 7.2.1.

Step 2: (Extraction of the atomic measure μ^* of Theorem 7.2.1) With $r > n$, solve the semidefinite program:

$$\begin{aligned} \inf_{\mathbf{y}\in\mathbb{R}^{s(r)}} \quad & \{\mathrm{trace}(\mathbf{M}_r(\mathbf{y})) : \\ \text{s.t.} \quad & y_\alpha = y^*_\alpha, \;\; \forall \alpha \in \mathbb{N}^d_n, \\ & \mathbf{M}_{r-t_j}(g_j\,\mathbf{y}) \succeq 0, \quad j = 0,\ldots,m\}. \end{aligned} \tag{7.8}$$

(7.8) is a semidefinite program that has an optimal solution because its feasible set is compact. The rationale behind Step 2 is provided by the fact that if $\mu^* \in \mathscr{M}(\mathbf{K})_+$ is an atomic measure with finite support then the rank of $\mathbf{M}_{\mu^*,n}$ stabilizes whenever $n \geq n_0$ for some n_0. Next, if $\mathbf{M}_r(\mathbf{y}) \succeq 0$ then $\mathrm{trace}(\mathbf{M}_r(\mathbf{y}))$ is the *nuclear* norm of $\mathbf{M}_r(\mathbf{y})$ which when minimized is known to induce optimal solutions with small rank. Of course other small-rank-inducing criteria can be used in lieu of $\mathrm{trace}(\mathbf{M}_r(\mathbf{y}))$. Let $L_\mathbf{y} : \mathbb{R}[\mathbf{x}]^* \to \mathbb{R}$ be the linear *Riesz functional*

$$p \left(= \sum_{\alpha} p_\alpha \mathbf{x}^\alpha \right) \quad \mapsto L_{\mathbf{y}}(p) := \sum_{\alpha} p_\alpha \, y_\alpha,$$

and observe that $\mathrm{trace}(\mathbf{M}_r(\mathbf{y})) = L_{\mathbf{y}}(\theta)$ where the polynomial

$$\mathbf{x} \mapsto \theta(\mathbf{x}) := \sum_{\alpha \in \mathbb{N}^d_r} \mathbf{x}^{2\alpha} \in \mathbb{R}_{2r}[\mathbf{x}]$$

is strictly positive on $\mathbb{R}^d$. It has been proved in Nie (2013) that if one chooses a randomly generated strictly positive polynomial θ of degree $2r$ and if one minimizes $L_{\mathbf{y}}(\theta)$ in (7.8) then generically there exists r such that

$$\mathrm{rank}\, \mathbf{M}_r(\mathbf{y}) = \mathrm{rank}\, \mathbf{M}_{r-v}(\mathbf{y})$$

at an optimal solution of (7.8). Then by a Flat Extension Theorem of Curto and Fialkow (2005), $\mathbf{y}$ is the vector of moments up to degree $2r$ of some measure μ supported on $\mathbf{K}$. In particular $\mathbf{y}^* = (y_\alpha)_{\alpha \in \mathbb{N}^d_{2n}}$ is the vector of moments of μ up to degree $2n$.

The potential and efficiency of the methodology is illustrated on two 2D nontrivial nonconvex design spaces $\mathbf{K}$ (the folium and Wynn's polygon) and one 3D (the sphere). As shown in Figure 7.1 for the folium, in Figure 7.2 for Wynn's polygon and in Figure 7.3 for the sphere, the red dots denote the optimal design in each case, all obtained with $n = 3$.

7.3 Inference from a Sample

We consider the setting described in Chapter 6, which is repeated here for convenience: μ is a measure on $\mathbb{R}^d$ which will be called the population measure; the associated Christoffel function can be called the population Christoffel function. Start with a sequence of $\mathbb{R}^d$-valued random variables $(X_i)_{i \in \mathbb{N}}$, which are independent and identically distributed according to μ. For any $N \in \mathbb{N}$, we let μ_N be the empirical measure associated with $X_1, \ldots, X_N$,

$$\mu_N = \frac{1}{n} \sum_{i=1}^{N} \delta_{X_i}, \tag{7.9}$$

where $\delta_{\mathbf{x}}$ denotes the Dirac measure supported on $\mathbf{x} \in \mathbb{R}^d$.

In this section we show how it is possible to combine the quantitative asymptotics given in Chapter 4 and the algebraic considerations of Chapter 5 with statistical approximation results described in Chapter 6 in order to infer

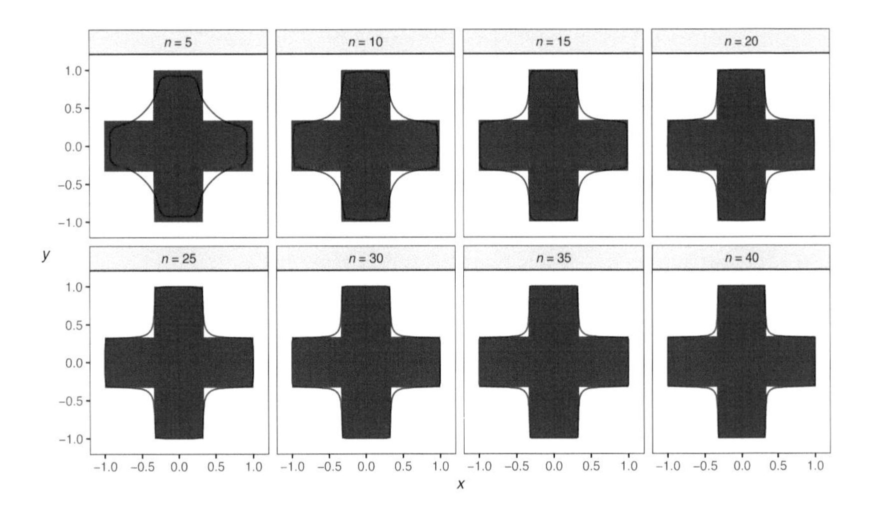

Figure 7.4 Illustration of the convergence of a Christoffel–Darboux sublevel set to the boundary of the support of a measure as the degree increases. The shaded area is S and the red line is the chosen sublevel set. Here the average value of the CD kernel is $\binom{n+2}{n}$ and the depicted level set is chosen to be $\frac{1}{2}\binom{n+3}{n}$.

properties of the population measure μ, such as density, support and its algebraic dimension, from the knowledge of only a sample.

7.3.1 Inferring the Support of a Measure

Throughout this section we assume that the population measure μ has bounded support S, such that $S = \mathrm{cl}(\mathrm{int}(S))$.

A Deterministic Result for Lebesgue Measure: Using the indications provided by Lemmas 4.3.1 and 4.3.2, choosing $C > 0$ and $q > d$, one could guess that the following set

$$S_n = \{\mathbf{x} \colon \mathbf{v}_n(\mathbf{x})^T \mathbf{M}_{\mu,n}^{-1} \mathbf{v}_n(\mathbf{x}) \leq Cn^q\}$$

should be close to S in a certain sense. This is indeed the case although the precise sense has to be specified. Figure 7.4 illustrates this phenomenon; we see that as the degree bound grows, a chosen sublevel set of the CD kernel gets close to the boundary of the support. This convergence seems to take place at different rates depending on the local geometry of the support.

The following result makes this intuition precise in the special case of the Lebesgue measure, as described in Lasserre and Pauwels (2019).

Assumption 7.3.1 We make the following assumptions.

(a) $S \subset \mathbb{R}^d$ is a compact set such that $\mathrm{cl}(\mathrm{int}(S)) = S$; μ_S is the uniform measure on S, that is, $\mu_S = \lambda_S/\lambda(S)$ where λ_S is the restriction of the Lebesgue measure to S.

(b) $(\delta_k)_{k\in\mathbb{N}}$ is a decreasing sequence of positive numbers converging to 0. For every $k \in \mathbb{N}$, let n_k be the smallest integer such that

$$2^{3-\frac{\delta_k n_k}{\delta_k+\mathrm{diam}(S)}} n_k^d \left(\frac{e}{d}\right)^d \exp\left(\frac{d^2}{n_k}\right) \le \alpha_k, \tag{7.10}$$

where $\mathrm{diam}(S)$ denotes the diameter of the set S and

$$\alpha_k := \frac{\delta_k^d \omega_d}{\lambda(S)} \frac{(n_k+1)(n_k+2)(n_k+3)}{(n_k+d+1)(n_k+d+2)(2n_k+d+6)}.$$

Note that n_k is well defined. Indeed, since δ_k is positive, the left-hand side of (7.10) goes to 0 as $n_k \to \infty$ while the right-hand side remains bounded for increasing values of n_k. Recall the definition of the Hausdorff distance $d_H(X,Y)$ between two compact sets X, Y:

$$d_H(X,Y) = \max\left\{\sup_{\mathbf{x}\in X}\inf_{\mathbf{y}\in Y} \mathrm{dist}(\mathbf{x},\mathbf{y}), \sup_{\mathbf{y}\in Y}\inf_{\mathbf{x}\in X} \mathrm{dist}(\mathbf{x},\mathbf{y})\right\}.$$

Theorem 7.3.2 *Let $S \subset \mathbb{R}^d$, μ_S, $\{\delta_k\}_{k\in\mathbb{N}}$, $\{\alpha_k\}_{k\in\mathbb{N}}$ and $\{n_k\}_{k\in\mathbb{N}}$ satisfy Assumption 7.3.1. For every $k \in \mathbb{N}$, let $S_k \subset \mathbb{R}^p$ be the set defined by*

$$S_k := \left\{\mathbf{x} \in \mathbb{R}^p : \; s(n_k)\, \Lambda_{n_k}^{\mu_S}(\mathbf{x}) \ge \alpha_k\right\}.$$

Then, as $k \to \infty$,

$$d_H(S_k, S) \to 0,$$
$$d_H(\partial S_k, \partial S) \to 0.$$

The preceding result can be generalized to positive densities, bounded from above and from below. The arguments combine Lemmas 4.3.2 and 4.3.1; see Lasserre and Pauwels (2019) for details.

Inference from a Sample: In a statistical context, one cannot compute K_n^μ or Λ_n^μ but rather one has access to $K_n^{\mu_N}$ based on the empirical measure. In this case it is possible to combine similar arguments to those in Theorem 7.3.2 with the concentration result of 6.3.1 to obtain high-probability bounds for support inference. We account for a simplified version of the main results of Vu et al. (2019). Throughout this subsection, we assume that μ is the restriction of the

Lebesgue measure to a compact support set S, with nonempty interior and whose boundary is a smooth hypersurface of $\mathbb{R}^d$.

Theorem 7.3.3 *Let $S \subset \mathbb{R}^d$ be compact with nonempty interior such that its boundary is a smooth embedded hypersurface and let μ be the restriction of the Lebesgue measure to S. Then, for any $\delta > 0$, there exist constants C_1, C_2, C_3 which depend on δ and can be computed from problem data, such that setting for all $N \in \mathbb{N}$,*

$$
\begin{aligned}
n_N &:= \left\lfloor C_1 N^{\frac{1}{d+2}} \right\rfloor, \\
\alpha_N &:= C_2 n_N^{\frac{3d}{4}}, \\
S_N &:= \{\mathbf{x} \in \mathbb{R}^d,\ K_{n_N}^{\mu_N} \leq \alpha_N\},
\end{aligned}
$$

it holds with probability at least $1 - \delta$ that

$$\max\{\, d_H(S, S_n),\ d_H(\partial S, \partial S_n)\,\} \leq \frac{C_3}{N^{\frac{1}{2d+4}}}.$$

It is important to emphasize that in Theorem 7.3.3 the estimator of the support S_N is computed from knowledge of only the sample $(\mathbf{x}_i)_{i=1}^N$. An explicit expression for the constants and a detailed proof can be found in Vu et al. (2019). This result generalizes to more general measures with positive density and a controlled rate of decay near the boundary of S. The main proof argument combines extensions of the quantitative estimates in Lemmas 4.3.2 and 4.3.1, which were also used to obtain Theorem 7.3.2, with the statistical concentration results described in Theorem 6.3.1. The smoothness assumption of the boundary of S allows us to control the supremum of the CD kernel on S, the Bernstein–Markov constant which appeared in Theorem 6.3.1.

We propose a numerical illustration in $\mathbb{R}^2$, inspired by Vu et al. (2019); we choose two different subsets of $\mathbb{R}^2$ which comply with Theorem 7.3.3. According to Theorem 7.3.3, the degree bound should be proportional to $N^{1/4}$. For each value of N, we implement the following procedure:

- Choose $n_N := \lfloor 2N^{1/4} \rfloor$.
- Evaluate the empirical Christoffel function at each input point.
- Choose the smallest value as a threshold and draw the corresponding level set.

The results are presented in Figure 7.5. It illustrates how the Christoffel–Darboux kernel is able to identify the support, its boundary and topological features for large enough sample sizes despite the randomness inherent to sampling.

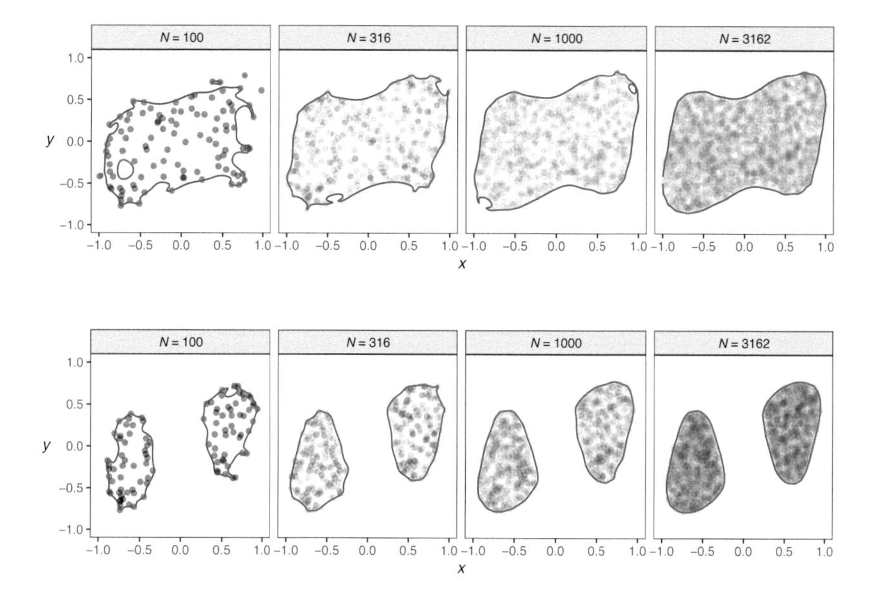

Figure 7.5 Experiment on synthetic data in the plane. The sample points are drawn uniformly on a chosen set with smooth boundary.The red line shows the boundary of the support estimated from the sample. For N large enough, the empirical CD kernel is able to identify the support.

7.3.2 Singular Support and Geometric Properties

In this section, we consider measures which comply with Assumption 6.3.3; see Chapter 5 for details. We recall that μ is supported on an algebraic set. We denote by V the Zariski closure of $S = \mathrm{supp}(\mu)$ endowed with the area measure σ_V. They satisfy the following constraints:

(a) V is an irreducible algebraic set,
(b) μ is absolutely continuous with respect to σ_V.

Theorem 6.3.4 asserts that, so long as $N \geq \mathbf{HF}(n)$, with probability 1, $\mathbf{M}_{\mu_N,n}$ and $\mathbf{M}_{\mu,n}$ have the same rank, equal to $\mathbf{HF}(n)$. They actually have the same kernel, so that in this case it is possible to recover the set of polynomials of degree up to n vanishing on S (or V) from the knowledge of only a sufficiently large sample; see also Proposition 5.2.3 for geometric details. These polynomials completely characterize V for large degrees, so that one has access with probability 1 to a complete characterization of V based on the knowledge of only a random sample.

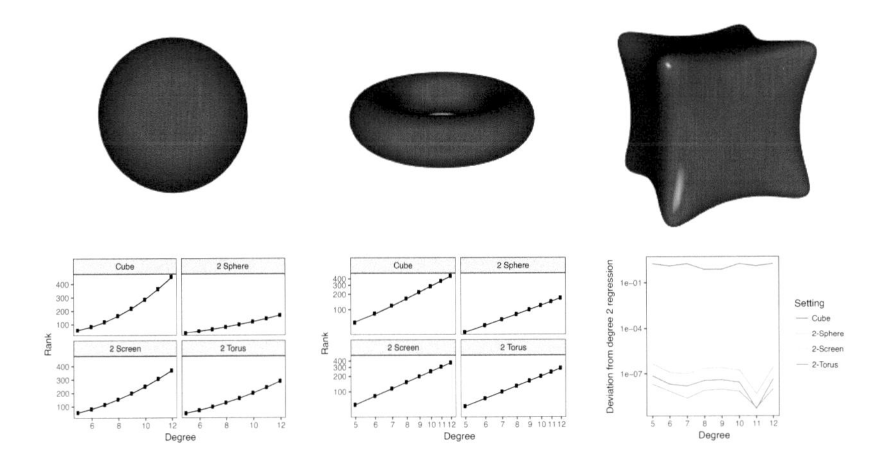

Figure 7.6 Top: A visualization of the two-dimensional surfaces considered in this example, the sphere, the torus and the TV screen. Bottom: Relation between the rank of the moment matrix and the corresponding degree bound. For different sets, the dots represent the measured rank and the curve is the degree-2 interpolation. On the left, the raw relation, we see that the cube has the highest rank. The same plot is in log log scale in the middle. The difference between measured rank and estimated degree-2 interpolation is hardly visible. On the right, we represent the residuals between degree-2 interpolation and measured ranks. The degree–rank relation is well interpolated for two-dimensional sets while this is not the case for the cube.

Let us illustrate Theorem 6.3.4 with the example of inference of algebraic dimension taken from Pauwels et al. (2021). It is known from algebraic geometry – see, for example, Cox et al. (2007, Chapter 9) – that for n large enough, $\mathbf{HF}(n)$ is a polynomial in n with degree the algebraic dimension of V. Hence, given a sample of size N, it is in principle possible to get access to the dimension of V by investigating variations of the rank of $\mathbf{M}_{\mu_N,n}$ as a function of n.

We perform the following numerical experiment:

- Sample 20 000 points on a chosen set $\Omega \subset \mathbb{R}^3$, from a density with respect to the area measure on Ω.
- For $n = 5, \dots, 12$, compute the rank of the empirical moment matrix: set $X \in \mathbb{R}^{20\,000 \times s(n)}$ as the design matrix representing each point in a polynomial basis (of size $s(d)$), such that the empirical moment matrix is given by $1/20\,000 X^T X$. We estimate the rank of X using singular-value thresholding (multivariate Chebyshev basis, threshold 10^{-10}).

- Fit a degree-2 regression polynomial interpolating the relation between the degree and the rank.

We choose four different subsets of $\mathbb{R}^3$: unit cube, unit sphere, TV screen, torus. The first one is three-dimensional while all the others are two-dimensional (see Figure 7.6). From Proposition 5.2.3, in the first case it is expected that the computed rank grows like a third-degree polynomial, while for the remaining cases it should grow like a quadratic. Hence the interpolation of the rank–degree relation should be of good quality for the last three cases and not for the first case. This is what we observed in Figure 7.6.

7.3.3 Density Estimation on Algebraic Sets

We illustrate the result presented in Theorem 5.3.4 with several multivariate datasets whose topological characteristics suggest mapping them to algebraic sets capturing symmetries. The CD kernel allows us to treat different algebraic supports using the same computational tool.

The first step consists in mapping the data of interest on an algebraic set whose topology reflects the intrinsic topology of the data, namely the circle for periodic data, the sphere for celestial data and the torus for bi-periodic data. Then we evaluate the empirical Christoffel function on the chosen set and use it as a proxy for density. We use the pseudo-inverse of the empirical moment matrix and evaluate the Christoffel function on a grid using (5.5) and (5.6). We then plot the contours of the estimate obtained on the grid to get a graphical representation of the estimated density.

The Christoffel function depends strongly on the geometry of the boundary of the support. The algebraic sets considered here *do not* have boundaries (as manifolds), and isotropy properties ensure that the Christoffel function associated with the *uniform* measure on these sets is *constant*.

Dragonfly Orientation on the Circle: The dataset was described in Batschelet (1981) and consists of measurements of the orientation of 214 dragonflies with respect to the azimuth of the sun. The orientation is an angle which has a periodicity and as such is naturally mapped to the circle. The dataset and the corresponding Christoffel function are shown in Figure 7.7 (left). As the degree increases, the Christoffel function captures regions densely populated by observations (high density) and regions without any observation (low density). As was already observed in Batschelet (1981), dragonflies tend to sit in a direction perpendicular to the sun.

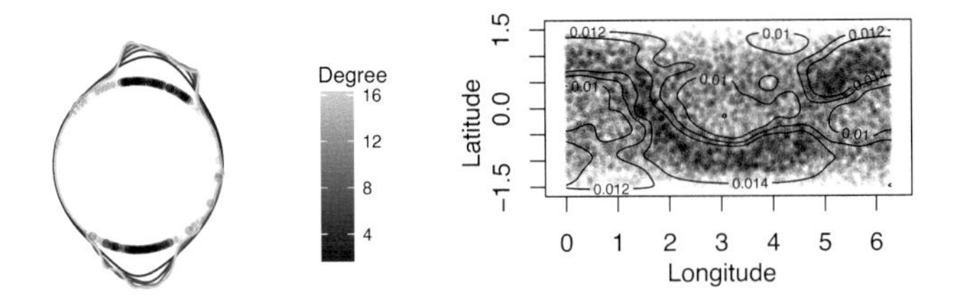

Figure 7.7 Left: Dragonfly orientation with respect to the sun, on the torus. The curves represent the empirical Christoffel function and the dots are observations. Right: Each point represents the observation of a double star on the celestial sphere, associated with longitude and latitude. The level sets represent the empirical Christoffel functions on the sphere in $\mathbb{R}^3$ (degree 8). The highlighted band corresponds to the Milky Way.

Double Stars on the Sphere: We reproduce the experiment performed in Cuevas et al. (2006b). The dataset is provided by the European Space Agency and was aquired by the Hipparcos satellite (Perryman et al., 1997). The data consist of the position of 12 176 double stars on the celestial sphere described by spherical coordinates. Double stars are of interest in astronomy because of their connection with the formation of single stars. A natural question is that of the uniformity of the distribution of these double stars on the celestial map. The dataset and corresponding Christoffel function are shown in Figure 7.7 (right) using equirectangular projection. Firstly we note that the displayed level lines nicely capture the geometry of the sphere without distortion at the poles. Secondly the Christoffel function allows us to detect a higher-density region (above 0.14) which corresponds to the Milky Way.

Amino-acid Dihedral Angles on the Bi-torus: We reproduce the manipulations performed in Lovell et al. (2003). Proteins are amino-acid chains with 3D structure described by ϕ and ψ the backbone dihedral angles of amino-acid residues. The 3D structure of a protein is extremely relevant as it relates to the molecular and biological function of a protein. Ramachandran plots consist of a scatter plot of these angles for different amino acids and allow us to visualize energetically allowed configuration for each amino acid.

It is worth emphasizing that being able to describe typical regions in Ramachandran plots is of great relevance as a tool for *protein structure validation* (Lovell et al., 2003). Since the data consist of angles, they have

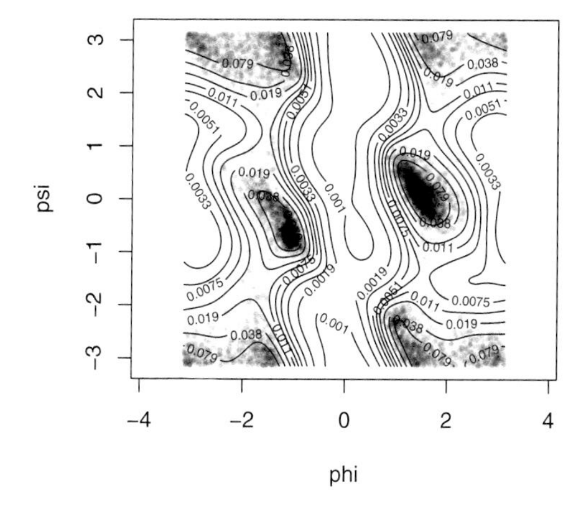

Figure 7.8 Each point represents two dihedral angles for a Glycine amino acid. These angles are used to describe the global three dimensional shape of a protein. They live on the bi-torus. The level sets are those of the empirical Christoffel functions evaluated on the sphere in $\mathbb{R}^4$. The degree is 4.

a bi-periodic structure and therefore naturally map to the bi-torus in $\mathbb{R}^4$. A Ramachandran plot for 7705 Glycine amino acids as well as the corresponding Christoffel function estimate are shown in Figure 7.8. The Christoffel function is able to identify highly populated areas (density above 0.08) and its level set fits nicely the specific geometry of the torus. We refer the reader to Lovell et al. (2003) for more details about this dataset.

7.3.4 Detection of Outliers

In this section we describe a heuristic to classify some points of a fixed cloud of data points as *potential outliers*. No rigorous asymptotic analysis is provided as the cloud of points is assumed to be fixed.

To better illustrate the method, recall Figure 1 of the Introduction (reproduced here as Figure 7.9). The cloud of 2D data points consists of $N = 1040$ points. As one may immediately see (because we have a 2D drawing), all points significantly outside the annulus (with a brown or red color rather than black) seem to be *anomalies* when compared with the large majority of black points inside (or very close to) the annulus. Therefore they may qualify as *outliers* if one considers that the annulus is a correct representative of the data points.

Of course the term "representative" is here used in a fuzzy manner. Indeed if the N points are drawn from a certain distribution μ, it could happen that the support of μ is not the plotted annulus but also contains a compact set A

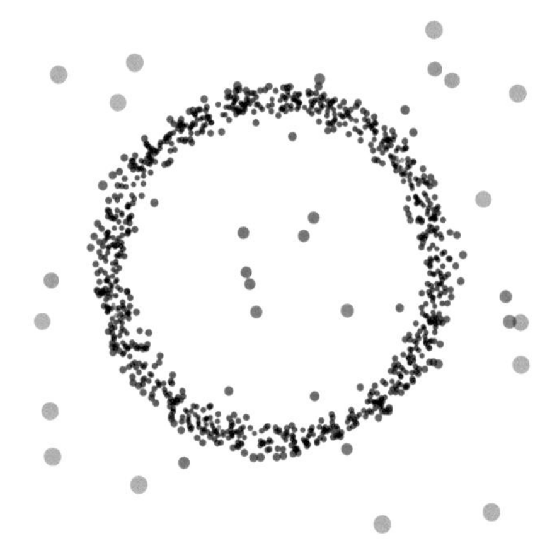

Figure 7.9 $N = 1040$ and $n = 8$; points with size and color proportional to the value of $1/\Lambda_n^{\mu_N}$.

outside the annulus, and with small measure $\mu(A)$. Then by sampling a lot more points, one might be able to observe more points clustering in (or close to) the additional compact set A; such points would not be outliers anymore.

However, we here assume that a decision on possible outliers has to be made on the basis of only the current N available data points. So let μ^N be the empirical measure associated with the cloud of points $(\mathbf{x}_i)_{i=1}^N$, that is,

$$\mu_N := \frac{1}{N}\sum_{i=1}^{N}\delta_{\mathbf{x}_i}.$$

Recall that the color and size of points in Figure 7.9 is proportional to $\Lambda_n^{\mu_N}$; that is, a point $\mathbf{x}_i$ has small size and is colored in black if $1/\Lambda_n^{\mu_N}(\mathbf{x}_i)$ is small whereas it has larger size and is colored in red if $1/\Lambda_n^{\mu_N}(\mathbf{x}_i)$ is large. So Figure 7.9 simply illustrates that a relatively high *score* $1/\Lambda_n^{\mu_N}(\mathbf{x}_i)$ is common to all points that are not inside or not close to the annulus, whereas *all* points inside or close to the annulus have a small score.

Again this is not surprising in view of results in Chapter 4 for a measure μ supported on a compact set $S \subset \mathbb{R}^d$. Indeed whenever $\mathbf{x} \notin S$, by Lemma 4.3.1, $n^d\,\Lambda_n^{\mu}(\mathbf{x}) \to 0$, as $n \to \infty$; the convergence is exponentially fast in n and the exact rate depends on the distance $d(\mathbf{x}, S)$ (the higher the distance, the higher the rate). On the other hand, the same quantity remains positive on average inside the support.

Table 7.1 *Description of the five network intrusion dataset constructed from KDD cup 1999 data following Williams et al. (2002) and Yamanishi et al. (2004)*

Dataset	http	smtp	ftp-data	ftp	others
Number of examples	567 498	95 156	30 464	4091	5858
Proportions of attacks	0.004	0.0003	0.023	0.077	0.016

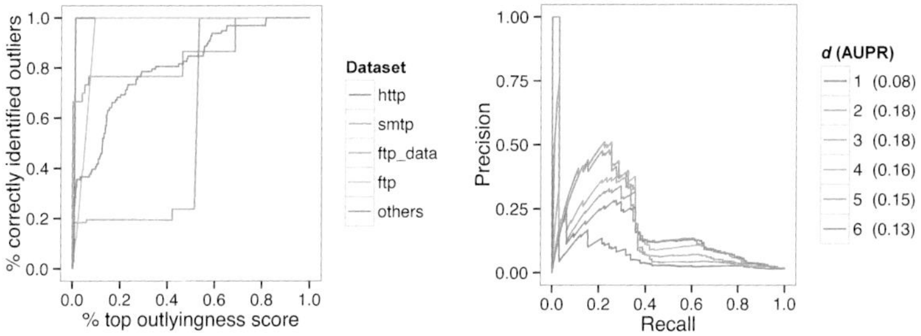

Figure 7.10 Left: Reproduction of results in Williams et al. (2002) with $\Lambda_3^{\mu_N}$-score. Right: Precision–recall curves for different values of n (dataset "others"). AUPR is the area under the precision-recall curve: the larger it is, the better the performance.

So as a simple heuristic whose rationale is just provided by the above discussion, we propose to

$$\textit{declare a point } \mathbf{x} \textit{ of the cloud as a potential outlier if } \Lambda_n^{\mu_N}(\mathbf{x}) < \tau,$$

where τ is some appropriate threshold. Notice the simplicity of the test as it depends only on the choice of the degree n and the threshold τ. For instance, a threshold proportional to $\binom{d+n}{n}^{-1}$ seems a reasonable choice as $\tau \int 1/\Lambda_n^{\mu_N} \, d\mu_N = 1$.

Example: Detection of Network Intrusions: We chose the *KDD cup 99* network intrusion dataset (available from Lichman, 2013) which consists of network connection data with labels describing whether they correspond to normal traffic or network intrusions. Following Williams et al. (2002) and Yamanishi et al. (2004), we construct five datasets consisting of labeled vectors in $\mathbb{R}^3$, the label indicating normal traffic or network attack. The content of these datasets is summarized in Table 7.1 and details on their construction are provided in Williams et al. (2002), Yamanishi et al. (2004) and in Lasserre and Pauwels (2016, Appendix C).

Williams et al. (2002) have compared different types of methods for outlier detection in the same experimental setting: methods based on robust estimation and Mahalanobis distance, mixture model based methods, and recurrent neural network based methods, see Williams et al. (2002, Figure 7).

On the left-hand side of Figure 7.10 we represent the same performance measure with our approach. We first compute $\Lambda_n^{\mu_N}(\mathbf{x})$ for each data point $\mathbf{x}$ and decide that $\mathbf{x}$ is a potential outlier if $\Lambda_n^{\mu_N}(\mathbf{x}) > \tau$, for some given threshold τ. We then display, for varying values of τ, the proportion of correctly identified outliers, with score above τ, as a function of the proportion of examples with score above the threshold (for different values of the threshold τ). The main comments are as follows.

- The detection procedure does indeed detect network intrusions with varying performances on the five datasets.
- Except for the "ftp-data dataset", the global shapes of the curves are very similar to results reported in Williams et al. (2002, Figure 7), indicating that the proposed approach is comparable to other dedicated methods for intrusion detection, at least for these four datasets.

In a second experiment, we investigate the effect of changing the degree n in $\Lambda_n^{\mu_N}$ on the performances in terms of outlier detection. We focus on the single dataset labelled "others" because it is the most heterogeneous in terms of data and outliers. We adopt a slightly different measure of performance and use precision–recall curves (see e.g. Davis and Goadrich, 2006) to measure performances in identifying network intrusions (the higher the curve, the better). Denote by AUPR the area under such curves. The right panel of Figure 7.10 represents these results. Firstly, the case $n = 1$, which corresponds to vanilla *Mahalanobis distance*, provides poor performances. Secondly, the global performances rapidly increase with n and then decrease and stabilize. As we have seen in Chapter 6, there is a tradeoff between the degree n and the size N of the sample.

7.3.5 Inversion of Affine Shuffling

This section illustrates how the affine invariance of the Christoffel function can be used efficiently and in a very simple manner to detect whether two clouds of points are in fact the same, modulo such an affine transformation and possible shuffling of labels.

Suppose that we are given two clouds of N points $\boldsymbol{\xi} = (\mathbf{x}_i)_{i=1}^N \subset \mathbb{R}^d$, $\boldsymbol{\xi}' = (\mathbf{z}_i)_{i=1}^N \subset \mathbb{R}^d$, and we want to check whether there is an affine mapping $\mathcal{A}\colon \mathbb{R}^d \to \mathbb{R}^d$ and some permutation $\sigma\colon \{1,\dots,N\} \to \{1,\dots,N\}$, such that $\mathbf{z}_i = \mathcal{A}\,\mathbf{x}(\sigma(i))$ for every $i \in \{1,\dots,N\}$. Notice that finding $\mathcal{A}$ (if it exists) is a nontrivial problem since the permutation σ is also unknown. In other words, if we associate a matrix $\mathbf{A} = [\mathbf{x}(1),\dots,\mathbf{x}(N)] \in \mathbb{R}^{d\times N}$ with the cloud $\boldsymbol{\xi}$ and a matrix $\mathbf{C} = [\mathbf{z}(1),\dots,\mathbf{z}(N)] \in \mathbb{R}^{d\times N}$ with the cloud $\boldsymbol{\xi}'$, then $\mathbf{C} = \mathcal{A}\,\hat{\mathbf{A}}$, where $\hat{\mathbf{A}}$ is obtained from $\mathbf{A}$ by permuting (shuffling) columns of $\mathbf{A}$ by σ.

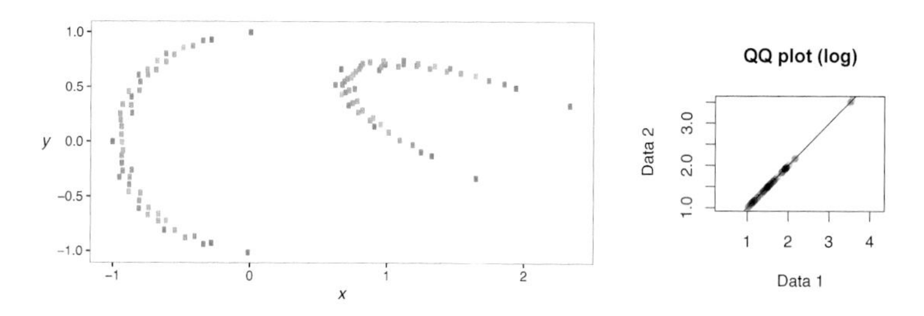

Figure 7.11 Affine matching. On the left, two datasets $\xi, \xi' \subset \mathbb{R}^2$, where ξ' is the image of ξ by an affine transformation. Colors indicate the correspondence between the two clouds recovered by matching Λ_n^μ and Λ_n^ν. The matching is illustrated on the right with a quantile plot of the Chritoffel function values for each dataset. For readability, a log transformation is applied and the first diagonal is represented. QQ: quantile–quantile.

Observe that the Christoffel functions Λ_n^μ and Λ_n^ν associated with the empirical measure

$$\mu := \frac{1}{N} \sum_{i=1}^{N} \delta_{\mathbf{x}_i} \quad \text{and} \quad \nu := \frac{1}{N} \sum_{i=1}^{N} \delta_{\mathbf{z}_i}$$

depend only on the respective moments of μ and ν. Therefore they are invariant under any permutation σ of labels. the labelling of points.

This suggests the following procedure:

- Form the vectors $\mathbf{u} := \Lambda_n^\mu(\mathbf{x}_i) \in \mathbb{R}^N$ and $\mathbf{v} := \Lambda_n^\nu(\mathbf{z}_i) \in \mathbb{R}^N$.
- Define $j = \sigma(i)$ if the rank of v_j is the same as the rank of u_i (e.g. when entries of $\mathbf{u}$ and $\mathbf{v}$ are ranked in increasing order).

If there is no "tie" in $\mathbf{u}$ and in $\mathbf{v}$ then this procedure returns the correct permutation σ. In case of ties, the procedure does not allow us to elicit completely the correspondence matching. Overall, the method is not garanteed to work but allows us to treat simple cases easily. An interesting topic is to investigate the robustness of this procedure to noise or to matching misspecification.

The procedure is illustrated in Figure 7.11 where a moon-shaped cloud of points $\xi \subset \mathbb{R}^2$ is deformed to ξ' by an affine transformation. The matching between points of ξ and ξ' is recovered by matching the corresponding Christoffel function values. On the right is a quantile plot for the correspondence between Christoffel function values.

7.4 Notes and Sources

Section 7.1: The linear Gaussian model is classical and can be found in most statistics textbooks. Statistical leverage scores have been historically used as a diagnosis tool for linear regression (Hoaglin and Welsch, 1978; Velleman and Welsch, 1981; Chatterjee and Hadi, 1986). These leverage scores characterize the importance of an observation and turn out to be relevant quantities for randomized subsampling in large-scale numerical linear algebra. Hence they emerged as a fundamental tool for matrix sketching and column sampling (Mahoney and Drineas, 2009; Mahoney, 2011; Drineas et al., 2012; Wang and Zhang, 2013) and play an important role in low-rank matrix approximation (Clarkson and Woodruff, 2013; Bach, 2013), kernel nonparametric regression (Alaoui and Mahoney, 2015; Rudi et al., 2015; Ma et al., 2015), random feature learning (Rudi and Rosasco, 2017) and quadrature (Bach, 2017). In the context of kernel nonparametric regression, the relation with the underlying density was investigated in Pauwels et al. (2018) with results similar to those outlined in Chapter 4, and Askari et al. (2018) investigate empirically the capacity to detect outliers. A precise characterization of the capacity of leverage scores to detect outliers was given using potential theory estimates in Beckermann et al. (2021) for one complex variable.

Section 7.2: Interestingly, even though they are central in the pioneering works of Kiefer and Wolfowitz (1959, 1960), Kiefer (1961), Kiefer and Wolfowitz (1965), neither term *Christoffel–Darboux kernel* nor *Christoffel function* is ever mentioned (as they were not yet standard in the sixties). Even if relatively straightforward, the explicit form (7.6) of a dual of the D-optimal design for $n > 1$ and its interpretation in computational geometry seem to be new. Most of the material regarding polynomial experimental design is from de Castro et al. (2019). However, in the case $n = 1$ the set $\{\mathbf{x} \colon K_n^{\mu^*}(\mathbf{x},\mathbf{x}) \leq s(n)\}$ is an ellipsoid and the link with the Löwner–John ellipsoid is described in e.g. Todd (2016, Section 2.1) when the set $\mathbf{K} \subset \mathbb{R}^d$ is a finite collection of points. The use of a log-det criterion to find a sublevel set of a polynomial (of degree larger than 2) (i) that contains the convex hull of set of points in $\mathbb{R}^d$ and (ii) with small volume (to mimick the Löwner–John ellipsoid in case $n = 1$) was proposed in Magnani et al. (2005). In general the (whenever finite) Lebesgue volume of a sublevel set $G = \{\mathbf{x} \colon g(\mathbf{x}) \leq 1\}$ for a given nonnegative polynomial g cannot be expressed in terms of the determinant of a Gram matrix $\mathbf{Q}_g$ of g, and the criterion $\log\det \mathbf{Q}_g$ is used as a proxy for the Lebesgue volume of G. However, in the case where g is homogeneous then an explicit expression of vol(G) was used in Lasserre (2015) to yield a higher-degree generalization of the Löwner–John ellipsoid (with a characterization of contacts points).

Section 7.3: This section is based on Lasserre and Pauwels (2016), Lasserre and Pauwels (2019) and Pauwels et al. (2021).

PART THREE

COMPLEMENTARY TOPICS

8
Further Applications

This chapter contains two clusters of recent results which amply illustrate the utility and effectiveness of Christoffel–Darboux kernels. The first application is concerned with approximation of discontinuous functions while the second application is concerned with spectral analysis of dynamical systems. We simply touch on the surface of these novel facets of Christoffel–Darboux analysis, offering full bibliographical references and only minimal sketches of proofs.

8.1 Approximation of Nonsmooth Functions

Recall the notation $\mathbb{R}[\mathbf{x}]$ (resp. $\mathbb{R}_n[\mathbf{x}]$) for the ring of polynomials in the variables $\mathbf{x} = (x_1, \ldots, x_d)$ (resp. its subspace of polynomials of total degree at most n). In this section, f denotes a bounded measurable function,

$$\begin{array}{llcl} f\colon & X & \to & Y, \\ & \mathbf{x} := (x_1,\, x_2, \ldots, x_{d-1}) & \mapsto & y, \end{array}$$

from a given compact set $X \subset \mathbb{R}^{d-1}$ to a given compact set $Y \subset \mathbb{R}$, with $d \geq 2$. We assume that X is equal to the closure of its interior.

Given $n \in \mathbb{N}$, let $\mathbf{v}_n(\mathbf{x}, y)$ be a basis of the vector space $\mathbb{R}_n[\mathbf{x}, y]$, and let

$$\mathbf{z} := (\mathbf{x}, y),$$

where $\mathbf{x} \in \mathbb{R}^{d-1}$ and $y \in \mathbb{R}$. Next, let μ be the Borel measure on $X \times Y$ defined by

$$d\mu(\mathbf{x}) := \mathbb{I}_X(\mathbf{x})\, \delta_{f(\mathbf{x})}(dy)\, d\mathbf{x}, \tag{8.1}$$

which is supported on the graph

$$\{(\mathbf{x}, f(\mathbf{x}))\colon \mathbf{x} \in X\} \subset X \times Y$$

of the function f, where $\mathbb{I}_X$ denotes the indicator function of X, which takes value 1 on X and 0 otherwise, and $\delta_{f(\mathbf{x})}$ denotes the Dirac measure at $f(\mathbf{x})$.

Its associated moment matrix of order $2n$ in the basis $\mathbf{v}_n$ reads

$$\mathbf{M}_{\mu,n} = \int \mathbf{v}_n(\mathbf{z})\mathbf{v}_n(\mathbf{z})^T d\mu(\mathbf{z}) . = \int_X \mathbf{v}_n(\mathbf{x}, f(\mathbf{x}))\mathbf{v}_n(\mathbf{x}, f(\mathbf{x}))^T d\mathbf{x}$$

where the integral is understood entry-wise.

For example, if $\mathbf{v}_n(\mathbf{x}, y)$ is the usual basis of monomials arranged in lexicographic order, then one has access to moments of the form

$$\int_X f(\mathbf{x})^{\alpha_0} x_1^{\alpha_1} \dots x_{d-1}^{\alpha_{d-1}} \, d\mathbf{x},$$

with $\alpha = (\alpha_0, \alpha_1, \dots, \alpha_{d-1}) \in \mathbb{N}^d$. But $\mathbf{v}_n$ could also be any orthonormal polynomial basis. In general, using a basis of Chebyshev or Legendre polynomials results in moments matrices with a much better numerical condition number.

Given the moment matrix of degree $2n$, we aim to compute an approximation f_n of the function f, with convergence guaranteed when degree n increases. As a simple remark from what has been described in previous chapters, the sequence of Christoffel–Darboux kernels associated with μ is an appropriate tool to approximate accurately its support, *hence the graph of f* in our case.

Recall that the CD kernel is a sum of squares polynomial $q_n(\mathbf{x}, y)$ of degree $2n$ in d variables. Equation (4.9) and Lemma 4.3.1 suggest that q_n should be small only on the graph of f. Hence, for every fixed $\mathbf{x} \in X$, define the following estimator:

$$f_n(\mathbf{x}) := \arg\min_{y \in Y} q_n(\mathbf{x}, y).$$

In principle f_n should be close to f in a certain sense. However, as the support of μ is the graph of a function, it is singular, which generates lack of regularity and numerical stability (see Chapter 5). To address this issue, consider an additional measure μ_0 on $\mathbb{R}^d$ which is absolutely continuous with respect to Lebesgue measure, hence with nonsingular associated moment matrix $\mathbf{M}_{\mu_0,n}$. For each $\beta > 0$, define the following *proxy* for the CD kernel of μ:

$$q_{\mu+\beta\mu_0,n}(\mathbf{z}) : \quad \mathbf{z} \mapsto \mathbf{v}_n(\mathbf{z})^T (\mathbf{M}_{\mu,n} + \beta \mathbf{M}_{\mu_0,n})^{-1} \mathbf{v}_n(\mathbf{z}). \tag{8.2}$$

The resulting regularized Christoffel–Darboux semialgebraic approximation $f_{n,\beta}$ is defined as follows:

$$\mathbf{x} \in X \mapsto f_{n,\beta}(\mathbf{x}) := \min\{\arg\min_{y \in Y} q_{\mu+\beta\mu_0,n}(\mathbf{x}, y)\}. \tag{8.3}$$

The following is the main result of Marx et al. (2020).

Theorem 8.1.1 *Assuming that μ_0 is absolutely continuous and choosing $\beta_n = 2^{3-\sqrt{n}}$, the following hold:*

(a) *If the set $S \subset X$ of continuity points of f is such that $X \setminus S$ has Lebesgue measure zero, then*

$$f_{n,\beta_n}(\mathbf{x}) \underset{n\to\infty}{\rightarrow} f(\mathbf{x})$$

for almost all $\mathbf{x} \in X$, and

$$\|f - f_{n,\beta_n}\|_{L^1(X)} \underset{n\to\infty}{\rightarrow} 0.$$

(b) *If f is Lipschitz on X, then*

$$\|f - f_{n,\beta_n}\|_{L^1(X)} = O(n^{-1/2}).$$

The proof relies on Lemma 4.3.1 and (4.9) combined with a Markov inequality argument.

We illustrate this result on three examples of discontinuous univariate functions taken from Eckhoff (1993) and also used in Marx et al. (2020). In this case, analytic moments of the measure μ supported on the graph of the function f are not available as input to our algorithm. Therefore instead of $\mathbf{M}_{\mu,n}$ we use the empirical moment matrix $\mathbf{M}_n$ computed by uniform sampling, that is,

$$\mathbf{M}_n := \frac{1}{N} \sum_{k=1}^{N} \mathbf{v}_n(\mathbf{x}_k, f(\mathbf{x}_k))\mathbf{v}_n(\mathbf{x}_k, f(\mathbf{x}_k))^T, \tag{8.4}$$

for N sufficiently large, that is, 10^3, and $\mathbf{v}_n$ the monomial basis vector. Semi-algebraic approximations of degree 10 are shown in Figure 8.1 for three benchmarks (Eckhoff 1993, Examples 65, 66, 67) of discontinuous functions f, appropriately scaled in $X = Y = [-1, 1]$. We observe that the estimated function is very close to the target function, except for Example 66 where the second rightmost discontinuity is not detected. In this example, increasing the degree of the approximations does not fix the issue, and we believe that this is due to the poor resolution of the monomial basis.

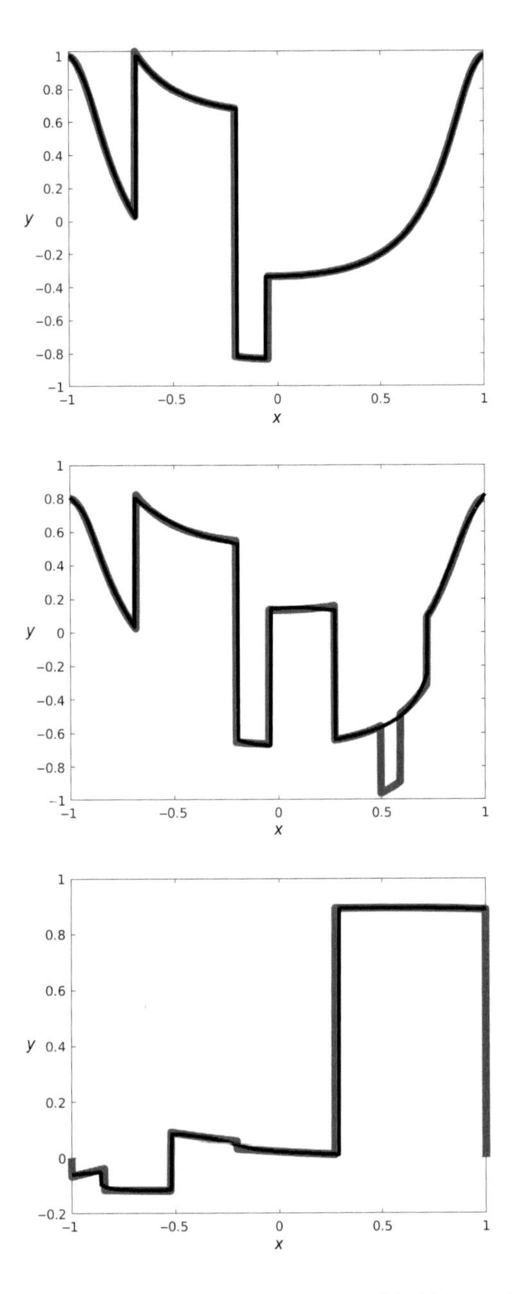

Figure 8.1 Degree 10 semialgebraic approximations (black) for the discontinuous univariate functions (red) of Examples 65 (top), 66 (middle) and 67 (bottom) of (Eckhoff 1993).

8.2 Spectral Analysis of Dynamical Systems

By its very nature, the Christoffel–Darboux kernel is a versatile spectral analysis tool. Here we do not touch on applications to quantum physics, signal processing or continuum mechanics. Instead, we report only on a recent advance of ergodic theory flavor, with CD analysis at its core. Details and proofs are contained in Korda et al. (2020). Some additional bibliographical and historical comments are included in the Notes and Sources section at the end of this chapter.

Specifically, we exploit the unitarity of the Koopman operator in the measure-preserving ergodic setting, by analyzing its fine spectral structure (i.e. Lebesgue decomposition) from a single trajectory. The CD kernel approach allows us to efficiently separate the point spectrum from the continuous one, and further on, to enter into the dichotomy between the singular continuous and the absolutely continuous spectrum. Moreover, this spectral analysis relies solely on quadrature techniques (with the help of convex optimization) derived from classical Cesàro-type renormalizations of a Fourier series. This allows for a detailed understanding of the spectrum derived from raw data and opens the door to approximations of the Koopman operator that explicitly take into account the continuous part, or even singular continuous part, of the spectrum. Following this scheme, a canonical finite-rank approximation of the Koopman operator is obtained, based on conditioning the data offered by measurements and exploiting the available grasp on its spectral measure.

On the numerical side, this method is simple to implement and readily applicable to high-dimensional systems since the computational complexity is fully determined only by the number of the moments N and in particular is independent of the dimension of the underlying state-space. To be more precise, the complexity is governed by the inversion (or Cholesky factorization) of an $N \times N$ hermitian positive-definite Toeplitz matrix which can be carried out with asymptotic complexity $O(N^2)$ or even $O(N \log^2(N))$ as opposed to $O(N^3)$ for a general matrix.

Let

$$\mathbf{x}^+ = T(\mathbf{x}),$$

be a discrete dynamical system, where $\mathbf{x}$ is the state of the system, $\mathbf{x}^+$ the successor state and T is the transition mapping defined on the state-space state X endowed with a positive Borel measure ν. We also assume that T is a measure-preserving bijection with ν the preserved measure. The *Koopman operator* $U \colon L^2(\nu) \to L^2(\nu)$ is defined as the composition operator $Uf = f \circ T, f \in L^2(\nu)$. The unitary operator U is a *linear* transformation which provides an equivalent description of the *nonlinear* dynamical system (8.2). The price to pay for this apparent simplification is to accept infinite dimensions, and for this reason effective finite-rank approximations of the Koopman operator U are crucial.

Functions $f \in L^2(\nu)$ are referred to as *observables* as they often represent physical measurements taken on the dynamical systems. The spectral measure of U decomposes as $E = E_{at} + E_{ac} + E_{sc}$, corresponding to a direct orthogonal sum decomposition of the underlying Hilbert space into its atomic, absolutely continuous and singular continuous parts. Let $f \in L^2(\nu)$ be a nonzero vector and denote by $\mu_f(\cdot) = \langle E(\cdot)f, f\rangle$ the spectral measure localized at f. Since the support of μ_f lies on the unit circle, the complex moments of this measure (or equivalently its Fourier coefficients) determine via the spectral theorem the compression of U onto the $*$-cyclic subspace generated by f. The main questions (certainly very familiar to the quantum physicist) are the computation of the moments $m_k = \int_{\mathbb{T}} e^{i2\pi\theta k}\, d\mu_f(\theta)$ from data and the reconstruction or approximation of the measure μ_f and operator U from these moments.

The given data is encoded in the form of M measurements (or snapshots) of the observable $f \in L^2(\nu)$ in the form

$$y_i = f(\mathbf{x}_i), \quad i = 1, \ldots, M.$$

We assume that the measure ν is *ergodic* and that the data (8.2) lie on a single trajectory, that is, $\mathbf{x}_{i+1} = T(\mathbf{x}_i)$. In this case, Birkhoff's Ergodic Theorem implies, for ν-almost all initial conditions $\mathbf{x}_1$,

$$\begin{aligned} m_k &= \int_{\mathbb{T}} e^{i2\pi\theta k}\, d\mu_f = \int_X (f \circ T^k)\bar{f}\, d\nu \\ &= \lim_{M\to\infty} \frac{1}{M-k} \sum_{i=1}^{M-k} (f \circ T^k(\mathbf{x}_i))\bar{f}(\mathbf{x}_i) \\ &= \lim_{M\to\infty} \frac{1}{M-k} \sum_{i=1}^{M-k} y_{i+k}\bar{y}_i. \end{aligned}$$

From now on we assume that the moments m_k, $k \in \{-N, \ldots, N\}$ have been computed and we focus on the reconstruction of the spectral measure $\mu := \mu_f$ from this finite data. A change of coordinates allows us to work on the unit interval $[0, 1]$ where we seek Lebesgue decomposition $\mu = \mu_{at} + \mu_{ac} + \mu_{sc}$. We assume without loss of generality that $\mu_{at}(\{0\}) = \mu_{at}(\{1\})$ and the absolutely continuous part of the form $d\mu_{ac} = \rho\, d\theta$ with the density $\rho \in L^1([0, 1], d\theta)$.

Recall that the CD kernel is defined for each positive integer $N \in \mathbb{N}$ and each $z \in \mathbb{C}$, $s \in \mathbb{C}$ by $K_N^{\mu}(z, s) = \sum_{j=0}^{N} P_j(z)\overline{P_j(s)}$, where P_js are the orthonormal polynomials associated with μ. Note that the first N orthonormal polynomials (and hence the kernel itself) can be determined from the first N moments

$(m_k)_{k=0}^N$ of the measure μ, provided the associated Toeplitz moment matrix is invertible. To ensure this is the case, we pass from the measure μ to $d\tilde{\mu} = d\mu + 1d\theta$, with the associated CD kernel denoted $\tilde{K}_N$.

Defining

$$\zeta_N(\theta) = \frac{N+1}{\tilde{K}_N(e^{i2\pi\theta}, e^{i2\pi\theta})} - 1,$$

we derive the following result from the Markov–Stieltjes ineqalities (Theorem 3.5.2) and Theorem 3.2.1.

Proposition 8.2.1 *If μ is a positive measure on $\mathbb{T}$ and $(m_k)_{k=0}^N$ its moments defined by* (8.2)*, then for all $\theta \in [0, 1]$,*

$$\lim_{N\to\infty} \zeta_N/(N+1) = \mu(\{e^{i2\pi\theta}\}).$$

Moreover, for Lebesgue-almost all $\theta \in [0, 1]$,

$$\lim_{N\to\infty} \zeta_N = \rho(\theta).$$

Once the above finite kernels are computed, one can use Cesàro sums or quadrature to approximate the distribution function of the measure μ, obtaining a weakly convergent sequence of approximations, denoted by $\hat{F}_N$. In order to detect presence of the singular spectrum in a given interval $[t, t+\epsilon]$, we use the *singularity indicator*

$$\Delta_{N,\epsilon}(t) := \frac{\hat{F}_N(t+\epsilon) - \hat{F}_N(t)}{F_{\zeta_N}(t+\epsilon) - F_{\zeta_N}(t)} - 1,$$

where $F_{\zeta_N}(t) = \int_0^t \zeta_N(\theta)\, d\theta$. In view of Proposition 8.2.1, one expects that $\Delta_N > 0$, in the limit as $N \to \infty$, if there a contribution of the singular spectrum in $[t, t+\epsilon]$ and $\Delta_N = 0$ otherwise, allowing us to detect the singular continuous part of the spectrum (since the atomic part can be singled out using Proposition 8.2.1.

As a byproduct of the above approximation scheme, the spectral measure E can be effectively evaluated as follows. We consider either the case of a singleton, that is, $E_{\{\theta_0\}}$, or interval $[a, b)$, that is, $E_{[a,b)}$. To this end, a careful choice of Fourier coefficients is in order. Specifically, for the singleton $\{\theta_0\}$, one possible choice is

$$\alpha_{k,N}^{\{\theta_0\}} = \begin{cases} \frac{1}{N+1} e^{-i2\pi k\theta_0} & k \in \{0, \ldots, N\}, \\ 0 & \text{otherwise}, \end{cases} \tag{8.5}$$

while for the interval $[a, b)$, one possible choice is

$$\alpha_{k,N}^{[a,b)} = \frac{1}{2}\alpha_{k,N}^{\{a\}} + \beta_{k,N}^{[a,b)} - \frac{1}{2}\alpha_{k,N}^{\{b\}}, \tag{8.6}$$

where

$$\beta_{k,N}^{[a,b)} = \begin{cases} \frac{N-|k|}{N}\frac{i}{2\pi k}(e^{-i2\pi bk} - e^{-i2\pi ak}) & k \neq 0, \\ b-a & k = 0. \end{cases}$$

The following theorem, based on a recent generalization of the Wiener–Wintner Ergodic Theorem (Lacey and Terwilleger, 2008), establishes ν-almost everywhere convergence of the spectral projections approximations.

Theorem 8.2.2 *Let* $\alpha_{k,N}^{\{\theta_0\}}$ *and* $\alpha_{k,N}^{[a,b)}$ *be given by* (8.5), *respectively* (8.6), *and let* $g \in L^2(\nu)$ *be given. Then for* ν*-almost all* $\mathbf{x} \in X$,

$$\lim_{N\to\infty} \sum_{k=-N}^{N} \alpha_{k,N}^{\{\theta_0\}} g(T^k(\mathbf{x})) = (E_{\{\theta_0\}}g)(\mathbf{x})$$

and

$$\lim_{N\to\infty} \sum_{k=-N}^{N} \alpha_{k,N}^{[a,b)} g(T^k(\mathbf{x})) = (E_{[a,b)}g)(\mathbf{x}).$$

It goes without saying that the spectral analysis technique sketched in this section applies to other similar frameworks, such as stationary time series. Some relevant numerical experiments involving real data extracted from some nasty dynamical systems are contained in Korda et al. (2020). It is notable that some qualitative distinctions between rather intractable dynamical systems were detected by the spectral analysis of their associated Koopman operator, and in the end, by the asymptotics of the respective Christoffel–Darboux kernels.

We import from Korda et al. (2020) a single example, related to the well-known Lorenz system of differential equations:

$$\dot{x_1} = 10(x_2 - x_1),$$

$$\dot{x_2} = x_1(28 - x_3) - x_2,$$

$$\dot{x_3} = x_1x_2 - \frac{8}{2}x_3.$$

Notice in Figure 8.2 the presence of singular continuous spectrum with respect to x_3.

8.3 Notes and Sources

Section 8.1: The material is essentially from Marx et al. (2020), which considers the generic problem of reconstructing an unknown function $f: X \to \mathbb{R}$

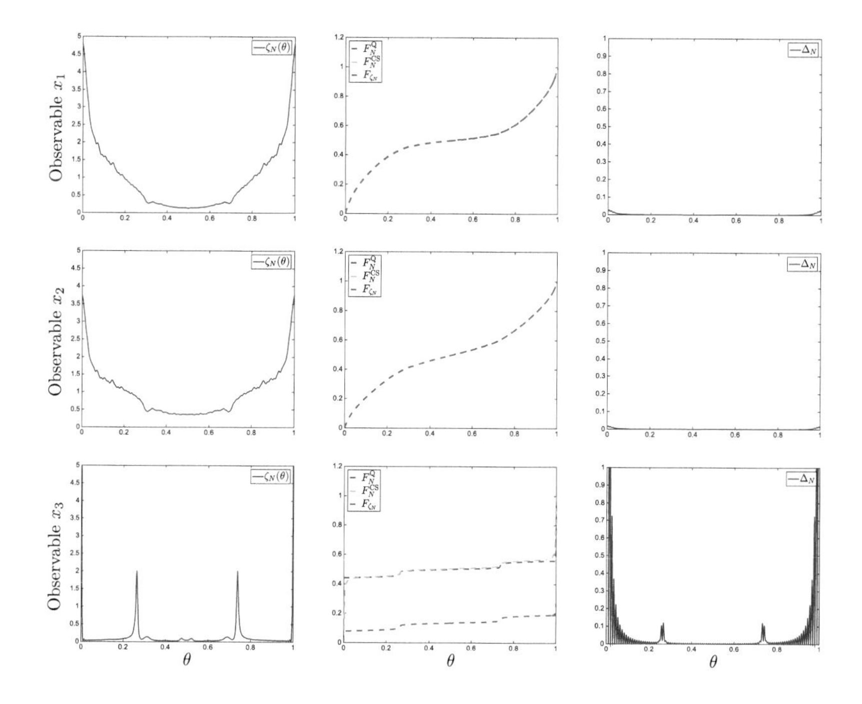

Figure 8.2 Lorenz system for $N = 100$. Left: Density approximation. Middle: Distribution function approximation. Right: Singularity indicator Δ_N.

from the sole knowledge of finitely many moments $\int_X \mathbf{x}^\alpha f(\mathbf{x})^k \, d\mathbf{x}$, $(\alpha, k) \in \Gamma$. For instance, in analysis or control of nonlinear PDE and optimal control problems such information is available via moments of the *occupation measure* associated with a classical solution f. Then finitely many such moments can be approximated, with arbitrary precision, via the Moment–SOS hierarchy (Lasserre, 2019) provided that the associated problem has algebraic data; that is, all coefficients of the partial differential equation (PDE) are polynomials and the domain is a basic semialgebraic set, the vector field of the ordinary differential equation (ODE) is defined by polynomials, and the state and control sets are basic semialgebraic. A detailed account of the Moment–SOS hierarchy in this context can be found in Henrion et al. (2020). Briefly, instead of searching for a function f on X, the basic idea is to rather (i) consider a measure μ on $X \times \mathbb{R}$ supported on the *graph* $\{(\mathbf{x}, f(\mathbf{x})) : \mathbf{x} \in X\}$ of f, and (ii) use the Christoffel function Λ_n^μ to approximate the support of μ (hence f). As we have seen throughout the book, Λ_n^μ is indeed a good candidate tool to identify the support of μ (hence f). Importantly, being semialgebraic and not necessarily continuous, the function $\mathbf{x} \mapsto \Lambda_n^\mu(\mathbf{x}, y(\mathbf{x}))$, where $y(\mathbf{x}) \in \arg\min_y \Lambda_n^\mu(\mathbf{x}, y)$, is able to approximate with good accuracy potential discontinuities of f (and avoiding Gibbs phenomenon). Similarly, for interpolation problems with a finite sample $(f(\mathbf{x}_k))_{k\in S}$ available, one may easily compute moments of the associated atomic measure μ supported on $\{(\mathbf{x}_k, f(\mathbf{x}) : k \in S\}$ and apply the above technique; for more details the interested reader is referred to Marx et al. (2020) and references therein.

Section 8.2: In his address at the International Mathematical Congress of Mathematicians, Rome, 1908, Poincaré made the bold statement that a complicated dynamics governed by nonlinear partial differential equations can be reduced to and analyzed by the novel (at that time) linear infinite-dimensional spectral methods advocated by Hilbert and Fredholm (Poincaré, 1975). His amazing insight became possible only after advances in the abstract spectral theory of unitary, or unbounded, self-adjoint operators. It was Carleman (1932), Koopman (1931), Koopman and Von Neumann (1932), and von Neumann (1932) who put on solid bases the linear operator reduction of nonlinear dynamical systems. Originally aimed at ergodic theory, the new method reached wider areas of applications, opportunely enhanced by the current high potential of computer simulations and accumulation of big data. The recent surge of interest in Carleman linearization, spectral analysis of the Koopman operator or Koopman–von Neumann mechanics is well charted in a recent collaborative volume (Mauroy et al., 2020). An account of the Koopman operator and its spectrum via kernel estimates is well described in Das and Giannakis (2019). A glimpse of connections to quantum mechanics can be found in Knill (1998), while the natural import of harmonic analysis techniques goes back to Wiener and Wintner (1941).

9

Transforms of Christoffel–Darboux Kernels

This chapter is devoted to a couple of natural transformations of CD kernels. The first reflects abstract perturbations of the generating measure and the second offers a specific "cloud" isolation procedure of a 2D measure, solely involving CD kernel operations. Here we do not provide full details of an array of classical transforms of orthogonal polynomials, and implicitly of CD kernels, going back independently to Christoffel, Darboux, Szegő and several other founders of approximation theory. The Notes and Sources section at the end of the chapter contain some bibliographical indications in this direction.

9.1 Perturbations of Christoffel–Darboux Kernels

Central to all questions we have touched on in the previous chapters is the dependence of the truncated Christoffel–Darboux kernels on the generating measure. In the theory of univariate orthogonal polynomials various perturbations and stability results concerning the CD kernel are well known; see the Notes and Sources section at the end of this chapter. A systematic study of perturbations of multivariate CD kernels was recently initiated by Beckermann et al. (2021).

Let μ denote a positive Borel measure, compactly supported by $\mathbb{C}^d$, and let $K_n^\mu(\cdot, \cdot)$ stand for its truncated CD kernels. In perturbation problems the following *cosine kernel* is of interest:

$$C_n^\mu(\mathbf{z}, \mathbf{w}) := \frac{K_n^\mu(\mathbf{z}, \mathbf{w})}{\sqrt{K_n^\mu(\mathbf{z}, \mathbf{z})}\sqrt{K_n^\mu(\mathbf{w}, \mathbf{w})}}. \tag{9.1}$$

Multi-point matrix analogs of these kernels can be defined as in the multi-point interpolation setting: for two ℓ-tuples $\mathbf{z}_1, \mathbf{z}_2, \ldots, \mathbf{z}_\ell, \mathbf{w}_1, \mathbf{w}_2, \ldots, \mathbf{w}_\ell$ of arbitrary points in $\mathbb{C}^d$, one introduces the $\ell \times \ell$ matrices

$$\mathbf{K}_n^\mu(\mathbf{z}_1, \mathbf{z}_2, \ldots, \mathbf{z}_\ell; \mathbf{w}_1, \mathbf{w}_2, \ldots, \mathbf{w}_\ell) := (K_n^\mu(\mathbf{z}_j, \mathbf{w}_k))_{j,k=1}^\ell,$$
$$\mathbf{C}_n^\mu(\mathbf{z}_1, \mathbf{z}_2, \ldots, \mathbf{z}_\ell; \mathbf{w}_1, \mathbf{w}_2, \ldots, \mathbf{w}_\ell) := (C_n^\mu(\mathbf{z}_j, \mathbf{w}_k))_{j,k=1}^\ell.$$

When working on singular supports, it is necessary to consider the Zariski closure $S(\mu)$ of the support of the measure μ. Then one proves that there exists an integer N, with the property

$$\det K_n^\mu(\mathbf{z}_1, \mathbf{z}_2, \ldots, \mathbf{z}_\ell; \mathbf{z}_1, \mathbf{w}_2, \ldots, \mathbf{z}_\ell) > 0, \tag{9.2}$$

whenever $n \geq N$ and $\mathbf{z}_1, \mathbf{z}_2, \ldots, \mathbf{z}_\ell$ are mutually distinct points belonging to $S(\mu)$. For a proof see Lemma 4.1 in Beckermann et al. (2021).

A first stability result is stated below.

Proposition 9.1.1 *Let μ, ν be two positive measures of compact support, close in moments. That is, for a positive integer N and $\epsilon \in (0,1)$, one has*

$$(1-\epsilon)\,\|p\|_{2,\mu}^2 \leq \|p\|_{2,\nu}^2 \leq (1+\epsilon)\,\|p\|_{2,\mu}^2$$

for all polynomials $p \in \mathbb{C}[\mathbf{z}_1, \ldots, \mathbf{z}_d]$ of degree less than or equal to N. Then, for all $\mathbf{z}, \mathbf{w} \in \mathbb{C}^d$,

$$(1-\epsilon)\,K_n^\nu(\mathbf{z},\mathbf{z}) \leq K_n^\mu(\mathbf{z},\mathbf{z}) \leq (1+\epsilon)K_n^\nu(\mathbf{z},\mathbf{z}), \tag{9.3}$$
$$|K_n^\mu(\mathbf{z},\mathbf{w}) - K_n^\nu(\mathbf{z},\mathbf{w})| \leq \epsilon\sqrt{K_n^\nu(\mathbf{z},\mathbf{z})}\sqrt{K_n^\nu(\mathbf{w},\mathbf{w})}, \tag{9.4}$$
$$|C_n^\mu(\mathbf{z},\mathbf{w}) - C_n^\nu(\mathbf{z},\mathbf{w})| \leq 2\epsilon. \tag{9.5}$$

Note that the measures μ and ν in the above proposition can be supported by an algebraic subset of $\mathbb{C}^d$. For the proof and a discussion of numerical analysis aspects of the above estimates see Section 3.2 in Beckermann et al. (2021).

The main perturbation result for CD kernels with respect to perturbation of a measure along its singular support follows.

Theorem 9.1.2 (Beckermann et al., 2021) *Let μ be a compactly supported measure, with Zariski closure $S(\mu)$ of its support. Consider $\sigma = \sum_{j=1}^\ell t_j \delta_{\mathbf{z}_j}$, $t_j > 0$, $\mathbf{z}_1, \ldots, \mathbf{z}_\ell \in S(\mu)$ be a finite-point mass additive summand to μ (with mutually distinct $\mathbf{z}_j$s).*

Let $n \geq N$ be as in (9.2), and consider the following matrices (depending on n)

$$\mathbf{C} := \mathbf{C}_n^{\mu}(\mathbf{z}_1, ..., \mathbf{z}_\ell; \mathbf{z}_1, ..., \mathbf{z}_\ell),$$

$$\widetilde{\mathbf{C}} := \mathbf{C}_n^{\mu}(\mathbf{z}_1, ..., \mathbf{z}_\ell, \mathbf{z}; \mathbf{z}_1, ..., \mathbf{z}_\ell, \mathbf{z}) = \begin{bmatrix} \mathbf{C} & \mathbf{b}^* \\ \mathbf{b} & 1 \end{bmatrix}, \ \mathbf{b} \in \mathbb{C}^{1\times\ell},$$

$$\operatorname{diag} \mathbf{D}\left(\frac{1}{\sqrt{t_j K_n^{\mu}(\mathbf{z}_j, \mathbf{z}_j)}}\right)_{j=1,\dots,\ell},$$

and the constants

$$\Sigma_m := 1 - \sum_{j=0}^{m-1}(-1)^j \mathbf{b}\,\mathbf{C}^{-1}(\mathbf{D}^2\mathbf{C}^{-1})^j \mathbf{b}^*, \quad m = 1, 2, \dots.$$

Then, for all $\mathbf{z} \in \mathbb{C}^d$,

$$\frac{K_n^{\mu+\sigma}(\mathbf{z}, \mathbf{z})}{K_n^{\mu}(\mathbf{z}, \mathbf{z})} = 1 - \mathbf{b}(\mathbf{D}^2 + \mathbf{C})^{-1}\mathbf{b}^* \tag{9.6}$$

and

$$\Sigma_1 \le \Sigma_3 \le \Sigma_5 \le \cdots \le \frac{K_n^{\mu+\sigma}(\mathbf{z}, \mathbf{z})}{K_n^{\mu}(\mathbf{z}, \mathbf{z})} \le \cdots \le \Sigma_4 \le \Sigma_2 \le \Sigma_0. \tag{9.7}$$

As a matter of fact, one has the estimate:

$$(-1)^m \left(\frac{K_n^{\mu+\sigma}(\mathbf{z}, \mathbf{z})}{K_n^{\mu}(\mathbf{z}, \mathbf{z})} - \Sigma_{m+1}\right) \le \frac{\|\mathbf{D}\mathbf{C}^{-1}\mathbf{D}\|}{1 + \|\mathbf{D}\mathbf{C}^{-1}\mathbf{D}\|}\, \mathbf{b}\,\mathbf{C}^{-1}(\mathbf{D}^2\mathbf{C}^{-1})^m\mathbf{b}^*.$$

In practice, one deals with points $\mathbf{z}_j$ lying on the unbounded connected component of $S(\mu)$, exterior to $\operatorname{supp}(\mu)$. Pluripotential estimates imply in this situation an exponential decay of $\|D\|$ as n tends to infinity. Also, $\|\mathbf{b}\| \le \sqrt{\ell}$ since $|C_n^{\mu}(\mathbf{z}, \mathbf{z}_j)| \le 1$. Hence, the uniform boundedness of C^{-1} assures a fast-decreasing gap between the alternating bounds appearing in the theorem.

Several one-dimensional cases, illuminated by function theory insights, validate the assumption on the uniform boundedness of $\mathbf{C}^{-1}$. We refer to Beckermann et al. (2021) for the proof of the theorem and a discussion of these one-dimensional frameworks.

To fix ideas, we specialize the above statement to a single point mass $\sigma = t_1\delta_{\mathbf{z}_1}$. Then

$$C = 1, \ \ b = C_n^{\mu}(\mathbf{z}, \mathbf{z}_1), \ \ D^2 = \frac{1}{t_1 K_n^{\mu}(\mathbf{z}_1, \mathbf{z}_1)}.$$

According to (9.6), we infer

$$\frac{K_n^{\mu+\sigma}(\mathbf{z}, \mathbf{z})}{K_n^{\mu}(\mathbf{z}, \mathbf{z})} = 1 - b(1 + D^2)^{-1}b^* = 1 - \frac{|C_n^{\mu}(\mathbf{z}, \mathbf{z}_1)|^2}{1 + \frac{1}{t_1 K_n^{\mu}(\mathbf{z}_1, \mathbf{z}_1)}},$$

and, from (9.7) for $m = 2$,

$$-\frac{1}{(t_1 K_n^{\mu}(\mathbf{z}_1, \mathbf{z}_1))^2} \leq \Sigma_3 - \Sigma_2 \leq \frac{K_n^{\mu+\sigma}(\mathbf{z}, \mathbf{z})}{K_n^{\mu}(\mathbf{z}, \mathbf{z})} - \Sigma_2$$
$$= \frac{K_n^{\mu+\sigma}(\mathbf{z}, \mathbf{z})}{K_n^{\mu}(\mathbf{z}, \mathbf{z})} - 1 + |C_n^{\mu}(\mathbf{z}, \mathbf{z}_1)|^2 \left(1 - \frac{1}{t_1 K_n^{\mu}(\mathbf{z}_1, \mathbf{z}_1)}\right) \leq 0.$$

For finite point mass measures μ, the quantities $t_j K_n^{\mu}(\mathbf{z}_j, \mathbf{z}_j)$ can be interpreted as leverage scores. See Beckermann et al. (2021) for some numerical experiments and further details.

9.2 Eliminating Outliers in a 2D Christoffel–Darboux Kernel

The same idea we have encountered in previous sections, of analyzing the fine structure of a point distribution by means of a function space supported by it, bears fruit in two real dimensions. All thanks to some profound facts borrowed from operator theory. Without entering into technical details, we follow the general argument in Putinar (2021a,b).

We start with a positive Borel measure μ compactly supported by $\mathbb{C}$, with infinite support, and we aim at extracting from its moments the "cloud" of μ (to be defined below), also encoded by the power moments of the uniformly distributed mass on it.

First we recall a few basic facts about the complex orthogonal polynomials associated with μ. The closure of complex polynomials in $L^2(\mu)$ is denoted $P^2(\mu)$, with associated orthogonal projection P. The multiplication M by the complex variable $z \in \mathbb{C}$ is a bounded linear transform of $L^2(\mu)$ which leaves invariant the subspace $P^2(\mu)$:

$$PMP = MP.$$

The linear operator $S = S_{\mu} = M|_{P^2(\mu)} \colon P^2(\mu) \longrightarrow P^2(\mu)$ is called *subnormal*. The spectrum of $M \colon L^2(\mu) \longrightarrow L^2(\mu)$ coincides with the closed support $\mathrm{supp}(\mu)$ of the measure μ, while the spectrum of S can be larger, containing in addition some connected components of $\mathbb{C} \setminus \mathrm{supp}(\mu)$.

The constant function $\mathbf{1}$ is a cyclic vector for S, producing the finite-dimensional filtration (Krylov subspaces):

$$\mathbb{C}_n[z] = \{f \in \mathbb{C}[z],\ \deg f \leq n\} = \mathrm{span}\{S^j \mathbf{1},\ 0 \leq j \leq n\}.$$

We denote by $P_n(z)$ the associated complex orthogonal polynomials:

$$\langle P_j, P_k \rangle = \int P_j \overline{P_k}\, d\mu = \delta_{jk},\ \ \deg P_k = k,\ \ j,k \geq 0.$$

The operator S has a distinguished Hessenberg matrix representation with respect to the orthonormal basis $(P_n)_{n=0}^{\infty}$ of $P^2(\mu)$,

$$\langle zP_j, P_k \rangle = h_{kj}, \quad j, k \geq 0,$$

observing the automatic vanishing relations

$$h_{jk} = 0, \quad j + 1 < k.$$

The adjoint operator is represented by the matrix

$$\langle S^* P_j, P_k \rangle = \langle M^* P_j, P_k \rangle = \langle P_j, SP_k \rangle = \overline{h_{jk}}.$$

The matrix representing S has the form:

$$H = \begin{bmatrix} h_{00} & h_{01} & h_{02} & h_{03} & \ldots \\ h_{10} & h_{11} & h_{12} & h_{13} & \ldots \\ 0 & h_{21} & h_{22} & h_{23} & \\ 0 & 0 & h_{32} & h_{33} & \ldots \\ \vdots & & \ddots & \ddots & \end{bmatrix}.$$

For every nonnegative integer n, one associates the *Christoffel–Darboux kernel*

$$K_n(z, w) = K_n^{\mu}(z, w) = \sum_{j=0}^{n} p_j(z)\overline{p_j(w)},$$

characterized by the identity

$$\langle K_n(z, w), f(w) \rangle = \begin{cases} f(z) & f \in \mathbb{C}_n[z], \\ 0 & \deg f > n. \end{cases}$$

Recall that the Christoffel function of order n is

$$\Lambda_n(z) = \frac{1}{K_n(z, z)} = \inf\{\|f\|^2, \; f(z) = 1, \; \deg f \leq n\}.$$

Note that the self-commutator $[S^*, S]$ is nonnegative

$$\begin{aligned} \langle [S^*, S]f, f \rangle &= \|Sf\|^2 - \|S^* f\|^2 \\ &= \|wf(w)\|^2 - \|P\overline{w}f(w)\|^2 \geq \|wf(w)\|^2 - \|\overline{w}f(w)\|^2 = 0. \end{aligned}$$

A theorem due to Berger and Shaw asserts that the trace $\mathrm{Tr}[S^*, S] < \infty$ is finite. This will be the gate to our algorithm. A second landmark contribution to the spectral theory of this class of (hyponormal) operators is encoded in the following trace formula (originating in works by Carey, Pincus and Helton, Howe):

$$\mathrm{Tr}[p(S, S^*), q(S, S^*)] = \frac{1}{\pi} \int_{\Sigma(\mu)} \left[\frac{\partial p}{\partial \overline{z}} \frac{\partial q}{\partial z} - \frac{\partial q}{\partial \overline{z}} \frac{\partial p}{\partial z} \right] dA(z), \quad p, q \in \mathbb{C}[z, \overline{z}]. \tag{9.8}$$

Although S and S^* do not commute, their order in the above functional calculus does not affect the trace. As usual, dA stands for the area measure. In (9.8) $\Sigma(\mu)$ is a measurable subset of the convex hull of $\mathrm{supp}(\mu)$ which we call the *cloud* of μ. Details can be found in Gustafsson and Putinar (2017).

Function theory enters into play, with the following notable result.

Theorem 9.2.1 (Thomson, 1991) *Let μ be a positive Borel measure, compactly supported on $\mathbb{C}$. There exists a Borel partition $\Delta_0, \Delta_1, \ldots$ of the closed support of μ with the following properties:*

(a) $P^2(\mu) = L^2(\mu_0) \oplus P^2(\mu_1) \oplus P^2(\mu_2) \oplus \cdots$, *where $\mu_j = \mu|_{\Delta_j}$ and $j \geq 0$.*
(b) *Every operator S_{μ_j}, with $j \geq 1$, is irreducible with spectral picture*

$$\sigma(S_{\mu_j}) \setminus \sigma_{\mathrm{ess}}(S_{\mu_j}) = G_j, \quad \text{simply connected,}$$

and

$$\mathrm{supp}\,(\mu_j) \subset \overline{G_j}, \qquad j \geq 1.$$

(c) *If $\mu_0 = 0$, then any element $f \in P^2(\mu)$ which vanishes $[\mu]$-a.e. on $G = \bigcup_j G_j$ is identically zero.*

The proof appeared in Thomson (1991) for L^p spaces, $1 \leq p < \infty$. A conceptually simpler proof appears in Brennan (2005). The central position of Thomson's Theorem was immediately recognized in Conway (1991) (published almost simultaneously with the original article).

Roughly speaking, Thomson's Theorem offers a decomposition of the measure μ into "light" components, singular with respect to area measure, and "heavy" ones, carrying or surrounding positive area regions. The *cloud* of the measure μ is the closure of the union of the latter, that is, of $G_1 \cup G_2 \cup G_3 \cup \cdots$ in the above notation.

The algorithm of eliminating *outliers* of μ is stated as a theorem below. We denote by $\hat{\sigma}$ the polynomial convex hull of a closed set $\sigma \subset \mathbb{C}$.

Theorem 9.2.2 *Let μ be a positive Borel measure with compact support σ in $\mathbb{C}$, with associated Hessenberg matrix $(h_{jk})_{j,k=0}^{\infty}$ and Christoffel–Darboux kernels $K_n(z, w), n \geq 0$. The moments of the area measure supported by the cloud of μ can be computed by the formula*

$$\frac{1}{\pi}\int_{\Sigma(\mu)} \frac{\partial R}{\partial \overline{z}}(z,\overline{z})dA(z)$$
$$= \lim_n \lim_N \int R(z,\overline{z})[zK_n(z,z) - \int K_n(z,\zeta)\zeta K_N(\zeta,z)d\mu(\zeta)]d\mu(z), \quad (9.9)$$

where $R \in \mathbb{C}[z,\overline{z}]$.

For fixed values of $n < N$ *the error* $\epsilon_{N,n} = \epsilon_{N,n}(\mu)$ *in the above limit satisfies*

$$\epsilon_{N,n}^2 \leq \frac{\text{Area}\,\hat{\sigma}}{\pi}\|\tilde{R}\|_{\infty,\sigma\times\sigma}^2 \left[\left(\sum_{j>n} s_j\right) + \sum_{j\leq n<N<k} |h_{jk}|^2\right],$$

where

$$s_j = h_{j+1,j}^2 - h_{j,j-1}^2 + \sum_{\ell<j<k}\left(|h_{\ell j}|^2 - |h_{jk}|^2\right)$$

and $\pi\sum_{j=0}^{\infty} s_j = \text{Area}\,\Sigma(\mu)$.

Note that the right-hand side of relation (9.9) depends only on the CD kernel of the original measure μ, while the output computes moments against the uniform mass distributed on the cloud.

The convergence of this procedure is geometric, for external point masses, as explained below.

Corollary 9.2.3 *Let* μ *be a positive measure of compact support and let* ν *be a finite atomic measure supported by the complement of the polynomial hull of* $\text{supp}(\mu)$. *There exists a constant* $\rho > 1$ *with the property*

$$\epsilon_{N,n}^2(\mu+\nu) \leq \epsilon_{N,n}^2(\mu) + O(\rho^{-n}), \; n \to \infty, \quad (9.10)$$

with the second term independent of $N > n$.

Example 9.2.4 We illustrate the algorithm by a simple toy example built on the beta distribution. The cloud will be the unit disk, and outliers will be distributed on two concentric circles of a larger radius. We change to polar coordinates $z = re^{it}$ with $r \geq 0$ and $t \in [-\pi,\pi]$. Let α, β be positive constants defining the rotationally invariant weight

$$w(z) = r^{\alpha-1}(1-r)^{\beta-1}.$$

The moments are

$$u_{k\ell} = \int_{\mathbb{D}} z^k \overline{z}^\ell w(z)dA(z) = 2\pi\delta_{k\ell}\int_0^1 r^{2k+1}r^{\alpha-1}(1-r)^{\beta-1}dr$$
$$= 2\pi\delta_{k\ell}B(2k+\alpha+1,\beta) = 2\pi\delta_{k\ell}\frac{\Gamma(2k+\alpha+1)\Gamma(\beta)}{\Gamma(\alpha+\beta+2k+1)}, \quad k,\ell \geq 0.$$

Let $R, \rho > 1$ and $\theta, \sigma \in (0, \pi)$. For a continuous function ϕ in the plane we define the measure ν as

$$\int \phi d\nu = \int_{-\theta}^{\theta} \phi(Re^{it})dt + \phi(\rho e^{i\sigma}) + \phi(\rho e^{-i\sigma}).$$

The moments are

$$\nu_{k\ell} = 2R^{k+\ell}\frac{\sin(k-\ell)\theta}{k-\ell} + 2\rho^{k+l}\cos(k-\ell)\sigma, \quad k, \ell \geq 0.$$

In case $k = \ell$ we define

$$\frac{\sin(k-\ell)\theta}{k-\ell}|_{k=\ell} = \theta.$$

The space $P^2(\chi_{\mathbb{D}} w dA)$ has the monomials as an orthogonal basis and each complex number of the open unit disk is a bounded point evaluation. On the other hand, the support of the measure ν is disjoint from the closed unit disk and does not disconnect the plane. Thus the measure $\mu = \chi_{\mathbb{D}} w dA + \nu$ fulfills the conditions in the statement of the algorithm. The moments of μ are

$$s_{k\ell} = 2\pi\delta_{k\ell}B(2k+\alpha+1, \beta) + 2R^{k+\ell}\frac{\sin(k-\ell)\theta}{k-\ell} + 2\rho^{k+l}\cos(k-\ell)\sigma, \quad k, \ell \geq 0.$$

These moments depend on six independent parameters α, β, R, ρ, θ, σ. In geometric terms, the measure μ consists of a nonuniform mass distribution on the unit disk, a couple of external point masses and a line integral along an external arc.

Normally at this point we should run the algorithm, that is, compute successively traces of commutators of the multiplier S_μ and its adjoint. Since we know from the start Thompson's decomposition of the measure μ, we infer on theoretical grounds that the moments of the cloud (endowed with Lebesgue measure) are

$$a_{k\ell} = \int_{\mathbb{D}} z^k \overline{z}^\ell dA(z) = \delta_{k\ell}\frac{\pi}{k+1}, \qquad k, \ell \geq 0.$$

Note that in these new moments the six parameters are erased.

Example 9.2.5 An even simpler example indicating how embedded outliers are eliminated is the following. Consider the unit disk $\mathbb{D}$ with uniform mass as the cloud and a collection of point masses located at a finite subset $F \subset \mathbb{D}$. The corresponding measure is

$$\mu = \chi_{\mathbb{D}} dA + d\nu,$$

where ν is a finite positive atomic measure supported on F.

The identity map onto Bergman's space

$$V\colon P^2(\mu) \longrightarrow L^2_a(\mathbb{D}), \quad Vf = f, \quad f \in P^2(\mu),$$

is continuous and invertible as a linear bounded operator. However, this map is not a unitary transform. Bounded point evaluations, detected by the associated Christoffel functions, exist for every $a \in \mathbb{D}$. Denote by P and Q the orthogonal projections of the Hilbert spaces $P^2(\mu)$ and $L^2_a(\mathbb{D})$, respectively, onto the subspaces of elements vanishing on the finite subset F. The projections $I - P$ and $I - Q$ have finite rank. Moreover, the restricted map

$$VP = QVP\colon PP^2(\mu) \longrightarrow QL^2(\mathbb{D})$$

is unitary, by definition of the measure μ.

Denote by $T = M_z$ the position operator (Hessenberg infinite matrix) acting on $P^2(\mu)$ and similarly let $S = M_z$ be the Bergman shift, acting on $L^2(\mathbb{D})$. Clearly $VT = SV$ and even $QVP(PTP) = (QSQ)QVP$, that is, the operators $T_1 = PTP$ and $S_1 = QSQ$ are unitarily equivalent. Consequently

$$\mathrm{Tr}[T_1^{*k}, T_1^{\ell}] = \mathrm{Tr}[S_1^{*k}, S_1^{\ell}], \qquad k, \ell \geq 0.$$

But T_1 is a finite-rank perturbation of T, and so is S_1 of S. Since the trace of a commutator is not affected by an additive finite-rank perturbation we infer

$$\mathrm{Tr}[T^{*k}, T^{\ell}] = \mathrm{Tr}[S^{*k}, S^{\ell}] = \frac{k\ell\delta_{k\ell}}{\pi} \int_D z^{k-1}\bar{z}^{\ell-1}\, dA(z), \qquad k, \ell \geq 0.$$

The latter are the normalized power moments of the area mass distribution on the disk. In conclusion our iterative procedure will eventually erase at the level of moments the influence of the additive perturbation ν. There is no difference in the above setting in replacing the disk by any bounded open subset of the complex plane.

More examples and comments are contained in Putinar (2021a,b).

Remark We stress that the notions of "cloud" and "outlier" used in this section are not identical to those invoked in previous chapters. More precisely, a sufficiently dense mass carried by a closed curve will produce a cloud, as described by Thomson's Theorem (Theorem 9.2.1). On the other hand, an additional mass supported by an open curve or isolated points is eliminated by our algorithm regardless of its position with respect to the clouds. In short, embedded exceptional outliers are erased by the moment operations described in Theorem 9.2.2. The reasons for this departure from the main cloud/outlier dichotomy are due to the major qualitative differences between real and complex Christoffel–Darboux kernels.

9.3 Notes and Sources

Section 9.1 Most of the material is from Beckermann et al. (2021). The perturbation effect of the generating measure, moment data or Jacobi matrix on orthogonal polynomials has been studied since the time of Christoffel and Darboux. It is no accident that their names are widely circulating today under the independent concepts of Christoffel transform and Darboux transform. As this topic has reached a status that deserves an independent monograph, we barely touch on a few significant sources of potential value and interest for the reader.

The numerical cost of passing from perturbations of moments to orthogonal polynomials is analyzed in Gautschi (1986) in the classical setting of measures supported by the real line. Adding one point mass to a given measure is an operation bearing the name of Uvarov's transform, resurrected and skillfully exploited by B. Simon and collaborators (Simon, 2005b).

A lucid observation of Mark Krein (1957) opened a wide area of iso-spectral transformations of Sturm–Liouville or Schrodinger operators by linking classical and independent works by Christoffel and Darboux. Roughly speaking, a second-order linear differential operator with rational coefficients is split into a product of two first-order linear operators. The reverse product of these factors gives rise to the so-called *Darboux transform*, leading to another differential operator which can be diagonalized by the spectral data of the original one (Samsonov and Ovcharov, 1995; Gómez-Ullate et al., 2010). The same splitting and switching of order of factors can be performed at the discrete level of Jacobi matrices, with no less spectacular results (Yoon, 2002; Bueno and Marcellán, 2004; Cantero et al., 2016). Darboux transforms continue to have high impact on the analysis of completely integrable dynamical systems (Matveev and Salle, 1991; Adler and van Moerbeke, 2001).

The Cauchy transform $F(z)$ of a positive measure defined on the real line is an analytic function in the upper half-plane, with values also in the upper half-plane, a so-called *Nevanlinna function*. A remarkable continued fraction expansion of $F(z)$ reveals a whole group of linear fractional transforms leaving invariant the class of Nevanlinna functions, and hence operating indirectly on positive measures. The result of such operations on the associated orthogonal polynomials appear in Peherstorfer (1992) and Zhedanov (1997). In this context one encounters Christoffel transforms, Szegő transforms, Geronimus transforms and a few other remarkable operations (Garza and Marcellán, 2009).

Section 9.2 The "cloud" of a planar measure, which we define in the last section of this chapter, has developed from some recent refined spectral analysis tools, combined with more classical complex function theory advances. To be more specific, the spectral theory of seminormal or hyponormal operators has its origin in the analysis of integral operators with a Cauchy-type kernel and quantum scattering theory. The interplay between concrete functional models acting on Lebesgue space and abstract theory of operator commutators led to a series of surprising results, ending with Connes' cyclic cohomology and multivariate index formulas. In a nutshell, Heisenberg's commutation relation

$$[H^*, H] = I,$$

which cannot be satisfied by bounded linear transforms H, is relaxed to

$$[T^*, T] \geq 0.$$

This time linear bounded operators T can well fulfill the positivity condition, such as the multiplier M_z on the space $P^2(\mu)$ (closure of complex polynomials) associated with a positive measure with compact support in $\mathbb{C}$. Point masses present in μ are detected by a simple property of the corresponding eigenvectors of M_z: they are annihilated by the commutator $[M_z^*, M_z]$. The continuum part of the support of the measure μ is then isolated by some natural limiting process relying only on the Christoffel–Darboux kernel. We refer the reader to Gustafsson and Putinar (2017) for some constructive aspects of the theory of hyponormal operators and for a guide through its history and basic references.

10

Spectral Characterization and Extensions of the Christoffel Function

In this chapter we analyze the (real) Christoffel function $\Lambda_n^\mu : \mathbb{R}^d \to \mathbb{R}_+$ associated with a finite positive Borel measure μ on a compact $\mathbf{\Omega} \subset \mathbb{R}^d$, for a *fixed* n. We describe alternative viewpoints by (a) its spectral interpretation on appropriate moment matrices, (b) its extension to $L^p(\mathbf{\Omega}, \mu)$ spaces, and (c) its extension via convex cones of polynomials positive on the support of μ, as follows.

(a) We first provide a simple *spectral* characterization of $\Lambda_n^\mu(\boldsymbol{\xi})$ associated with μ on $\mathbf{\Omega} \subset \mathbb{R}^d$, in terms of its moment matrix $\mathbf{M}_{\mu,n}$ and the moment matrix $\mathbf{M}_n(\delta_{\boldsymbol{\xi}})$ associated with the Dirac measure $\delta_{\boldsymbol{\xi}}$.

(b) We next consider its natural extension to Lebesgue $L^k(\mathbf{\Omega}, \mu)$ spaces

$$\boldsymbol{\xi} \mapsto \Lambda_{n,k}^\mu(\boldsymbol{\xi}) := \inf_{p \in \mathbb{R}_n[\mathbf{x}]} \left\{ \int_{\mathbf{\Omega}} |p(\mathbf{x})|^k \, d\mu : \; p(\boldsymbol{\xi}) = 1 \right\}, \quad \boldsymbol{\xi} \in \mathbb{R}^d$$

(so that $\Lambda_n^\mu = \Lambda_{n,2}^\mu$), and interpret its reciprocal as the $L^j(\mathbf{\Omega}, \mu)$ norm (with $1/k + 1/j = 1$) of a linear functional $\ell_{\boldsymbol{\xi}} \in L^j(\mathbf{\Omega}, \mu)$. The latter is the Hahn–Banach extension to $L^k(\mathbf{\Omega}, \mu)$ of the *point evaluation* linear functional $\ell_{\boldsymbol{\xi}}^n$ on $\mathbb{R}_n[\mathbf{x}]$, $p \mapsto \ell_{\boldsymbol{\xi}}^n(p) = p(\boldsymbol{\xi})$. (Recall that, in general, point evaluation on $L^2(\mathbf{\Omega}, \mu)$ does not make sense.) Namely, for $\boldsymbol{\xi} \in \mathbf{\Omega}$,

$$\frac{1}{\Lambda_{n,k}^\mu(\boldsymbol{\xi})^{1/k}} = \inf_{f \in L^j(\mathbf{\Omega},\mu)} \{\|f\|_j : \; f(p) = p(\boldsymbol{\xi}), \forall p \in \mathbb{R}_n[\mathbf{x}]\}.$$

In other words, the function $\ell_{\boldsymbol{\xi}} \in L^j(\mathbf{\Omega}, \mu)$ "mimics" the Dirac measure at $\boldsymbol{\xi}$ when acting on polynomials of degree at most n, and in particular, if $k = 2$, then

$$\mathbf{x} \mapsto \ell_{\boldsymbol{\xi}}(\mathbf{x}) = K_n^\mu(\boldsymbol{\xi}, \mathbf{x}), \quad \forall \mathbf{x} \in \mathbf{\Omega},$$

which has a sharp peak around the point $\mathbf{x} = \boldsymbol{\xi}$, as expected.

(c) Finally we specialize to measures on compact basic semialgebraic sets $\boldsymbol{\Omega} = \{\mathbf{x} \in \mathbb{R}^d : g_j(\mathbf{x}) \geq 0,\ j = 1, \ldots, m\}$ (for some $(g_j) \subset \mathbb{R}[\mathbf{x}]$), and consider the natural extension

$$\boldsymbol{\xi} \mapsto \kappa_n(\boldsymbol{\xi}) := \inf_{p \in \mathscr{Q}_{2n}(\boldsymbol{\Omega})} \left\{ \int_{\boldsymbol{\Omega}} p\, d\mu : p(\boldsymbol{\xi}) = 1 \right\}, \quad \boldsymbol{\xi} \in \mathbb{R}^d,$$

where $\mathscr{Q}_{2n}(\boldsymbol{\Omega})$ is the (degree-$2n$ truncated) quadratic module generated by the g_j (a convex subcone of $\mathscr{P}_{2n}(\boldsymbol{\Omega})$, the convex cone of polynomials of degree at most $2n$, nonnegative on $\boldsymbol{\Omega}$). (Of course one readily obtains $\kappa_n(\boldsymbol{\xi}) \leq \Lambda_n^{\mu}(\boldsymbol{\xi})$ for all n.) In this case, remarkably, the function $\kappa(\boldsymbol{\xi})$ simply relates to the Christoffel functions Λ_n^{μ} and $\Lambda_n^{\phi_j}$, $j = 1, \ldots, m$, where $d\phi_j = g_j\, d\mu$ on $\boldsymbol{\Omega} \cap \{\mathbf{x} : g_j \geq 0\}$. Such an extension is in the spirit of the extension in Schmüdgen (2017) were the author uses $\mathscr{P}_{2n}(\boldsymbol{\Omega})$ instead of $\mathscr{Q}_{2n}(\boldsymbol{\Omega})$. When using the convex cone $\mathscr{P}_{2n}(\boldsymbol{\Omega})$, the extension of the Christoffel function is related to the notion of *maximal masses* introduced in Schmüdgen (2017). However, in the univariate case $\boldsymbol{\Omega} = [-1, 1]$, extensions with both $\mathscr{P}_{2n}(\boldsymbol{\Omega})$ and $\mathscr{P}_{2n}(\boldsymbol{\Omega})$ coincide.

All the above results are obtained by tools from convex optimization and convex conic duality.

10.1 A Spectral Characterization of the Christoffel Function

The notation $\Sigma[\mathbf{x}]$ ($\subset \mathbb{R}[\mathbf{x}]$) stands for the convex cone of SOS polynomials: that is, polynomials that are sums of squares. Similarly, $\Sigma_n[\mathbf{x}] \subset \mathbb{R}_{2n}[\mathbf{x}]$ stands for its subset of SOS polynomials of degree at most $2n$. Let $\mathbf{v}_n(\mathbf{x})$ denote the vector which forms the usual monomial basis of $\mathbb{R}_n[\mathbf{x}]$. Then a polynomial $p \in \mathbb{R}_n[\mathbf{x}]$ is given by

$$\mathbf{x} \mapsto p(\mathbf{x}) = \sum_{\alpha \in \mathbb{N}_n^d} p_\alpha\, \mathbf{x}^\alpha = \langle \mathbf{p}, \mathbf{v}_n(\mathbf{x}) \rangle = \mathbf{p}^T \mathbf{v}_n(\mathbf{x}),$$

for some real vector $\mathbf{p} = (p_\alpha) \in \mathbb{R}^{s(n)}$. Next, recall that for two real symmetric matrices $\mathbf{A}, \mathbf{B}$, the notation $\mathbf{A} \succeq \mathbf{B}$ (resp. $\mathbf{A} \succ \mathbf{B}$) stands for $\mathbf{A} - \mathbf{B}$ is positive semidefinite (resp. positive definite). The scalar

$$\lambda_{\min}(\mathbf{A}, \mathbf{B}) := \min\{\, \lambda : \exists \mathbf{x} \neq 0 \text{ s.t. } \mathbf{A}\,\mathbf{x} = \lambda\, \mathbf{B}\,\mathbf{x} \,\}$$

denotes the smallest *generalized* eigenvalue of the pair $(\mathbf{A}, \mathbf{B})$.

Let μ be a finite Borel measure on a compact set $\mathbf{\Omega} \subset \mathbb{R}^d$ and assume that its moment matrix satisfies $\mathbf{M}_{\mu,n} \succ 0$ for all n. For the Dirac measure $\delta_{\boldsymbol{\xi}}$ at a point $\boldsymbol{\xi} \in \mathbb{R}^d$, its associated moment matrix is denoted by $\mathbf{M}_{\boldsymbol{\xi},n}$.

Recall from (4.4) and (4.7) that for every $n \in \mathbb{N}$, the Christoffel function $\Lambda_n^\mu : \mathbb{R}^d \to \mathbb{R}_+$ associated with μ has the variational formulation

$$\boldsymbol{\xi} \mapsto \Lambda_n^\mu(\boldsymbol{\xi}) = \min_{p \in \mathbb{R}_n[\mathbf{x}]} \left\{ \int_{\mathbf{\Omega}} p^2 \, d\mu \colon \, p(\boldsymbol{\xi}) = 1 \right\}, \quad \boldsymbol{\xi} \in \mathbb{R}^d, \tag{10.1}$$

which also reads

$$\Lambda_n^\mu(\boldsymbol{\xi}) = \min_{\mathbf{p} \in \mathbb{R}^{s(n)}} \{ \mathbf{p}^T \mathbf{M}_{\mu,n} \, \mathbf{p} : \, \mathbf{p}^T \mathbf{v}_n(\boldsymbol{\xi}) = 1 \}. \tag{10.2}$$

Problem (10.2) is a convex quadratic optimization problem for which efficient techniques are available. At an optimal solution $\mathbf{p}^* \in \mathbb{R}^{s(n)}$, the necessary Karush–Kuhn–Tucker (KKT)-optimality condition reads

$$p^*(\boldsymbol{\xi}) = 1\,; \quad \mathbf{M}_{\mu,n} \, \mathbf{p}^* = \lambda \, \mathbf{v}_n(\boldsymbol{\xi}), \quad \text{for some } \lambda.$$

Multiplying by $\mathbf{p}^*$ yields $\Lambda_n^\mu(\boldsymbol{\xi}) = \lambda \, \mathbf{v}_n(\boldsymbol{\xi})^T \mathbf{p}^* = \lambda$, and therefore as $\mathbf{M}_{\mu,n}$ is nonsingular,

$$\mathbf{p}^* = \Lambda_n^\mu(\boldsymbol{\xi}) \, \mathbf{M}_{\mu,n}^{-1} \, \mathbf{v}_n(\boldsymbol{\xi}), \tag{10.3}$$

so that the polynomial minimizer $p^* \in \mathbb{R}_n[\mathbf{x}]$ reads

$$\begin{aligned}
\mathbf{x} \mapsto p^*(\mathbf{x}) = \mathbf{v}_n(\mathbf{x})^T \mathbf{p}^* &= \Lambda_n^\mu(\xi) \, \mathbf{v}_n(\mathbf{x})^T \mathbf{M}_{\mu,n}^{-1} \, \mathbf{v}_n(\xi) \\
&= \Lambda_n^\mu(\xi) \sum_{\alpha \in \mathbb{N}_n^d} P_\alpha(\mathbf{x}) \, P_\alpha(\xi) && (10.4) \\
&= \frac{K_n^\mu(\mathbf{x}, \xi)}{K_n^\mu(\xi, \xi)}, \quad \forall \mathbf{x} \in \mathbb{R}^d, && (10.5)
\end{aligned}$$

where $(P_\alpha)_{\alpha \in \mathbb{N}^d} \subset \mathbb{R}[\mathbf{x}]$ is any family of polynomials that are orthonormal with respect to μ, and $K_n^\mu(\mathbf{x}, \mathbf{y})$ is the Christoffel–Darboux kernel defined in earlier chapters.

So evaluating Λ_n^μ at a point $\mathbf{x} \in \mathbb{R}^d$ may be done in several ways, depending on which type of information is available:

(a) via the kernel K_n^μ if the $(P_\alpha)_{\alpha \in \mathbb{N}_n^d}$ are available, or

(b) via the inverse $\mathbf{M}_{\mu,n}^{-1}$ if $\mathbf{M}_{\mu,n}$ is available, or

(c) numerically, by solving the quadratic optimization problem (10.2).

We also have an alternative spectral characterization since Λ_n^μ can be viewed as minimizing the generalized Rayleigh quotient $\mathbf{p}^T \mathbf{M}_{\mu,n} \mathbf{p} / \mathbf{p}^T \mathbf{M}_n(\delta_{\xi}) \mathbf{p}$ over $\mathbf{p} \in \mathbb{R}^{s(n)}$. However, some care is needed because $\mathbf{M}_{\xi,n}$ is not invertible.

Lemma 10.1.1 *If $\Lambda_n^{\mu}(\boldsymbol{\xi})$ is the Christoffel function defined in* (10.1) *then*

$$\Lambda_n^{\mu}(\boldsymbol{\xi}) \;=\; \lambda_{\min}(\mathbf{M}_{\mu,n}, \mathbf{M}_{\xi,n}). \tag{10.6}$$

In addition,

$$\Lambda_n^{\mu}(\boldsymbol{\xi}) = \max\{\gamma:\; \gamma\,\mathbf{M}_{\xi,n} \;\preceq \mathbf{M}_{\mu,n}\}, \tag{10.7}$$

$$\Lambda_n^{\mu}(\boldsymbol{\xi})^{-1} = \min\{\gamma:\; \mathbf{M}_{\xi,n} \;\preceq \gamma\,\mathbf{M}_{\mu,n}\}. \tag{10.8}$$

Proof Let $\mathbf{p}^* \in \mathbb{R}^{s(n)}$ be the optimal solution of (10.2). Then by (10.3),

$$\begin{aligned}
\mathbf{M}_{\mu,n}\,\mathbf{p}^* &= \Lambda_n^{\mu}(\boldsymbol{\xi})\,\mathbf{v}_n(\boldsymbol{\xi}) \;=\; \Lambda_n^{\mu}(\boldsymbol{\xi})\,\mathbf{v}_n(\boldsymbol{\xi})\,(\mathbf{v}_n(\boldsymbol{\xi})^T\mathbf{p}^*)\\
&= \Lambda_n^{\mu}(\boldsymbol{\xi})\,\left(\mathbf{v}_n(\boldsymbol{\xi})\,\mathbf{v}_n(\boldsymbol{\xi})^T\right)\,\mathbf{p}^*\\
&= \Lambda_n^{\mu}(\boldsymbol{\xi})\,\mathbf{M}_{\xi,n}\,\mathbf{p}^*,
\end{aligned}$$

which shows that $\Lambda_n^{\mu}(\boldsymbol{\xi})$ is a generalized eigenvalue of the pair $(\mathbf{M}_{\mu,n}, \mathbf{M}_{\xi,n})$ with associated eigenvector $\mathbf{p}^*$. Next, let $0 \neq \mathbf{q} \in \mathbb{R}^{s(n)}$ be a generalized eigenvector of the pair $(\mathbf{M}_{\mu,n}, \mathbf{M}_{\xi,n})$ with eigenvalue θ, that is,

$$\mathbf{M}_{\mu,n}\,\mathbf{q} = \theta\,\mathbf{M}_{\xi,n}\,\mathbf{q} \;=\; \theta\,\mathbf{v}_n(\boldsymbol{\xi})\,\mathbf{v}_n(\boldsymbol{\xi})^T\mathbf{q}.$$

Then necessarily $\theta \neq 0$ and $\mathbf{v}_n(\boldsymbol{\xi})^T\mathbf{q} \neq 0$ because $\mathbf{M}_{\mu,n}$ is nonsingular. Rescale $\mathbf{q}$ so that $\mathbf{v}_n(\boldsymbol{\xi})^T\mathbf{q} = 1 = q(\boldsymbol{\xi})$. Then

$$\begin{aligned}
&\mathbf{M}_{\mu,n}\,\mathbf{q} = \theta\,\mathbf{M}_{\xi,n}\,\mathbf{q}\\
\Rightarrow &\int q^2\,d\mu = \mathbf{q}^T\mathbf{M}_{\mu,n}\,\mathbf{q}\\
&\qquad = \theta\,\mathbf{q}^T\mathbf{v}_n(\boldsymbol{\xi})\mathbf{v}_n(\boldsymbol{\xi})^T\mathbf{q} \;=\; \theta\,q(\boldsymbol{\xi})^2 \;=\; \theta,
\end{aligned}$$

and therefore $\theta \geq \Lambda_n^{\mu}(\boldsymbol{\xi})$. Next, to prove (10.7), let

$$\rho \;:=\; \sup\{\gamma:\; \gamma\,\mathbf{M}_{\xi,n} \;\preceq \mathbf{M}_{\mu,n}\}. \tag{10.9}$$

The above optimization problem is a semidefinite program whose dual reads

$$\rho^* \;=\; \inf_{\mathbf{X}\succeq 0}\,\{\langle \mathbf{M}_{\mu,n}, \mathbf{X}\rangle:\; \langle \mathbf{M}_{\xi,n}, \mathbf{X}\rangle \;=\; 1\}. \tag{10.10}$$

As both (10.9) and (10.10) have a feasible solution, then by weak duality, $\rho \leq \rho^*$, $\rho < \infty$ and $\rho^* > -\infty$. Next, the Slater condition[1] holds for (10.9) because as $\mathbf{M}_{\mu,n} \succ 0$, $\gamma = 0$ is a strictly feasible solution. Therefore, by a standard result in convex conic programming, $\rho = \rho^*$ and (10.10) has an optimal solution $\mathbf{X}^* \succeq 0$. In addition, (10.10) is homogeneous with only one

[1] For a convex optimization problem $\inf_{\mathbf{x}}\{f(\mathbf{x}):\, g_j(\mathbf{x}) \leq 0\, j = 1,\ldots,m\}$ where f, g_j are convex functions, the Slater condition holds if there exists a strictly feasible solution $\mathbf{x}_0$, that is, such that $g_j(\mathbf{x}_0) < 0$ for all $j = 1,\ldots,m$.

constraint and therefore by Barvinok (2002, Corollary 13.2, p. 84), it has a rank-1 optimal solution $\mathbf{X}^* = \mathbf{q}\mathbf{q}^T$. Hence

$$\rho = \rho^* = \langle \mathbf{M}_{\mu,n}, \mathbf{q}\mathbf{q}^T \rangle = \mathbf{q}^T \mathbf{M}_{\mu,n}\, \mathbf{q} = \int q^2 d\mu,$$

$$1 = \langle \mathbf{M}_{\xi,n}, \mathbf{q}^T \mathbf{q} \rangle = \mathbf{q}^T \mathbf{v}_n(\boldsymbol{\xi})\, \mathbf{v}_n(\boldsymbol{\xi})^T \mathbf{q} = (\mathbf{v}_n(\boldsymbol{\xi})^T \mathbf{q})^2 = q(\boldsymbol{\xi})^2,$$

and therefore $\rho^* \geq \Lambda_n^\mu(\boldsymbol{\xi})$. On the other hand, $\rho^* \leq \Lambda_n^\mu(\boldsymbol{\xi})$ because for every $p \in \mathbb{R}_n[\mathbf{x}]$ with coefficient vector $\mathbf{p}$ and such that $p(\boldsymbol{\xi}) = 1$, $\mathbf{X} := \mathbf{p}\mathbf{p}^T$ is feasible for (10.10), in particular for $\mathbf{p} := \mathbf{p}^*$ (optimal solution of (10.2)) with value $\langle \mathbf{M}_{\mu,n}, \mathbf{p}\mathbf{p}^T \rangle = \Lambda_n^\mu(\boldsymbol{\xi})$. Hence (10.7) follows. Finally (10.8) is a straightforward reformulation of (10.7). □

10.2 Extension to $L^k(\boldsymbol{\Omega}, \mu)$ Spaces

In this section we consider an extension of the Christoffel function associated with a measure μ on a compact subset $\boldsymbol{\Omega} \subset \mathbb{R}^d$. To simplify notation, we have deleted the subscript $\mathbb{R}$ as we consider only real polynomials. We consider an embedding of $\mathbb{R}[\mathbf{x}]$ into $L^k(\boldsymbol{\Omega}, \mu)$ spaces, $k \geq 1$, and not only the Hilbert space $L^2(\boldsymbol{\Omega}, \mu)$ as is usually the case when dealing with the Christoffel function. Then with $k \in \mathbb{N}$, (10.1) becomes

$$\boldsymbol{\xi} \mapsto \Lambda_{n,k}^\mu(\boldsymbol{\xi}) := \min_{p \in \mathbb{R}_n[\mathbf{x}]} \left\{ \int_{\boldsymbol{\Omega}} |p|^k \, d\mu \colon p(\boldsymbol{\xi}) = 1 \right\}, \quad \boldsymbol{\xi} \in \mathbb{R}^d, \tag{10.11}$$

for every $n \in \mathbb{N}$. (With this notation $\Lambda_n^\mu = \Lambda_{n,2}^\mu$.)

Extensions to $L^k(\boldsymbol{\Omega}, \mu)$ spaces have been already considered to provide asymptotic results in the same vein as for the classical setting $k = 2$; see, for example, Levin and Lubinsky (2015) and Zhou (2016).

The goal of this section is different as we consider such extensions to provide a simple interpretation of the reciprocal of the Christoffel function (generalized to $L^k(\boldsymbol{\Omega}, \mu)$ spaces). Namely, it is the $L^j(\boldsymbol{\Omega}, \mu)$-norm (with $1/k + 1/j = 1$) of a linear functional on $L^k(\boldsymbol{\Omega}, \mu)$ that mimics the Dirac measure up to moments of order n. This functional is nothing less than the (Hahn–Banach) extension to $L^j(\boldsymbol{\Omega}, \mu)$ of the *point evaluation* functional on $\mathbb{R}_n[\mathbf{x}]$ (when $\mathbb{R}_n[\mathbf{x}]$ is viewed as a subspace of $L^k(\boldsymbol{\Omega}, \mu)$).

The notation $\mathbb{R}_{n,k}[\mathbf{x}]$ is to emphasize that one now considers $\mathbb{R}_n[\mathbf{x}]$ as a subspace of $L^k(\boldsymbol{\Omega}, \mu)$. Let $1 \leq k < \infty$ be fixed, and for every $\boldsymbol{\xi} \in \mathbb{R}^d$, let $\ell_{\boldsymbol{\xi}}^n \in \mathbb{R}_{n,k}[\mathbf{x}]^*$ be the (point evaluation at $\boldsymbol{\xi}$) linear form $p \mapsto \ell_{\boldsymbol{\xi}}^n(p) = p(\boldsymbol{\xi})$, for all $p \in \mathbb{R}_{n,k}[\mathbf{x}]$. Its representative is the vector $\mathbf{v}_n(\boldsymbol{\xi}) = (\boldsymbol{\xi}^\alpha)_{\alpha \in \mathbb{N}_n^d} \in \mathbb{R}^{s(n)}$. Then the dual norm of $\ell_{\boldsymbol{\xi}}^n$ reads

$$\|\ell_{\boldsymbol{\xi}}^n\|_* := \sup_{p \in \mathbb{R}_{n,k}[\mathbf{x}]} \left\{ |p(\boldsymbol{\xi})| : \left(\int_{\mathbf{\Omega}} |p|^k \, d\mu \right)^{1/k} \leq 1 \right\}.$$

Therefore

$$\|\ell_{\boldsymbol{\xi}}^n\|_* \geq \frac{|p(\boldsymbol{\xi})|}{\|p\|_k}, \quad \forall p \in \mathbb{R}_{n,k}[\mathbf{x}],$$

and so, equivalently,

$$\frac{1}{\|\ell_{\boldsymbol{\xi}}^n\|_*} \leq \frac{\|p\|_k}{|p(\boldsymbol{\xi})|}, \quad \forall p \in \mathbb{R}_{n,k}[\mathbf{x}],$$

that is,

$$\frac{1}{\|\ell_{\boldsymbol{\xi}}^n\|_*} = \inf_{p \in \mathbb{R}_{n,k}[\mathbf{x}]} \{ \|p\|_k : \, p(\boldsymbol{\xi}) = 1 \} = \Lambda_{n,k}^{\mu}(\boldsymbol{\xi})^{1/k}.$$

In other words, $\Lambda_{n,k}^{\mu}(\boldsymbol{\xi})^{1/k} \, \|\ell_{\boldsymbol{\xi}}^n\|_* = 1$. In particular, the Christoffel function $\Lambda_{n,2}^{\mu}(\boldsymbol{\xi})$ is just $1/\|\ell_{\boldsymbol{\xi}}^n\|_*^2$, and

$$\|\ell_{\boldsymbol{\xi}}^n\|_*^2 = \sum_{\alpha \in \mathbb{N}_d^n} P_\alpha(\boldsymbol{\xi})^2 = \|(P_\alpha(\boldsymbol{\xi}))_{\alpha \in \mathbb{N}_d^n}\|^2,$$

where the right-hand side is called the *Christoffel polynomial*.

Next, the linear form $\ell_{\boldsymbol{\xi}}^n \in \mathbb{R}_{n,k}[\mathbf{x}]^*$ is bounded and by the Hahn–Banach Theorem it has an extension to the whole $L^k(\mathbf{\Omega}, \mu)$ denoted $\ell_{\boldsymbol{\xi}}$ (hence $\ell_{\boldsymbol{\xi}} \in L^j(\mathbf{\Omega}, \mu)$ where $\frac{1}{k} + \frac{1}{j} = 1$) with norm

$$\|\ell_{\boldsymbol{\xi}}\|_j = \|\ell_{\boldsymbol{\xi}}^n\|_* = (\Lambda_{n,k}^{\mu}(\boldsymbol{\xi}))^{-1/k}. \tag{10.12}$$

There are possibly other extensions of $\ell_{\boldsymbol{\xi}}^n$ in $L_j(\mathbf{\Omega}, \mu)$ which may have smaller norm. However, the result below shows that in fact this not the case.

Lemma 10.2.1 *Let $\mathbf{\Omega} \subset \mathbb{R}^d$ be compact with nonempty interior, $\boldsymbol{\xi} \in \mathbb{R}^d$, and let $1 \leq k \in \mathbb{N}$ and $\frac{1}{k} + \frac{1}{j} = 1$. Then*

$$\Lambda_{n,k}^{\mu}(\boldsymbol{\xi})^{-1/k} = \|\ell_{\boldsymbol{\xi}}\|_j = \inf_{f \in L^j(\mathbf{\Omega}, \mu)} \left\{ \|f\|_j : \int_{\mathbf{\Omega}} \mathbf{x}^\alpha \, f \, d\mu = \boldsymbol{\xi}^\alpha, \alpha \in \mathbb{N}_n^d \right\} \tag{10.13}$$

and $\ell_{\boldsymbol{\xi}}$ is an optimal solution of the above optimization problem.

Proof Let

$$\theta := \inf_{f \in L^j(\mathbf{\Omega}, \mu)} \{ \|f\|_j : \, f(p) = p(\boldsymbol{\xi}), \forall p \in \mathbb{R}_{n,k}[\mathbf{x}] \}.$$

Then $\theta \leq \|\ell_{\xi}\|_j$ and therefore by (10.12) $\theta \cdot \Lambda^{\mu}_{n,k}(\xi)^{1/k} \leq 1$. On the other hand, let $p \in \mathbb{R}_{n,k}[\mathbf{x}]$ be arbitrary with $p(\xi) = 1$, and let $f \in L^j(\mathbf{\Omega}, \mu)$ be such that $f(q) = q(\xi)$ for all $q \in \mathbb{R}_{n,k}[\mathbf{x}]$. Then

$$\|p\|_k \cdot \|f\|_j \geq \int_{\mathbf{\Omega}} p\, f\, d\mu = f(p) = p(\xi) = 1,$$

which implies $\theta \cdot \|p\|_k \geq 1$ for all $p \in \mathbb{R}_{n,k}[\mathbf{x}]$ with $p(\xi) = 1$. Therefore $\Lambda^{\mu}_{n,k}(\xi)^{1/k}\, \theta \geq 1$, which in turn implies $\Lambda^{\mu}_{n,k}(\xi)^{1/k}\, \theta = 1$. That ℓ_{ξ} is an optimal solution is because from its definition $\ell_{\xi}(p) = p(\xi)$ for all $p \in \mathbb{R}_{n,k}[\mathbf{x}]$, and therefore ℓ_{ξ} is a feasible solution with value $\Lambda^{\mu}_{n,k}(\xi)^{-1/k}$. □

The above results have the following interpretation.

Theorem 10.2.2 *Let $\mathbf{\Omega} \subset \mathbb{R}^d$ be compact with nonempty interior, and let $n \in \mathbb{N}$ and $1 \leq k \in \mathbb{N}$ be fixed.*

(a) *A dual of the convex optimization problem* (10.11) *is the convex optimization problem*

$$\rho^* = \min_{f \in L^j(\mathbf{\Omega},\mu)} \left\{ \|f\|_j : \int \mathbf{x}^{\alpha}\, f\, d\mu = \xi^{\alpha}, \alpha \in \mathbb{N}^d_n \right\} \tag{10.14}$$

with optimal value $\rho^* = \Lambda^{\mu}_{n,k}(\xi)^{-1/k} = \|\ell_{\xi}\|_j$, the $L^j(\mathbf{\Omega}, \mu)$-norm of some $\ell_{\xi} \in L_j(\mathbf{\Omega}, \mu)$ whose restriction to $\mathbb{R}_{n,k}[\mathbf{x}]$ is the evaluation map $p \mapsto \ell_{\xi}(p) = p(\xi)$. The duality is more precisely

$$\|p\|_k \cdot \|f\|_j \geq 1,$$

for any pair $(p, f) \in \mathbb{R}_{n,k}[\mathbf{x}] \times L^j(\mathbf{\Omega}, \mu)$ of feasible solutions to (10.11) *and* (10.14)*, and in addition strong duality holds because* (10.11) *(resp.* (10.14)*) has an optimal solution $p^* \in \mathbb{R}_{n,k}[\mathbf{x}]$ (resp. $\ell_{\xi} \in L^j(\mathbf{\Omega}, \mu)$) with $\|p^*\|_k\, \|\ell_{\xi}\|_j = 1$.*

(b) *Moreover, for every $1 < k < \infty$,*

$$|\ell_{\xi}(\mathbf{x})| = \frac{|p^*(\mathbf{x})|^{k-1}}{\|p^*\|_k^k}, \quad \forall \mathbf{x} \in \mathbb{R}^d, \tag{10.15}$$

so that for all $k = 2s + 1 \in \mathbb{N}$, $s \in \mathbb{N}$, the function $\mathbf{x} \mapsto \ell_{\xi}(\mathbf{x})$ is an SOS polynomial of degree $2ns$.

Proof (a) Follows from Lemma 10.2.1. To obtain (b), observe that

$$\int_{\mathbf{\Omega}} p^*\, \ell_{\xi}\, d\mu = \ell_{\xi}(p^*) = p^*(\xi) = 1 = \|p^*\|_k \cdot \|\ell_{\xi}\|_j.$$

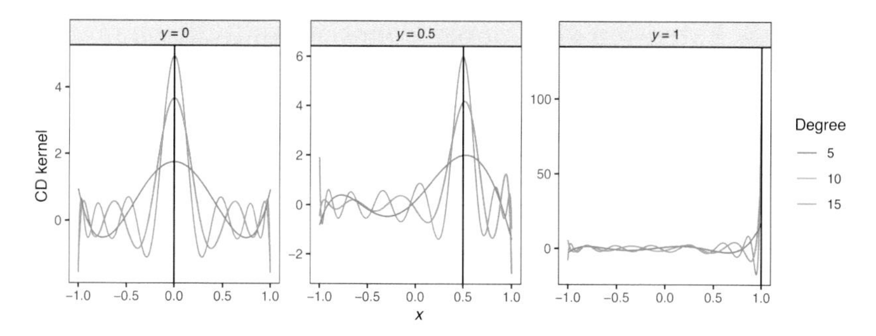

Figure 10.1 Univariate $x \mapsto K_n^{\mu}(x, y)$, for different values of y and various degrees n. As n increases, the CD kernel approximates Dirac delta measures.

It turns out that equality in the Hölder inequality holds if and only if $\gamma\,|\ell_{\xi}|^j = \kappa\,|p^*|^k$ for some scalars γ, κ not both zero; see Dunford and Schwartz (1958, 3.9.42, p.173). Therefore

$$|\ell_{\xi}(\mathbf{x})| \;=\; \gamma\,|p^*(\mathbf{x})|^{k/j}, \qquad \mu\text{-a.e. in } \mathbf{\Omega},$$

for some $\gamma > 0$, and so

$$\frac{1}{\|p^*\|_k} \;=\; \|\ell_{\xi}\|_j \;=\; \gamma\left(\int_{\mathbf{\Omega}} |p^*|^k\, d\mu\right)^{1/j} = \gamma\,\|p^*\|_k^{k/j} \;=\; \gamma\,\|p^*\|_k^{k-1},$$

from which one obtains $\gamma = \|p^*\|_k^{-k}$. Hence

$$|\ell_{\xi}(\mathbf{x})| \;=\; \frac{|p^*(\mathbf{x})|^{k-1}}{\|p^*\|_k^k} \;=\; \frac{|p^*(\mathbf{x})|^{k-1}}{\Lambda_{n,k}^{\mu}(\xi)}, \qquad \mu\text{-a.a. } \mathbf{x} \in \mathbf{\Omega}.$$

In particular, if $k = 2$, then combining with (10.4) and (10.5), we have

$$\ell_{\xi}(\mathbf{x}) \;=\; \sum_{\alpha \in \mathbb{N}_d^n} P_{\alpha}(\xi)\, P_{\alpha}(\mathbf{x}) = K_n^{\mu}(\mathbf{x}, \xi).$$

Also if $k - 1$ is even, then ℓ_{ξ} is an SOS polynomial of degree $2ns$. □

Theorem 10.2.2 states that the reciprocal of the Christoffel function is the $L^j(\mathbf{\Omega}, \mu)$ norm of the linear functional $\ell_{\xi} \in L^j(\mathbf{\Omega}, \mu)$ that mimics the Dirac measure δ_{ξ} as long as one considers only moments up to order n. This is illustrated in Figure 10.1 for $k = 2$ and $n = 1$, where μ is the Lebesgue measure on $\mathbf{\Omega} = [-1, 1]$.

10.3 Extension via Convex Cones of Positivity on Ω

In (10.1), instead of minimizing $\int p^2 d\mu$ over $p \in \mathbb{R}_n[\mathbf{x}]$, one may also consider minimizing over $p \in \mathscr{P}_{2n}(\mathbf{\Omega})$, where $\mathscr{P}_{2n}(\mathbf{\Omega})$ is the convex cone of polynomials of degree at most $2n$ that are nonnegative on $\mathbf{\Omega}$, or even on some appropriate smaller convex cone $\mathscr{Q}_{2n}(\mathbf{\Omega}) \subset \mathscr{P}_{2n}(\mathbf{\Omega})$, more practical for computational purposes.

10.3.1 Using the Convex Cone $\mathscr{P}_{2n}(\Omega)$

Let μ be a finite positive Borel measure supported on a compact set $\mathbf{\Omega} \subset \mathbb{R}^d$ with nonempty interior. Then the dual cone $\mathscr{P}_{2n}(\mathbf{\Omega})^* \subset \mathbb{R}^{s(2n)}$ is the set of vectors in $\mathbb{R}^{s(2n)}$ that have a *representing* measure on $\mathbf{\Omega}$. That is, $\mathbf{s} = (s_\alpha)_{\alpha\in\mathbb{N}^d_{2n}} \in \mathscr{P}_{2n}(\mathbf{\Omega})^*$ if and only if there exists a finite positive Borel measure ϕ on $\mathbf{\Omega}$ such that $s_\alpha = \int_{\mathbf{\Omega}} \mathbf{x}^\alpha \, d\phi$ for all $\alpha \in \mathbb{N}^d_{2n}$. Equivalently, $\mathbf{s}$ has a representing measure on $\mathbf{\Omega}$.

For an arbitrary finite signed Borel measure ϕ, let $\boldsymbol{\phi}_{2n} = (\phi_\alpha)_{\alpha\in\mathbb{N}^d_{2n}}$ be the moments of ϕ up to order $2n$. In particular, $\mathbf{v}_{2n}(\boldsymbol{\xi}) = (\boldsymbol{\xi}^\alpha)_{\alpha\in\mathbb{N}^d_{2n}} = (\boldsymbol{\delta}_{\boldsymbol{\xi}})_{2n}$. Consider the optimization problem

$$\begin{aligned} \tau_n(\boldsymbol{\xi}) := & \inf_{p\in\mathscr{P}_{2n}(\mathbf{\Omega})} \left\{ \int_{\mathbf{\Omega}} p \, d\mu : \; p(\boldsymbol{\xi}) = 1 \right\} \\ = & \min_{p\in\mathscr{P}_{2n}(\mathbf{\Omega})} \{ \langle \mathbf{p}, \boldsymbol{\mu}_{2n} \rangle : \; \langle \mathbf{p}, \mathbf{v}_{2n}(\boldsymbol{\xi}) \rangle = 1 \}. \end{aligned} \tag{10.16}$$

This is a linear conic optimization problem with associated dual

$$\sup_{\lambda} \{ \lambda : \; (\boldsymbol{\mu} - \lambda \, \boldsymbol{\delta}_{\boldsymbol{\xi}})_{2n} \in \mathscr{P}_{2n}(\mathbf{\Omega})^* \}. \tag{10.17}$$

Obviously in (10.16) one may replace the equality constraint $p(\boldsymbol{\xi}) = 1$ with the inequality constraint $p(\boldsymbol{\xi}) \geq 1$ and so (10.16) has a strictly feasible solution $p(\boldsymbol{\xi}) > 1$, which implies that the Slater condition holds for (10.16). Moreover $\tau_n(\boldsymbol{\xi}) \geq 0$ and so, by a standard result in conic optimization, both (10.16) and (10.17) have same optimal value and (10.17) has an optimal solution λ^*. Moreover, if $\mathbf{\Omega}$ is compact with nonempty interior and μ is absolutely continuous with respect to Lebesgue measure on $\mathbf{\Omega}$ (with a strictly positive density), then the Slater condition also holds for (10.17) and so (10.16) also has an optimal solution $p^* \in \mathscr{P}_{2n}(\mathbf{\Omega})$. Hence we have proved the following result.

Lemma 10.3.1 *Let $\mathbf{\Omega}$ be compact with nonempty interior and let μ be absolutely continuous with respect to Lebesgue measure on $\mathbf{\Omega}$, with a density strictly positive on $\mathbf{\Omega}$. Then $\tau_n(\boldsymbol{\xi})$ is the largest scalar λ such that $(\boldsymbol{\mu} - \lambda \, \boldsymbol{\delta}_{\boldsymbol{\xi}})_{2n} \in$*

$\mathscr{P}_{2n}(\boldsymbol{\Omega})^*$, that is, the finite sequence $(\mu_\alpha - \lambda\,\boldsymbol{\xi}^\alpha)_{\alpha\in\mathbb{N}^d_{2n}}$ has a representing measure on $\boldsymbol{\Omega}$.

Next observe that $\tau_n(\boldsymbol{\xi})$ depends only on the moments $\boldsymbol{\mu}_{2n}$, and not on μ. Therefore there are many other measures ϕ on $\boldsymbol{\Omega}$ with the same moments $\boldsymbol{\phi}_{2n} = (\phi_\alpha)_{\alpha\in\mathbb{N}^d_{2n}} = \boldsymbol{\mu}_{2n}$. However, with $\mathscr{M}(\boldsymbol{\Omega})_+$ being the set of finite Borel measures on $\boldsymbol{\Omega}$, let

$$\rho_n(\boldsymbol{\xi}) := \max_{\phi\in\mathscr{M}(\boldsymbol{\Omega})_+} \{\phi(\{\boldsymbol{\xi}\}) : \boldsymbol{\phi}_{2n} = \boldsymbol{\mu}_{2n}\}, \quad \boldsymbol{\xi}\in\boldsymbol{\Omega}.$$

Then, as shown in Schmüdgen (2017), $\rho_n(\boldsymbol{\xi}) = \tau_n(\boldsymbol{\xi})$. In other words $\tau_n(\boldsymbol{\xi})$ "selects" a measure ϕ^* on $\boldsymbol{\Omega}$ with $\boldsymbol{\phi}^*_{2n} = \boldsymbol{\mu}_{2n}$, and with maximal mass at $\boldsymbol{\xi}$.

10.3.2 Using a Tractable Convex Cone $\mathscr{Q}_{2n}(\Omega) \subset \mathscr{P}_{2n}(\Omega)$

The function $\tau_n(\boldsymbol{\xi})$ in (10.16) is essentially abstract in nature as there is no tractable characterization of $\mathscr{P}_{2n}(\boldsymbol{\Omega})$ in general; a notable exception is $\boldsymbol{\Omega} = [a,b]$ in the univariate case. Therefore in this section we specialize to compact basic *semialgebraic* sets $\boldsymbol{\Omega}$ of the form

$$\boldsymbol{\Omega} = \{\mathbf{x}\in\mathbb{R}^d : g_j(\mathbf{x}) \geq 0, j = 1,\ldots,m\} \tag{10.18}$$

for some polynomials $(g_j) \subset \mathbb{R}[\mathbf{x}]$ and instead consider a smaller cone $\mathscr{Q}_{2n}(\boldsymbol{\Omega}) \subset \mathscr{P}_{2n}(\boldsymbol{\Omega})$ of positivity on $\boldsymbol{\Omega}$, defined by

$$\mathscr{Q}_{2n}(\boldsymbol{\Omega}) := \left\{ \sigma_0 + \sum_{j=1}^m \sigma_j\, g_j : \sigma_j \in \Sigma[\mathbf{x}],\ \deg(\sigma_j\, g_j) \leq 2n \right\}, \tag{10.19}$$

which is a *truncated* version of the *quadratic module*

$$\mathscr{Q}(\boldsymbol{\Omega}) := \left\{ \sum_{j=0}^m \sigma_j\, g_j : \sigma_j \in \Sigma[\mathbf{x}] \right\}$$

associated with the polynomials g_js.

Remark For every integer n, $\mathscr{Q}_{2n}(\boldsymbol{\Omega}) \subset \mathscr{P}_{2n}(\boldsymbol{\Omega})$ and the inclusion is strict if $n > 1$. Moreover, although in general it is an intractable problem to check whether $p \in \mathscr{P}_{2n}(\boldsymbol{\Omega})$, it is computationally *tractable* to check whether $p \in \mathscr{Q}_{2n}(\boldsymbol{\Omega})$ as this can be done by solving a semidefinite program. Indeed, write

$$\mathbf{M}_{\mathbf{x},n} = \mathbf{v}_n(\mathbf{x})\,\mathbf{v}_n(\mathbf{x})^T = \sum_{\alpha\in\mathbb{N}^d_{2n}} \mathbf{B}_\alpha\,\mathbf{x}^\alpha$$

for appropriate real symmetric matrices $\mathbf{B}_\alpha$. Then a polynomial $p \in \mathbb{R}_{2n}[\mathbf{x}]$, $\mathbf{x} \mapsto p(\mathbf{x}) := \sum_\alpha p_\alpha \, \mathbf{x}^\alpha$, is an SOS of degree $2n$ (i.e. $p \in \Sigma_n[\mathbf{x}]$) if and only if there exists a real symmetric matrix $\mathbf{X} \succeq 0$ such that

$$\langle \mathbf{X}, \mathbf{B}_\alpha \rangle \;=\; p_\alpha\,, \quad \forall \alpha \in \mathbb{N}^d_{2n}\,. \tag{10.20}$$

The set of real symmetric matrices $\mathbf{X} \succeq 0$ that satisfy (10.20) is convex and is called a *spectrahedron* (the intersection of an affine linear space with the cone of positive semidefinite matrices). A semidefinite program is a conic convex optimization with (i) a linear criterion and (ii) a spectrahedron as feasible set. Up to arbitrary fixed precision, a semidefinite program can be solved efficiently, that is, in polynomial time in its input size. For more details the interested reader is referred to, for example, Anjos and Lasserre (2011, Chapter 1).

For every $j = 1, \ldots, m$, let μ_j be the measure on $\mathbf{\Omega}$ with density g_j with respect to μ, that is,

$$\mu_j(B) \;=\; \int_{\mathbf{\Omega} \cap B} g_j \, d\mu, \quad \forall B \in \mathcal{B}(\mathbb{R}^d).$$

With $\boldsymbol{\xi} \in \mathbb{R}^d$ fixed and arbitrary, consider the optimization problem

$$\kappa_n(\boldsymbol{\xi}) \;:=\; \min_{p \in \mathcal{Q}_{2n}(\mathbf{\Omega})} \; \{ \int_{\mathbf{\Omega}} p \, d\mu \, : \, p(\boldsymbol{\xi}) \;=\; 1 \,\}, \tag{10.21}$$

which is a tractable version of (10.16). Of course, in view of $\mathcal{Q}_{2n}(\mathbf{\Omega}) \subset \mathcal{P}_{2n}(\mathbf{\Omega})$, $\kappa_n(\boldsymbol{\xi}) \geq \tau_n(\boldsymbol{\xi})$ for all n, and all $\boldsymbol{\xi}$.

We next show that the function $\boldsymbol{\xi} \mapsto \kappa_n(\boldsymbol{\xi})$ simply relates to the Christoffel functions Λ^μ_n and $\Lambda^{\mu_j}_n$, $j = 1, \ldots, m$.

Theorem 10.3.2 *Let $\kappa_n(\boldsymbol{\xi})$ be as in* (10.21). *Then*

$$\kappa_n(\boldsymbol{\xi}) \;=\; \min \left[\Lambda^\mu_n(\boldsymbol{\xi}), \; \min_{j:\, g_j(\boldsymbol{\xi})>0} \frac{1}{g_j(\boldsymbol{\xi})} \, \Lambda^{\mu_j}_{n-d_j}(\boldsymbol{\xi}) \right], \quad \boldsymbol{\xi} \in \mathbb{R}^d, \tag{10.22}$$

where $\Lambda^\mu_n(\boldsymbol{\xi})$ (resp. $\Lambda^{\mu_j}_{n-d_j}(\boldsymbol{\xi})$) is the Christoffel function associated with μ (resp. μ_j).

Proof In view of the definition (10.19) of $\mathcal{Q}_n(\mathbf{\Omega})$, an equivalent formulation of (10.21) reads

$$\begin{aligned}\kappa_n(\boldsymbol{\xi}) = \inf_{\mathbf{X}_j} \quad & \left\{ \langle \mathbf{X}_0, \mathbf{M}_{\mu,n} \rangle + \sum_{j=1}^m \langle \mathbf{X}_j, \mathbf{M}_{\mu_j, n-d_j} \rangle : \right. \\ \text{s.t.} \quad & \langle \mathbf{X}_0, \mathbf{M}_{\boldsymbol{\xi},n} \rangle + \sum_{j=1}^m g_j(\boldsymbol{\xi}) \, \langle \mathbf{X}_j, \mathbf{M}_{\boldsymbol{\xi},n-d_j} \rangle \;=\; 1, \\ & \left. \mathbf{X}_j \succeq 0, \; j = 0, \ldots, m \right\},\end{aligned} \tag{10.23}$$

with $d_j = \lceil \deg(g_j)/2 \rceil$, $j = 0, \ldots, m$. Problem (10.23) is a semidefinite program and its dual reads

$$\eta^* = \sup_\lambda \; \{\lambda\colon\; \lambda\, \mathbf{M}_{\xi,n} \preceq \mathbf{M}_{\mu,n};\; \lambda\, g_j(\boldsymbol{\xi})\, \mathbf{M}_{\xi,n-d_j} \preceq \mathbf{M}_{\mu_j,n-d_j}, j = 1,\ldots,m\}$$

(and, by weak duality, $\kappa_n(\boldsymbol{\xi}) \geq \eta^*$). Equivalently, with $g_0 = 1$ and $d_0 = 0$,

$$\eta^* = \min_{j=0,\ldots,m} \eta_j^*$$

with

$$\eta_j^* = \sup_\lambda \{\,\lambda\colon\; \lambda\, g_j(\boldsymbol{\xi})\, \mathbf{M}_{\xi,n-d_j} \preceq \mathbf{M}_{\mu_j,n-d_j}\}$$
$$= \begin{cases} \frac{1}{g_j(\boldsymbol{\xi})} \sup_\lambda \{\,\lambda\colon\; \lambda\, \mathbf{M}_{\xi,n-d_j} \preceq \mathbf{M}_{\mu_j,n-d_j}\} & \text{if } g_j(\boldsymbol{\xi}) > 0, \\ +\infty & \text{otherwise,} \end{cases}$$

for $j = 0, \ldots, m$. Therefore, by Lemma 10.1.1,

$$\eta^* = \min\left[\Lambda_n^\mu(\boldsymbol{\xi}),\; \min_{j\colon g_j(\boldsymbol{\xi})>0} \frac{1}{g_j(\boldsymbol{\xi})}\, \Lambda_{n-d_j}^{\mu_j}(\boldsymbol{\xi})\right].$$

Finally with $\varepsilon > 0$ sufficiently small and $\mathbf{X}_0 := \mathbf{I}$, $\mathbf{X}_j := \varepsilon\, \mathbf{I}$, $j = 1, \ldots, m$,

$$\langle \mathbf{X}_0, \mathbf{M}_{\xi,n}\rangle + \sum_{j=1}^m g_j(\boldsymbol{\xi}) \langle \mathbf{X}_j, \mathbf{M}_{\xi,n-d_j}\rangle = a > 0.$$

Then $(\mathbf{X}_0/a, \ldots, \mathbf{X}_m/a)$ is a strictly feasible solution of (10.23), which shows that Slater's condition holds for (10.23). Therefore, by standard convex duality, $\eta^* = \kappa_n(\boldsymbol{\xi})$. □

Observe that $p^2 \in \mathscr{Q}_{2n}(\boldsymbol{\Omega})$ whenever $p \in \mathbb{R}_n[\mathbf{x}]$, and $p(\boldsymbol{\xi})^2 = 1$ if $p(\boldsymbol{\xi}) = 1$. Therefore

$$\Lambda_n^\mu(\boldsymbol{\xi}) \geq \kappa_n(\boldsymbol{\xi}) \geq \tau_n(\boldsymbol{\xi}), \quad \forall \boldsymbol{\xi} \in \mathbb{R}^d.$$

Interestingly, formula (10.22) for the optimal value $\kappa_n(\boldsymbol{\xi})$ reflects the influence of the boundary $\partial\boldsymbol{\Omega}$ through the Christoffel functions associated with the measures μ_j.

Example 10.3.3 Let $d = 1$ and let μ be the uniform distribution on $\boldsymbol{\Omega} := [-1, 1]$ and let $x \mapsto g(x) := 1 - x^2$ so that $\boldsymbol{\Omega} = \{x \in \mathbb{R}\colon g(x) \geq 0\}$. Let $d\mu_1 = g\, d\mu$ on $\boldsymbol{\Omega}$. Figure 10.2 shows the functions Λ_3^μ and $\Lambda_2^{\mu_1}$.

10.4 Multi-point Interpolation

The standard Christoffel function Λ_n^μ can be seen as the optimal value of a *polynomial interpolation* problem with the single point $\boldsymbol{\xi} \in \mathbb{R}^d$. It is therefore

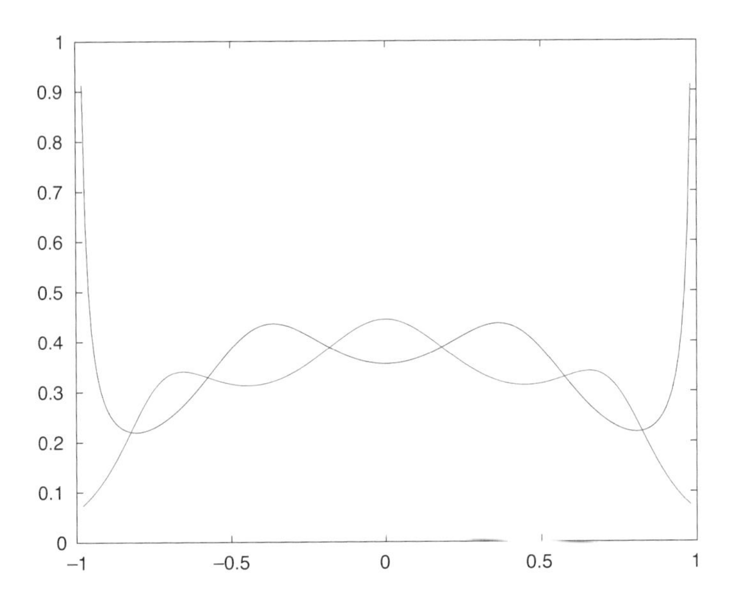

Figure 10.2 Christoffel function Λ_3^{μ} (blue) and $\Lambda_2^{\mu_1}\, g^{-1}$ (red).

natural to consider its extension to multi-point polynomial interpolation. That is, with $\{\boldsymbol{\xi}_1, \dots, \boldsymbol{\xi}_t\} \subset \mathbb{R}^d$ and $\mathbf{a} = (a_1, \dots, a_t) \in \mathbb{R}^t$ fixed, let

$$\Lambda_n^{\mu}(\boldsymbol{\xi}_1, \dots, \boldsymbol{\xi}_t; \mathbf{a}) := \min_{p \in \mathbb{R}_n[\mathbf{x}]} \left\{ \int_{\Omega} p^2 \, d\mu : \; p(\boldsymbol{\xi}_i) = a_i, i = 1, \dots, t \right\} \tag{10.24}$$

be a multi-point extension of (10.1); if n is sufficiently large there is always a feasible solution $p \in \mathbb{R}_n[\mathbf{x}]$ (take the interpolation polynomials at the points $\boldsymbol{\xi}_i$, $i = 1, \dots, t$). Equivalently,

$$\Lambda_n^{\mu}(\boldsymbol{\xi}_1, \dots, \boldsymbol{\xi}_t; \mathbf{a}) = \min_{\mathbf{p} \in \mathbb{R}^{s(n)}} \{ \mathbf{p}^T \mathbf{M}_{\mu,n}\, \mathbf{p} : \; \mathbf{p}^T \mathbf{v}_n(\boldsymbol{\xi}_i) = a_i, \; i \leq t \}, \tag{10.25}$$

which is again a convex quadratic optimization problem, but now with t linear constraints.

Proposition 10.4.1 *The multi-point Christoffel function defined in* (10.24) *is the quadratic form in* $\mathbf{a}$ *defined by*

$$\Lambda_n^{\mu}(\boldsymbol{\xi}_1, \dots, \boldsymbol{\xi}_t; \mathbf{a}) = \mathbf{a}^T \, \tilde{K}_n^{-1} \, \mathbf{a}, \tag{10.26}$$

where $\tilde{K}_n \in \mathbb{R}^{t \times t}$ *is the real symmetric matrix* $(K_n^{\mu}(\boldsymbol{\xi}_i, \boldsymbol{\xi}_j))_{1 \leq i,j \leq t}$.

If $t = 1$ *and* $\mathbf{a} = a_1 = 1$ *one retrieves the standard Christoffel function* $\Lambda_n^{\mu}(\boldsymbol{\xi})$.

Proof At an optimal solution $\mathbf{p}^* \in \mathbb{R}^{s(n)}$ the KKT-necessary optimality conditions read

$$p^*(\boldsymbol{\xi}_j) = a_j^2,\ j = 1,\dots,t; \quad \mathbf{M}_{\mu,n}\,\mathbf{p}^* = \sum_{j=1}^{t} \lambda_j^*\,\mathbf{v}_n(\boldsymbol{\xi}_j),$$

for some $\boldsymbol{\lambda}^* \in \mathbb{R}^t$. Hence $\mathbf{p}^* = \sum_{j=1}^{n} \lambda_j^*\,\mathbf{M}_{\mu,n}^{-1}\,\mathbf{v}_n(\boldsymbol{\xi}_j)$, and in particular,

$$\Lambda_n^{\mu}(\boldsymbol{\xi}_1,\dots,\boldsymbol{\xi}_t;\mathbf{a}) = \sum_{j=1}^{t} \lambda_j^*\,\mathbf{v}_n(\boldsymbol{\xi}_j)^T\mathbf{p}^* = \mathbf{a}^T\boldsymbol{\lambda}^*.$$

Next, recall that $\mathbf{v}_n(\mathbf{x})^T\mathbf{M}_{\mu,n}^{-1}\mathbf{v}_n(\boldsymbol{\xi}_j) = K_n^{\mu}(\mathbf{x},\boldsymbol{\xi}_j)$. Hence

$$\mathbf{x} \mapsto p^*(\mathbf{x}) = \sum_{j=1}^{t} \lambda_j^*\,K_n^{\mu}(\mathbf{x},\boldsymbol{\xi}_j), \quad \forall \mathbf{x} \in \mathbb{R}^d,$$

and so, in particular,

$$a_\ell = p^*(\boldsymbol{\xi}_\ell) = \sum_{j=1}^{t} \lambda_j^*\,K_n^{\mu}(\boldsymbol{\xi}_\ell,\boldsymbol{\xi}_j) = \left(\tilde{K}_n\,\boldsymbol{\lambda}^*\right)_\ell, \quad \ell = 1,\dots,t,$$

which yields the desired result $\boldsymbol{\lambda}^* = \tilde{K}_n^{-1}\,\mathbf{a}$. □

Spectral Characterization: We next provide a generalized eigenvalue interpretation of the multi-point problem (10.24).

Definition 10.4.2 Let $\mathscr{S}(\boldsymbol{\xi}_1,\dots,\boldsymbol{\xi}_t;\,\mathbf{a}) \subset \mathbb{R}[\mathbf{x}]$ be the set defined by

$$\mathscr{S}(\boldsymbol{\xi}_1,\dots,\boldsymbol{\xi}_t;\,\mathbf{a}) := \{q \in \mathbb{R}_n[\mathbf{x}]:\ q(\boldsymbol{\xi}_i) = a_i, i = 1,\dots,t\}.$$

Then, for a signed Borel measure ϕ on $\{\boldsymbol{\xi}_1,\dots,\boldsymbol{\xi}_t\}$, define

$$\begin{aligned}\lambda_{\min}^{\boldsymbol{\xi}_1,\dots,\boldsymbol{\xi}_t;\mathbf{a}}(\mathbf{M}_{\mu,n},\mathbf{M}_{\phi,n}) := \min_{\lambda}\{\lambda: \quad & \exists q \in \mathscr{S}(\boldsymbol{\xi}_1,\dots,\boldsymbol{\xi}_t;\,\mathbf{a}) \\ \text{s.t.} \quad & \mathbf{M}_{\mu,n}\,\mathbf{q} = \lambda\,\mathbf{M}_{\phi,n}\,\mathbf{q}\},\end{aligned} \tag{10.27}$$

which is a constrained version of the *generalized eigenvalue* for the pair of moment matrices $(\mathbf{M}_{\mu,n},\mathbf{M}_{\phi,n})$.

(When $t = 1$ then $\lambda_{\min}^{\boldsymbol{\xi};1}(\mathbf{M}_{\mu,n},\mathbf{M}_{\boldsymbol{\xi},n}) = \lambda_{\min}(\mathbf{M}_{\mu,n},\mathbf{M}_{\boldsymbol{\xi},n}) = \Lambda_n^{\mu}(\boldsymbol{\xi})$.) Next define the set

$$\Phi(\boldsymbol{\xi}_1,\dots,\boldsymbol{\xi}_t;\,\mathbf{a}) := \left\{\sum_{i=1}^{t} \theta_i\,\delta_{\boldsymbol{\xi}_i} :\ \sum_{i=1}^{t} a_i^2\,\theta_i = 1\right\} \tag{10.28}$$

of signed measures with support in $\{\boldsymbol{\xi}_1,\dots,\boldsymbol{\xi}_t\}$. Note that in the case where $t = 1$ and $a_i = 1$, then $\Phi(\boldsymbol{\xi};\,1) = \delta_{\boldsymbol{\xi}}$.

Lemma 10.4.3 *If $p^* \in \mathbb{R}_n[\mathbf{x}]$ is an optimal solution of* (10.24) *then*

$$\Lambda_n^\mu(\boldsymbol{\xi}_1, \ldots, \boldsymbol{\xi}_t;\, \mathbf{a}) \;=\; \lambda_{\min}^{\boldsymbol{\xi}_1,\ldots,\boldsymbol{\xi}_t;\,\mathbf{a}}(\mathbf{M}_{\mu,n}, \mathbf{M}_{\phi^*,n}) \qquad (10.29)$$

for some $\phi^* \in \Phi(\boldsymbol{\xi}_1, \ldots, \boldsymbol{\xi}_t;\, \mathbf{a})$.

Proof Let $\tau = \Lambda_n^\mu(\boldsymbol{\xi}_1, \ldots, \boldsymbol{\xi}_t;\, \mathbf{a})$. Then by the KKT optimality conditions

$$p^*(\boldsymbol{\xi}_i) \;=\; a_i\,,\; i = 1, \ldots, t; \quad \mathbf{M}_{\mu,n}\,\mathbf{p}^* \;=\; \sum_{i=1}^t \lambda_i^*\,\mathbf{v}_n(\boldsymbol{\xi}_i),$$

for some vector $\boldsymbol{\lambda}^* \in \mathbb{R}^t$. Write $\lambda_i^* = \tau\, a_i\, \theta_i^*$, for all $i = 1, \ldots, t$. Then

$$\tau \;=\; \langle \mathbf{p}^*, \mathbf{M}_{\mu,n}\,\mathbf{p}^*\rangle \;=\; \tau \sum_{i=1}^t a_i\,\theta_i^*\, \underbrace{\mathbf{v}_n(\boldsymbol{\xi}_i)^T\mathbf{p}^*}_{=a_i} \;=\; \tau \sum_i a_i^2\,\theta_i^*,$$

and so $\sum_i a_i^2\,\theta_i^* = 1$. Next,

$$\begin{aligned}
\mathbf{M}_{\mu,n}\,\mathbf{p}^* &= \tau \sum_{i=1}^t a_i\,\theta_i^*\,\mathbf{v}_n(\boldsymbol{\xi}_i)\,\underbrace{\mathbf{v}_n(\boldsymbol{\xi}_i)^T\mathbf{p}^*}_{=a_i}\,\frac{1}{a_i}\\
&= \tau \sum_{i=1}^t \theta_i^*\,\underbrace{\mathbf{v}_n(\boldsymbol{\xi}_i)\,\mathbf{v}_n(\boldsymbol{\xi}_i)^T}_{\mathbf{M}_{\xi,n}}\;\mathbf{p}^*\\
&= \tau\,\mathbf{M}_{\phi^*,n}\,\mathbf{p}^*,
\end{aligned}$$

with $\phi^* := \sum_{i=1}^t \theta_i^*\delta_{\boldsymbol{\xi}_i} \in \Phi(\boldsymbol{\xi}_1, \ldots, \boldsymbol{\xi}_t;\, \mathbf{a})$. As $p^* \in \mathscr{S}(\boldsymbol{\xi}_1, \ldots, \boldsymbol{\xi}_t;\, \mathbf{a})$ it follows that $\tau \geq \lambda_{\min}^{\boldsymbol{\xi}_1,\ldots,\boldsymbol{\xi}_t;\,\mathbf{a}}(\mathbf{M}_{\mu,n}, \mathbf{M}_{\phi^*,n})$. Next, suppose that $\psi \in \Phi(\boldsymbol{\xi}_1, \ldots, \boldsymbol{\xi}_t;\, \mathbf{a})$ and $q \in \mathscr{S}(\boldsymbol{\xi}_1, \ldots, \boldsymbol{\xi}_t;\, \mathbf{a})$ satisfy

$$\mathbf{M}_{\mu,n}\,\mathbf{q} \;=\; \tau_\psi\,\mathbf{M}_{\psi,n}\,\mathbf{q}; \quad \tau_\psi \;<\; \tau\; (= \Lambda_n^\mu(\boldsymbol{\xi}_1, \ldots, \boldsymbol{\xi}_t;\, \mathbf{a})).$$

Then, using $\mathbf{M}_{\psi,n} = \sum_i \theta_i\,\mathbf{v}_n(\boldsymbol{\xi}_i)\mathbf{v}_n(\boldsymbol{\xi}_i)^T$, we have

$$\Lambda_n^\mu(\boldsymbol{\xi}_1, \ldots, \boldsymbol{\xi}_t;\, \mathbf{a}) \;\leq \mathbf{q}^T\mathbf{M}_{\mu,n}\,\mathbf{q} \;=\; \tau_\psi \sum_{i=1}^t \theta_i\, q(\boldsymbol{\xi}_i)^2 \;=\; \tau_\psi \sum_{i=1}^t a_i^2\theta_i \;=\; \tau_\psi,$$

which yields a contradiction. □

Multi-point Extension Using the Convex Cone $\mathscr{P}_{2n}(\Omega)$: The multi-point analog of $\tau_n(\boldsymbol{\xi})$ in (10.16) reads

$$\tau_n(\boldsymbol{\xi}_1, \ldots, \boldsymbol{\xi}_t;\, \mathbf{a}_2) \;:=\; \inf_{p\in\mathscr{P}_{2n}(\boldsymbol{\Omega})} \left\{ \int_{\boldsymbol{\Omega}} p\, d\mu\colon\; p(\boldsymbol{\xi}_i) = a_i^2,\; i = 1, \ldots, t \right\}, \quad (10.30)$$

a linear conic optimization problem with t linear constraints (where the notation $\mathbf{a}_2$ stands for the vector $(a_i^2) \in \mathbb{R}_+^t$). We prefer to write $p(\boldsymbol{\xi}_i) = a_i^2$ (i) because $p \in \mathscr{P}_{2n}(\boldsymbol{\Omega})$ is nonnegative and (ii) for a meaningful comparison with $p \in \mathbb{R}_n[\mathbf{x}]$ in (10.24); p in (10.30) has degree $2n$ and should be considered as "equivalent" to the square of a polynomial in $\mathbb{R}_n[\mathbf{x}]$.

Recall that $\mathscr{P}_{2n}(\boldsymbol{\Omega})^* \subset \mathbb{R}^{s(2n)}$ is the space of $s(2n)$-vectors which have a representing measure on $\boldsymbol{\Omega}$. As a linear conic problem, (10.30) has a dual that reads

$$\sup_{\boldsymbol{\lambda}} \left\{ \mathbf{a}_2^T \boldsymbol{\lambda} : \; \boldsymbol{\mu}_{2n} - \sum_{i=1}^{t} \lambda_i \, \mathbf{v}_{2n}(\boldsymbol{\xi}_i) \in \mathscr{P}_{2n}(\boldsymbol{\Omega})^* \right\}. \tag{10.31}$$

Under the standard interior point condition in conic programming, both (10.30) and (10.31) have the same optimal value (which is finite since $\int p d\mu \geq 0$) and both have an optimal solution $p^* \in \mathscr{P}_{2n}(\boldsymbol{\Omega})$ and $\boldsymbol{\lambda}^* \in \mathbb{R}^t$, respectively. For instance as in Lemma 10.3.1, assume that $\boldsymbol{\Omega}$ is compact with nonempty interior, μ is absolutely continuous with respect to the Lebesgue measure on $\boldsymbol{\Omega}$, and, in addition, assume that (10.30) has a feasible solution $p \in \operatorname{int}(\mathscr{P}_{2n}(\boldsymbol{\Omega}))$. Then under such conditions,

$$\tau_n(\boldsymbol{\xi}_1, \ldots, \boldsymbol{\xi}_t; \mathbf{a}) = \mathbf{a}_2^T \boldsymbol{\lambda}^* \quad \text{and} \quad \left(\boldsymbol{\mu} - \sum_{i=1}^{t} \lambda_i^* \, \boldsymbol{\delta}_{\boldsymbol{\xi}_i} \right)_{2n} \in \mathscr{P}_{2n}(\boldsymbol{\Omega})^*, \tag{10.32}$$

where the last statement says that the finite sequence $(\mu_\alpha - \sum_{i=1}^t \lambda_i^* \boldsymbol{\xi}_i^\alpha)_{\alpha \in \mathbb{N}_{2n}^d}$ has a representing (positive) measure on $\boldsymbol{\Omega}$.

In other words, given $0 \neq \boldsymbol{\lambda} \in \mathbb{R}^t$, let $\phi_{\boldsymbol{\lambda}}$ be the signed measure $\sum_{i=1}^t \lambda_i \, \delta_{\boldsymbol{\xi}_i}$ on $\mathbb{R}^d$, and assume that μ is absolutely continuous with respect to the Lebesgue measure on $\boldsymbol{\Omega}$. Observe that $\mu - \phi_{\boldsymbol{\lambda}}$ is a *signed* measure. (To see that it is *not* a positive measure, just observe that if $\lambda_i^* > 0$ for some i, then $(\mu - \phi_{\boldsymbol{\lambda}})(\{\boldsymbol{\xi}_i\}) = -\lambda_i < 0$, and there is at least one $\lambda_i^* > 0$; otherwise the "sup" in (10.30) is infinite.)

Then $\tau_n(\boldsymbol{\xi}_1, \ldots, \boldsymbol{\xi}_t; \mathbf{a}_2)$ maximizes $\mathbf{a}_2^T \boldsymbol{\lambda}$
over all $\boldsymbol{\lambda}$ such that $(\boldsymbol{\mu} - \boldsymbol{\phi}_{\boldsymbol{\lambda}})_{2n}$ has a representing measure.

Multi-point Extension Using the Convex Cone $\mathscr{Q}_{2n}(\Omega)$: Let $\mathbf{a} := (a_1^2, \ldots, a_t^2) \in \mathbb{R}^s$. The multi-point counterpart of the function $\kappa_n(\boldsymbol{\xi})$ in (10.21) reads

$$\kappa_n(\boldsymbol{\xi}_1, \ldots, \boldsymbol{\xi}_t; \mathbf{a}) := \min_{p \in \mathscr{Q}_{2n}(\boldsymbol{\Omega})} \left\{ \int_{\boldsymbol{\Omega}} p \, d\mu : \; p(\boldsymbol{\xi}_i) = a_i^2, \; i = 1, \ldots, t \right\}. \tag{10.33}$$

Next, for any $\phi \in \Phi(\boldsymbol{\xi}_1, \ldots, \boldsymbol{\xi}_t; \mathbf{a})$, let $d\phi_j := g_j\, d\phi$ whereas $d\mu_j := g_j\, d\mu$, and define

$$\mathbb{T}^0_\phi = \sup_\theta \{\theta\colon\ \theta\, \mathbf{M}_{\phi,n} \preceq \mathbf{M}_{\mu,n}\}, \tag{10.34}$$

$$\mathbb{T}^j_\phi = \sup_\theta \{\theta\colon\ \theta\, \mathbf{M}_{\phi_j,n-d_j} \preceq \mathbf{M}_{\mu_j,n-d_j}\} \tag{10.35}$$

for all $j = 1, \ldots, m$.

Theorem 10.4.4 *Let $\kappa_n(\boldsymbol{\xi}_1, \ldots, \boldsymbol{\xi}_t; \mathbf{a})$ be as in (10.33) and let Φ be the set $\Phi(\boldsymbol{\xi}_1, \ldots, \boldsymbol{\xi}_t; \mathbf{a})$ defined in (10.28). Then*

$$\begin{aligned}
\kappa_n(\boldsymbol{\xi}_1, \ldots, \boldsymbol{\xi}_t; \mathbf{a}) &= \sup_{\phi\in\Phi} \sup_\lambda \{\lambda\colon\ \lambda\, \mathbf{M}_{\phi,n} \preceq \mathbf{M}_{\mu,n}, \\
&\qquad\qquad \lambda\, \mathbf{M}_{\phi_j,n-d_j} \preceq \mathbf{M}_{\mu_j,n-d_j}, \\
&\qquad\qquad \forall j = 1, \ldots, m\} \qquad (10.36)\\
&= \sup_{\phi\in\Phi} \min_{j=0,\ldots,m} \mathbb{T}^j_\phi \qquad (10.37)\\
&= \sup_{\phi\in\Phi} \min_{p\in\mathcal{Q}_{2n}(\boldsymbol{\Omega})} \left\{ \int_{\boldsymbol{\Omega}} p\, d\mu\colon\ \int p\, d\phi = 1 \right\}. \qquad (10.38)
\end{aligned}$$

In particular, with $\kappa_n(\boldsymbol{\xi})$ as in (10.21),

$$\kappa_n(\boldsymbol{\xi}_1, \ldots, \boldsymbol{\xi}_t; \mathbf{a}) \geq \max[\, a_1^2\, \kappa_n(\boldsymbol{\xi}_1), \ldots, a_t^2\, \kappa_n(\boldsymbol{\xi}_t)\,]. \tag{10.39}$$

Proof From the definition of $\mathcal{Q}_{2n}(\boldsymbol{\Omega})$ (and recalling that $g_0 = 1$ and $d_0 = 0$), (10.33) reads

$$\begin{aligned}
\kappa_n(\boldsymbol{\xi}_1, \ldots \boldsymbol{\xi}_t; \mathbf{a}) = \min_{\mathbf{X}_0,\ldots,\mathbf{X}_m \succeq 0} \Bigg\{ & \sum_{j=0}^m \langle \mathbf{X}_j, \mathbf{M}_{\mu_j,n-d_j} \rangle\colon \\
\text{s.t.}\ & \sum_{j=0}^m g_j(\boldsymbol{\xi}_i)\, \langle \mathbf{X}_j, \mathbf{M}_{\boldsymbol{\xi}_i,n-d_j} \rangle = a_i^2, \\
& \forall i = 1, \ldots, t \Bigg\}.
\end{aligned} \tag{10.40}$$

Its dual becomes

$$\rho = \sup_{\theta_i} \left\{ \sum_{i=1}^t a_i^2\, \theta_i\colon\ \sum_{i=1}^t \theta_i\, g_j(\boldsymbol{\xi}_i)\, \mathbf{M}_{\boldsymbol{\xi}_i,n-d_j} \preceq \mathbf{M}_{\mu_j,n-d_j}, j \leq m \right\}.$$

Equivalently (as $\rho \neq 0$),

$$\rho = \sup_{\phi\in\Phi} \sup_\lambda \{\lambda\colon\ \lambda\, \mathbf{M}_{\phi_j,n-d_j} \preceq \mathbf{M}_{\mu_j,n-d_j}, j \leq m\},$$

which is (10.36), and also $\rho = \sup_{\phi\in\Phi} \min_{j=0,\ldots,m} \mathbb{T}^j_\phi$, which is (10.37).

To obtain (10.38) observe that the dual of the inner sup reads

$$\min_{\mathbf{X}_j \succeq 0} \left\{ \sum_{j=0}^{m} \langle \mathbf{M}_{\mu_j, n-d_j}, \mathbf{X}_j \rangle : \sum_{j=0}^{m} \langle \mathbf{M}_{\phi_j, n-d_j}, \mathbf{X}_j \rangle = 1 \right\}, \tag{10.41}$$

or, equivalently,

$$\min_{p \in \mathscr{Q}_{2n}(\boldsymbol{\Omega})} \left\{ \int p \, d\mu : \int p \, d\phi = 1 \right\},$$

and therefore,

$$\rho = \sup_{\phi \in \Phi} \min_{p \in \mathscr{Q}_{2n}(\boldsymbol{\Omega})} \left\{ \int p \, d\mu : \int p \, d\phi = 1 \right\},$$

which is the desired result (10.38). Finally (10.39) is straightforward. Indeed, in (10.38), with $\phi = a_i^{-2} \, \delta_{\boldsymbol{\xi}_i} \in \Phi$, one obtains

$$\rho \geq \min_{p \in \mathscr{Q}_{2n}(\boldsymbol{\Omega})} \left\{ \int p \, d\mu : p(\boldsymbol{\xi}_i) = a_i^2 \right\} = a_i^2 \, \kappa_n(\boldsymbol{\xi}_i).$$

□

10.5 Notes and Sources

Section 10.1 The spectral characterization of the standard Christoffel function, and its extensions in Section 10.3 based on $\mathscr{P}_{2n}(\boldsymbol{\Omega})$ or the (truncated) quadratic module $\mathscr{Q}_{2n}(\boldsymbol{\Omega})$ associated with generators of $\boldsymbol{\Omega}$, are obtained by standard tools of convex optimization.

Section 10.2 Our treatment of the Christoffel function on $L^p(\boldsymbol{\Omega}, \mu)$ spaces (for general compact $\boldsymbol{\Omega} \subset \mathbb{R}^d$) via duality is new, whereas its asymptotic properties have been already considered and solved in Levin and Lubinsky (2015) for the univariate case or on $\boldsymbol{\Omega} = [-1, 1]$ or the unit circle, and recently for more general situations in $\mathbb{R}$ or $\mathbb{C}$ by Zhou (2016), using Totik's polynomial inverse image method (Totik, 2010, 2012). To quote Zhou "To deal with more general supports we need some notions from potential theory .... In particular, we need the concept of the equilibrium measure of a compact set K on the complex plane."

Section 10.3 The extension of the Christoffel function by using $\mathscr{P}_{2n}(\boldsymbol{\Omega})$ was isolated by Marcel Riesz in one of his famous moment problem notes (Riesz, 2013). Maximal masses in the truncated moment problem were investigated very early by Chebyshev and Markov, and resurrected in modern language by Akhiezer and Krein; see comments in Akhiezer (1965). The multivariate framework with $\mathscr{P}_{2n}(\mathbf{\Omega})$ is due to Schmüdgen (2017). In particular, Lemma 10.3.1 and its link with maximal masses are from Schmüdgen (2017, §18.4).

In the univariate case $\mathbf{\Omega} = [-1, 1]$ one retrieves results obtained by Schmüdgen (2017) with $\mathscr{P}_{2n}(\mathbf{\Omega})$. This is because in the univariate case $\mathbf{\Omega} = [-1, 1]$ with generator $x \mapsto g(x) = 1 - x^2$, the convex cones $\mathscr{P}_{2n}(\mathbf{\Omega})$ and $\mathscr{Q}_{2n}(\mathbf{\Omega})$ coincide. For instance if $\mathbf{\Omega} = [-1, 1]$ then Theorem 10.3.2 is in Schmüdgen (2017).

As already mentioned, the convex cone $\mathscr{Q}_{2n}(\mathbf{\Omega})$ is computationally tractable (as opposed to the intractable $\mathscr{P}_{2n}(\mathbf{\Omega})$). This distinguishing feature is central in the Moment–SOS hierarchy to solve instances of the *Generalized Moment Problem* whose list of important applications is almost endless. For more details the interested reader is referred to Henrion et al. (2020) and Lasserre (2019).

Section 10.4 The multi-point interpolation extensions and their interpretation are new.

References

Aamari, E. and Levrard, C. 2019. Nonasymptotic rates for manifold, tangent space and curvature estimation. *Ann. Statist.*, **47**(1), 177–204.

Adler, M. and van Moerbeke, P. 2001. Darboux transforms on band matrices, weights, and associated polynomials. *Int. Math. Res. Not.*, 935–984.

Ahiezer, N. I. 1965. *Lektsii po teorii approksimatsii*, 2nd edition. Izdat. "Nauka", Moscow.

Akhiezer, N. I. 1965. *The Classical Moment Problem and Some Related Questions in Analysis*, trans. N. Kemmer. Hafner, New York.

Alaoui, A. and Mahoney, M. 2015. Fast randomized kernel ridge regression with statistical guarantees. In *Advances in Neural Information Processing Systems*, NIPS, pp. 775–783.

Alpay, D. (ed.). 2003. *Reproducing Kernel Spaces and Applications*. Operator Theory: Advances and Applications, vol. 143. Birkhäuser, Basel.

Anjos, M. and Lasserre, J. B. (eds.). 2011. *Handbook of Semidefinite, Conic and Polynomial Optimization*. International Series in Operations Research and Management Science, vol. 166. Springer, New York, NY.

Appell, P. 1890. Sur une classe de polynômes à deux variables et le calcul approché des intégrales doubles. *Ann. Fac. Sci. Toulouse Sci. Math. Sci. Phys.*, **4**(2), H1–H20.

Aronszajn, N. 1950. Theory of reproducing kernels. *Trans. Amer. Math. Soc.*, **68**, 337–404.

Askari, A., Yang, F. and El Ghaoui, L. 2018. Kernel-based outlier detection using the inverse Christoffel function. arXiv preprint arXiv:1806.06775.

Bach, F. 2013. Sharp analysis of low-rank kernel matrix approximations. In *Proceedings of the 26th Annual Conference on Learning Theory*, PMLR, pp. 185–209.

Bach, F. 2017. On the equivalence between kernel quadrature rules and random feature expansions. *J. Mach. Learn. Res.*, **18**(21), 1–38.

Baran, M. 1988. Siciak's extremal function of convex sets in $\mathbf{C}^N$. *Ann. Polon. Math.*, **48**(3), 275–280.

Baran, M. 1992. Bernstein type theorems for compact sets in $\mathbf{R}^n$. *J. Approx. Theory*, **69**(2), 156–166.

Baran, M., Białas-Cież, L. and Milówka, B. 2013. On the best exponent in Markov inequality. *Potential Anal.*, **38**(2), 635–651.

Barvinok, A. 2002. *A Course on Convexity*. American Mathematical Society, Providence, R.I.

Batschelet, E. 1981. *Circular Statistics in Biology*. Academic Press, Cambridge, MA.

Bayer, C. and Teichmann, J. 2006. The proof of Tchakaloff's theorem. *Proc. Amer. Math. Soc.*, **134**(10), 3035–3040.

Beckermann, B., Putinar, M., Saff, E. B. and Stylianopoulos, N. 2021. Perturbations of Christoffel–Darboux kernels: detection of outliers. *Found. Comp. Math.*, **21**(1), 71–124.

Bedford, E. and Taylor, B. A. 1986. The complex equilibrium measure of a symmetric convex set in $\mathbf{R}^n$. *Trans. Amer. Math. Soc.*, **294**(2), 705–717.

Belkin, M. and Niyogi, P. 2008. Towards a theoretical foundation for Laplacian-based manifold methods. *J. Comput. System Sci.*, **74**(8), 1289–1308.

Berman, R. J., Boucksom, S. and Witt Nyström, D. 2011. Fekete points and convergence towards equilibrium measures on complex manifolds. *Acta Math.*, **207**(1), 1–27.

Berman, R. J. 2009. Bergman kernels and equilibrium measures for line bundles over projective manifolds. *Amer. J. Math.*, **131**(5), 1485–1524.

Bleher, P., Lyubich, M. and Roeder, R. 2020. Lee–Yang–Fisher zeros for the DHL and 2D rational dynamics, II. Global pluripotential interpretation. *J. Geom. Anal.*, **30**(1), 777–833.

Bloom, T. 1997. Orthogonal polynomials in $\mathbb{C}^n$. *Indiana Univ. Math. J.*, **46**(2), 427–452.

Bloom, T. and Levenberg, N. 2003. Weighted pluripotential theory in $\mathbb{C}^N$. *Amer. J. Math.*, **125**(1), 57–103.

Bloom, T. and Shiffman, B. 2007. Zeros of random polynomials on $\mathbb{C}^m$. *Math. Res. Lett.*, **14**(3), 469–479.

Bloom, T., Levenberg, N., Piazzon, F. and Wielonsky, F. 2015. Bernstein–Markov: a survey. *Dolomites Res. Notes Approx.*, **8**(Special Issue), 75–91.

Bochnak, J., Coste, M. and Roy, M.-F. 1998. *Real Algebraic Geometry*. Ergebnisse der Mathematik und ihrer Grenzgebiete (3) [Results in Mathematics and Related Areas (3)], vol. 36. Springer, Berlin. Translated from the 1987 French original, revised by the authors.

Bos, L. P. 1989. Asymptotics for the Christoffel function for the equilibrium measure on a ball in $\mathbf{R}^m$. In *Approximation Theory VI, Vol. I (College Station, TX, 1989)*. Academic Press, Boston, MA, pp. 97–100.

Bos, L. P. 1994. Asymptotics for the Christoffel function for Jacobi like weights on a ball in $\mathbf{R}^m$. *New Zealand J. Math.*, **23**(2), 99–109.

Bos, L. P., Della Vecchia, B. and Mastroianni, G. 1998. On the asymptotics of Christoffel functions for centrally symmetric weight functions on the ball in $\mathbb{R}^d$. In *Proceedings of the Third International Conference on Functional Analysis and Approximation Theory, Vol. I (Acquafredda di Maratea, 1996)*. I, no. 52. Sede della Società Palermo, pp. 277–290.

Bos, L. P., Brudnyi, A. and Levenberg, N. 2010. On polynomial inequalities on exponential curves in $\mathbb{C}^n$. *Constr. Approx.*, **31**(1), 139–147.

Breiding, P., Kališnik, S., Sturmfels, B. and Weinstein, M. 2018. Learning algebraic varieties from samples. *Rev. Mat. Complut.*, **31**(3), 545–593.

Brennan, Dzh. È. 2005. Thomson's theorem on mean-square polynomial approximation. *Algebra i Analiz*, **17**(2), 1–32.

Brudnyi, A. 2008. On local behavior of holomorphic functions along complex submanifolds of $\mathbb{C}^N$. *Invent. Math.*, **173**(2), 315–363.

Bubenik, P. 2015. Statistical topological data analysis using persistence landscapes. *J. Mach. Learn. Res.*, **16**(1), 77–102.

Bueno, M. I. and Marcellán, F. 2004. Darboux transformation and perturbation of linear functionals. *Linear Algebra Appl.*, **384**, 215–242.

Burns, D., Levenberg, N., Ma'u, S. and Révész, Sz. 2010. Monge–Ampère measures for convex bodies and Bernstein–Markov type inequalities. *Trans. Amer. Math. Soc.*, **362**(12), 6325–6340.

Butzer, P. L. and Fehér, F. (eds.). 1981. *E. B. Christoffel: The Influence of his Work on Mathematics and the Physical Sciences*. Birkhäuser, Basel–Boston, MA. Including expanded versions of lectures given at the International Christoffel Symposium held in Aachen and Monschau, November 8–11, 1979.

Cantero, M. J., Marcellán, F., Moral, L. and Velázquez, L. 2016. Darboux transformations for CMV matrices. *Adv. Math.*, **298**, 122–206.

Carleman, T. 1932. Application de la théorie des équations intégrales linéaires aux systèmes d'équations différentielles non linéaires. *Acta Math.*, **59**(1), 63–87.

Carlsson, G. 2009. Topology and data. *Bull. Amer. Math. Soc.*, **46**(2), 255–308.

Chatterjee, S. and Hadi, A.S. 1986. Influential observations, high leverage points, and outliers in linear regression. *Statis. Sci.*, **1**(3), 379–393.

Chazal, F., Cohen-Steiner, D. and Mérigot, Q. 2011. Geometric inference for probability measures. *Found. Comput. Math.*, **11**(6), 733–751.

Chazal, F., Glisse, M., Labruère, C. and Michel, B. 2014. Convergence rates for persistence diagram estimation in topological data analysis. In *International Conference on Machine Learning*. PMLR, pp. 163–171.

Chevalier, J. 1976. Estimation du support et du contour du support d'une loi de probabilité. *Ann. Inst. Henri Poincaré Probab. Stat.*, **12**(4), 339–364.

Clarkson, K. L. and Woodruff, D. P. 2013. Low rank approximation and regression in input sparsity time. In *ACM Symposium on Theory of Computing*. ACM, pp. 81–90.

Coman, D. and Poletsky, E. A. 2010. Polynomial estimates, exponential curves and Diophantine approximation. *Math. Res. Lett.*, **17**(6), 1125–1136.

Conway, J. B. 1991. *The Theory of Subnormal Operators*. Mathematical Surveys and Monographs, vol. 36. American Mathematical Society, Providence, RI.

Cox, D., Little, J. and O'Shea, D. 2007. *Ideals, Varieties, and Algorithms: An Introduction to Computational Algebraic Geometry and Commutative Algebra*. Springer Science and Business Media, Berlin.

Cucker, F. and Smale, S. 2002. On the mathematical foundations of learning. *Bull. Amer. Math. Soc.*, **39**(1), 1–49.

Cuevas, A. and Fraiman, R. 1997. A plug-in approach to support estimation. *Ann. Statist.*, **25**(6), 2300–2312.

Cuevas, A., González-Manteiga, W. and Rodríguez-Casal, A. 2006a. Plug-in estimation of general level sets. *Aust. N. Z. J. Stat.*, **48**(1), 7–19.

Cuevas, A., González-Manteiga, W. and Rodríguez-Casal, A. 2006b. Plug-in estimation of general level sets. *Aust. N. Z. J. Stat.*, **48**(1), 7–19.

Curto, R. and Fialkow, L.A. 2005. Truncated K-moment problems in several variables. *J. Operator Theory*, **54**, 189–226.

Daras, N. J. 2014. Markov-type inequalities with applications in multivariate approximation theory. In *Topics in Mathematical Analysis and Applications*. Springer Optimization and its Applications, vol. 94. Springer, Cham, pp. 277–314.

Das, S. and Giannakis, D. 2019. Delay-coordinate maps and the spectra of Koopman operators. *J. Stat. Phys.*, **175**(6), 1107–1145.

Davis, J. and Goadrich, M. 2006. The relationship between Precision-Recall and ROC curves. In *Proceedings of the 23rd International Conference on Machine Learning*. Association for Computing Machnery, pp. 233–240.

de Branges, L. 1968. *Hilbert Spaces of Entire Functions*. Prentice-Hall, Englewood Cliffs, N.J.

de Castro, Y., Gamboa, F., Henrion, D., Hess, R. and Lasserre, J. B. 2019. Approximate optimal designs for multivariate polynomial regression. *Ann. Statist.*, **47**, 127–155.

Demailly, J.-P. 1985. Mesures de Monge–Ampère et caractérisation géométrique des variétés algébriques affines. *Mém. Soc. Math. Fr. (N.S.)*, **19**, 124.

Demailly, J.-P. 2013. Applications of pluripotential theory to algebraic geometry. In *Pluripotential Theory*. Lecture Notes in Mathematics, vol. 2075. Springer, Heidelberg, pp. 143–263.

DeVore, R. A. 1972. *The Approximation of Continuous Functions by Positive Linear Operators*. Lecture Notes in Mathematics, vol. 293. Springer, Berlin.

Devroye, L. and Wise, G. L. 1980. Detection of abnormal behavior via nonparametric estimation of the support. *SIAM J. Appl. Math.*, **38**(3), 480–488.

Dinew, S. 2019. Lectures on pluripotential theory on compact Hermitian manifolds. In *Complex Non-Kähler Geometry*. Lecture Notes in Mathemtaics, vol. 2246. Springer, Cham, pp. 1–56.

Donner, K. 1982. *Extension of Positive Operators and Korovkin Theorems*. Lecture Notes in Mathematics, vol. 904. Springer, berlin.

Drineas, P., Magdon-Ismail, M., Mahoney, M. W. and Woodruff, D. P. 2012. Fast approximation of matrix coherence and statistical leverage. *J. Mach. Learn. Res.*, **13**, 3475–3506.

Dubois, D. W. and Efroymson, G. 1970. Algebraic theory of real varieties. I. In *Studies and Essays (Presented to Yu-why Chen on his 60th Birthday, April 1, 1970)*. Mathematical research Center, National Taiwan University, Taipei, pp. 107–135.

Dunford, N. and Schwartz, J. 1958. *Linear Operators Part I: General Theory*. Interscience, New York, NY.

Dunkl, C. F. and Xu, Y. 2014. *Orthogonal Polynomials of Several Variables*, 2nd edn. Encyclopedia of Mathematics and its Applications, vol. 155. Cambridge University Press, Cambridge.

Durrett, R. 2019. *Probability: Theory and Examples*, Vol. 49. Cambridge University Press, Cambridge.

Eckhoff, K. S. 1993. Accurate and efficient reconstruction of discontinuous functions from truncated series expansions. *Math. Comp.*, **61**(204), 745–763.

Edelsbrunner, H. and Harer, J. 2008. Persistent homology-a survey. *Contemp. Math.*, **453**, 257–282.

Fefferman, C., Mitter, S. K. and Narayanan, H. 2016. Testing the manifold hypothesis. *J. Amer. Math. Soc.*, **29**(4), 983–1049.

Foias, C. and Frazho, A. E. 1990. *The Commutant Lifting Approach to Interpolation Problems*. Operator Theory: Advances and Applications, vol. 44. Birkhäuser, Basel.

Freud, G. 1969. *Orthogonale Polynome*. Birkhäuser, Basel–Stuttgart. Lehrbücher und Monographien aus dem Gebiete der Exakten Wissenschaften, Mathematische Reihe, Band 33.

Gaier, D. 1987. *Lectures on Complex Approximation*, trans. Renate McLaughlin. Birkhäuser Boston, Boston, MA.

Garza, L. and Marcellán, F. 2009. Szegö transformations and rational spectral transformations for associated polynomials. *J. Comput. Appl. Math.*, **233**(3), 730–738.

Gautschi, W. 1986. On the sensitivity of orthogonal polynomials to perturbations in the moments. *Numer. Math.*, **48**(4), 369–382.

Geffroy, J. 1964. Sur un probleme d'estimation géométrique. *Publ. Inst. Statist. Univ. Paris*, **13**, 191–210.

Genovese, C. R., Perone-Pacifico, M., Verdinelli, I. and Wasserman, L. 2012a. Manifold estimation and singular deconvolution under Hausdorff loss. *Ann. Statist.*, **40**(2), 941–963.

Genovese, C. R., Perone-Pacifico, M., Verdinelli, I. and Wasserman, L. 2012b. Minimax manifold estimation. *J. Mach. Learn. Res.*, **13**(1), 1263–1291.

Geronimo, J. S. and Woerdeman, H. 2007. Two variable orthogonal polynomials on the bicircle and structured matrices. *SIAM J. Matrix Anal. Appl.*, **29**(3), 796–825.

Geronimo, J. S. and Woerdeman, H. J. 2004. Positive extensions, Fejér–Riesz factorization and autoregressive filters in two variables. *Ann. of Math. (2)*, **160**(3), 839–906.

Ghrist, R. 2008. Barcodes: the persistent topology of data. *Bull. Amer. Math. Soc.*, **45**(1), 61–75.

Gómez-Ullate, D., Kamran, N. and Milson, R. 2010. Exceptional orthogonal polynomials and the Darboux transformation. *J. Phys. A*, **43**(43), 434016, 16.

Gorbachuk, M. L. and Gorbachuk, V. I. 1997. *M. G. Krein's lectures on entire operators*. Operator Theory: Advances and Applications, vol. 97. Birkhäuser, Basel.

Grant, M. and Boyd, S. 2014. *CVX: Matlab Software for Disciplined Convex Programming, version 2.1*. CVX Research. Available at: http://cvxr.com/cvx/

Gröbner, W. 1948. Über die Konstruktion von Systemen orthogonaler Polynome in einune zwei-dimensionalen Bereichen. *Monatsh. Math.*, **52**, 38–54.

Gustafsson, B., Putinar, M., Saff, E. B. and Stylianopoulos, N. 2009. Bergman polynomials on an archipelago: estimates, zeros and shape reconstruction. *Adv. Math.*, **222**(4), 1405–1460.

Gustafsson, B. and Putinar, M. 2017. *Hyponormal Quantization of Planar Domains: Exponential Transform in Dimension Two*. Lecture Notes in Mathematics, vol. 2199. Springer, Cham.

Hein, M. and Audibert, J.-Y. 2005. Intrinsic dimensionality estimation of submanifolds in Rd. In *Proceedings of the 22nd International Conference on Machine Learning*. Association for Computing Machinery, pp. 289–296.

Hein, M., Audibert, J.-Y. and Von Luxburg, U. 2005. From graphs to manifolds–weak and strong pointwise consistency of graph Laplacians. In *International Conference on Computational Learning Theory*. COLT 2005. Springer, pp. 470–485.

Hellinger, E. 1922. Zur Stieltjesschen Kettenbruchtheorie. *Math. Ann.*, **86**(1–2), 18–29.

Hellinger, E. and Toeplitz, O. 1953. *Integralgleichungen und Gleichungen mit unendlichvielen Unbekannten*. Chelsea, New York, NY.

Henrion, D., Korda, M. and Lasserre, J. B. 2020. *The Moment-SOS Hierarchy: Lectures in Probability, Statistics, Computational Geometry and Nonlinear PDEs*. World Scientific, Singapore.

Herglotz, G., Schur, I., Pick, G., Nevanlinna, R. and Weyl, H. 1991. *Ausgewählte Arbeiten zu den Ursprüngen der Schur-Analysis*. Teubner-Archiv zur Mathematik [Teubner Archive on Mathematics], vol. 16. B. G. Teubner Verlagsgesellschaft mbH, Stuttgart. Gewidmet dem großen Mathematiker Issai Schur (1875–1941). [Dedicated to the great mathematician Issai Schur (1875–1941)], Edited and with a foreword and afterword by Bernd Fritzsche and Bernd Kirstein, With contributions by W. Ledermann and W. K. Hayman, With English, French and Russian summaries.

Hilbert, D. 1920. Gaston Darboux. 1842–1917 *Acta Math.*, **42**(1), 269–273.

Hilbert, D. 1953. *Grundzüge einer allgemeinen Theorie der linearen Integralgleichungen*. Chelsea, New York, NY.

Hoaglin, D. C. and Welsch, R. E. 1978. The hat matrix in regression and ANOVA. *Amer. Statist.*, **32**(1), 17–22.

Hoel, P. G. 1961/62. Some properties of optimal spacing in polynomial estimation. *Ann. Inst. Statist. Math.*, **13**, 1–8.

Hoel, P. G. and Levine, A. 1964. Optimal spacing and weighting in polynomial prediction. *Ann. Math. Statist.*, **35**, 1553–1560.

Kiefer, J. 1961. Optimum designs in regression problems. II. *Ann. Math. Statist.*, **32**, 298–325.

Kiefer, J. and Wolfowitz, J. 1959. Optimum designs in regression problems. *Ann. Math. Statist.*, **30**, 271–294.

Kiefer, J. and Wolfowitz, J. 1960. The equivalence of two extremum problems. *Canadian J. Math.*, **12**, 363–366.

Kiefer, J. and Wolfowitz, J. 1965. On a theorem of Hoel and Levine on extrapolation designs. *Ann. Math. Statist.*, **36**, 1627–1655.

Kim, A. K H. and Zhou, H. H. 2015. Tight minimax rates for manifold estimation under Hausdorff loss. *Electron. J. Stat.*, **9**(1), 1562–1582.

Klimek, M. 1991. *Pluripotential Theory*. London Mathematical Society Monographs, New Series, vol. 6. Clarendon Press, Oxford.

Knill, O. 1998. A remark on quantum dynamics. *Helv. Phys. Acta*, **71**(3), 233–241.

Kolmogorov, A. N. 1941. Stationary sequences in Hilbert's space. *Vestnik Moskovskogo Gosudarstvennogo Universiteta. Matematika [Moscow Univ. Math. Bull.]*, **2**, 40pp.

Koopman, B. O. 1931. Hamiltonian systems and transformation in Hilbert space. *Proc. Natl. Acad. Sci. USA*, **17**(5), 315–318.

Koopman, B. O. and Von Neumann, J. 1932. Dynamical systems of continuous spectra. *Proc Natl Acad. Sci. USA*, **18**(3), 255–263.

Koornwinder, T. 1975. Two-variable analogues of the classical orthogonal polynomials. In *Theory and Application of Special Functions (Proc. Advanced Sem., Math. Res. Center, Univ. Wisconsin, Madison, Wis., 1975)*. Academic Press, New York, pp. 435–495.

Korda, M., Putinar, M. and Mezić, I. 2020. Data-driven spectral analysis of the Koopman operator. *Appl. Comput. Harmon. Anal.*, **48**(2), 599–629.

Krein, M. G. 1957. On a continual analogue of a Christoffel formula from the theory of orthogonal polynomials. *Dokl. Akad. Nauk SSSR (N.S.)*, **113**, 970–973.

Krein, M. G. 1951. The ideas of P. L. Čebyšev and A. A. Markov in the theory of limiting values of integrals and their further development. *Uspekhi Mat. Nauk (N.S.)*, **6**(4 (44)), 3–120.

Kroó, A. 2015. Christoffel functions on convex and starlike domains in $\mathbb{R}^d$. *J. Math. Anal. Appl.*, **421**(1), 718–729.

Kroó, A. and Lubinsky, D. S. 2013a. Christoffel functions and universality in the bulk for multivariate orthogonal polynomials. *Canad. J. Math.*, **65**(3), 600–620.

Kroó, A. and Lubinsky, D. S. 2013b. Christoffel functions and universality on the boundary of the ball. *Acta Math. Hungar.*, **140**(1–2), 117–133.

Lacey, M. and Terwilleger, E. 2008. A Wiener–Wintner theorem for the Hilbert transform. *Ark. Mat.*, **46**(2), 315–336.

Lam, T. Y. 1984. An introduction to real algebra. *Rocky Mountain J. Math.*, **14**(4), 767–814.

Lasserre, J. B. 2015. A generalization of Löwner–John's Ellipsoid theorem. *Math. Program. Ser. A*, **152**(1), 559–591.

Lasserre, J. B. 2019. The Moment–SOS Hierarchy. In B. Sirakov, P. Ney de Sousa and M. Viana (eds.), *Proceedings of the International Congress of Mathematicians (ICM 2018)*. World Scientific, Singapore, pp. 3773–3794.

Lasserre, J. B. and Pauwels, E. 2016. Sorting out typicality with the inverse moment matrix SOS polynomial. In D. D. Lee, M. Sugiyama, U. V. Luxburg, I. Guyon and R. Garnett (eds.), *Advances in Neural Information Processing Systems*. Curran Associates, New York, NY, pp. 190–198.

Lasserre, J. B. and Pauwels, E. 2019. The empirical Christoffel function with applications in data analysis. *Adv. Comput. Math.*, **45**(3), 1439–1468.

Levin, E. and Lubinsky, D. S. 2015. Christoffel functions, L_p universality, and Paley-Wiener spaces. *J. Anal. Math.*, **125**, 243–283.

Levina, E. and Bickel, P. 2004. Maximum likelihood estimation of intrinsic dimension. *Advances in neural information processing systems*, **17**, 777–784.

Lichman, J. 2013. *UCI Machine Learning Repository*. School of Information and Computer Sciences, University of California, Irvine, CA. Available at: http://archive.ics.uci.edu/ml.

Liesen, J. and Strakoš, Z. 2013. *Krylov Subspace Methods: Principles and Analysis*. Numerical Mathematics and Scientific Computation. Oxford University Press, Oxford.

Lippmann, G., Poincaré, H., Appell, P., Lavisse, E., Volterra, V., Belugou, L., Picard, R E., Lèvy, L., Guichard, C. and Darboux, G. 1912. Le jubilé de M Gaston Darboux. *Revue internationale de l'enseignement*, **6**, 97–125.

Lovell, S. C., Davis, I. W., Arendall III, W. B., De Bakker, P. IW., Word, J.M., Prisant, M. G., Richardson, J. S. and Richardson, D. C. 2003. Structure validation by Cα geometry: ϕ, ψ and Cβ deviation. *Proteins*, **50**(3), 437–450.

Ma, P., Mahoney, M. W. and Yu, B. 2015. A statistical perspective on algorithmic leveraging. *J. Mach. Learn. Res.*, **16**(1), 861–911.

Magnani, A., Lall, S. and Boyd, S. 2005. Tractable fitting with convex polynomials via sum-of-squares. In *Proceedings of the 44th IEEE Conference on Decision and Control*. Curran Associates, New York, NY, pp. 1672–1677.

Mahoney, M. W. 2011. Randomized algorithms for matrices and data. *Found. Trends Mach. Learn.*, **3**(2), 123–224.

Mahoney, M. W. and Drineas, P. 2009. CUR matrix decompositions for improved data analysis. *Proc. Natl Acad. Sci USA*, **106**(3), 697–702.

Mammen, E. and Tsybakov, A. B. 1995. Asymptotical minimax recovery of sets with smooth boundaries. *Ann. Statist*, 502–524.

Marx, S., Pauwels, E., Weisser, T., Henrion, D. and Lasserre, J. B. 2021. Tractable semi-algebraic approximation using Christoffel–Darboux kernel. *Constr. Approx.*, **54**, 391–429.

Máté, A., Nevai, P. and Totik, V. 1987. Strong and weak convergence of orthogonal polynomials. *Amer. J. Math.*, **109**(2), 239–281.

Máté, A., Nevai, P. and Totik, V. 1991. Szegö's extremum problem on the unit circle. *Ann. of Math. (2)*, **134**(2), 433–453.

Matveev, V. B. and Salle, M. A. 1991. *Darboux Transformations and Solitons*. Springer Series in Nonlinear Dynamics. Springer, Berlin.

Mauroy, A., Mezić, I. and Susuki, Yoshihiko. 2020. *The Koopman Operator in Systems and Control*. Lecture Notes in Control and Information Sciences, vol. 484. Springer, Cham.

Molchanov, I. S. 1998. A limit theorem for solutions of inequalities. *Scand. J. Stat.*, **25**(1), 235–242.

Nevai, P. 1986. Géza Freud, orthogonal polynomials and Christoffel functions: A case study. *J. Approx. Theory*, **48**(1), 3–167.

Nie, J. 2013. Certifying convergence of Lasserre's hierarchy via flat truncation. *Math. Program. Ser. A*, **142**(1–2), 485–510.

Nikolski, N. 2019. *Hardy Spaces*, French edn. Cambridge Studies in Advanced Mathematics, vol. 179. Cambridge University Press, Cambridge.

Niyogi, P., Smale, S. and Weinberger, S. 2008. Finding the homology of submanifolds with high confidence from random samples. *Discrete Comput. Geom.*, **39**(1–3), 419–441.

Niyogi, P., Smale, S. and Weinberger, S. 2011. A topological view of unsupervised learning from noisy data. *SIAM J. Comput.*, **40**(3), 646–663.

Paulsen, V. I. and Raghupathi, M. 2016. *An Introduction to the Theory of Reproducing Kernel Hilbert Spaces*. Cambridge Studies in Advanced Mathematics, vol. 152. Cambridge University Press, Cambridge.

Pauwels, E., Bach, F. and Vert, J.-P. 2018. Relating leverage scores and density using regularized christoffel functions. In *Advances in Neural Information Processing Systems*. MIT Press, Cambridge, MA, pp. 1663–1672.

Pauwels, E., Putinar, M. and Lasserre, J. B. 2021. Data analysis from empirical moments and the Christoffel function. *Found. Comput. Math.*, **21**(1), 243–273.

Pawłucki, W. and Pleśniak, W. 1986. Markov's inequality and C^{∞} functions on sets with polynomial cusps. *Math. Ann.*, **275**(3), 467–480.

Peherstorfer, F. 1992. Finite perturbations of orthogonal polynomials. *J. Comput. Appl. Math.*, **44**(3), 275–302.

Perryman, M., Lindegren, L., Kovalevsky, J., Hoeg, E., Bastian, U., Bernacca, P. et al. 1997. The Hipparcos Catalogue. Astron. Astrophys., **500**, 501–504.

Piazzon, F. 2018. The extremal plurisubharmonic function of the torus. *Dolomites Res. Notes Approx.*, **11**(Special Issue Norm Levenberg), 62–72.

Piazzon, F. 2019a. Laplace Beltrami operator in the Baran metric and pluripotential equilibrium measure: the ball, the simplex, and the sphere. *Comput. Methods Funct. Theory*, **19**(4), 547–582.

Piazzon, F. 2019b. Pluripotential numerics. *Constr. Approx.*, **49**(2), 227–263.

Poincaré, H. 1975. L'avenir des mathématiques. *Scientia (Milano)*, **110**(5-8), 357–368. Abridged text of a paper read at the Fourth International Congress of Mathematicians, Rome, 1908, with introductions in Italian and English.

Polonik, W. 1995. Measuring mass concentrations and estimating density contour clusters-an excess mass approach. *Ann. Statist.*, **23**(3), 855–881.

Prestel, A. and Delzell, C. N. 2001. *Positive Polynomials: From Hilbert's 17th Problem to Real Algebra*. Springer Monographs in Mathematics. Springer, Berlin.

Prymak, A. and Usoltseva, O. 2019. Christoffel functions on planar domains with piecewise smooth boundary. *Acta Math. Hungar.*, **158**(1), 216–234.

Putinar, M. 1993. Positive polynomials on compact semi-algebraic sets. *Indiana Univ. Math. J.*, **42**, 969–984.

Putinar, M. 2021a. Moment estimates of the cloud of a planar measure. *Acta Appl. Math.*, https://doi.org/10.1007/s10440-021-00443-0.

Putinar, M. 2021b. Spectral Analysis of 2D outlier layout. *J. Spectral Theory*, **11**, 821–845.

Rényi, A. and Sulanke, R. 1963. Über die konvexe Hülle von n zufällig gewählten Punkten. *Probab. Theory. Related Fields*, **2**(1), 75–84.

Ricci, P. E. 1978. Čebyšev polynomials in several variables. *Rend. Mat. (6)*, **11**(2), 295–327.

Riesz, F. and Sz.-Nagy, B. 1990 [1955]. *Functional Analysis*, trans. L. F. Boron. Dover Books on Advanced Mathematics. Dover, New York, NY.

Riesz, M. 2013 [1988]. *Collected Papers*, ed. L. Garding and L. Hörmander. Springer Collected Works in Mathematics. Springer, Heidelberg.

Rodríguez Casal, A. 2007. Set estimation under convexity type assumptions. *Ann. Inst. Henri Poincaré Probab. Stat.*, **43**(6), 763–774.

Rosenblum, M. and Rovnyak, J. 1997 [1985]. *Hardy Classes and Operator Theory*. Dover, Mineola, NY.

Ross, J. and Nyström, D. W. 2019. Applications of the duality between the homogeneous complex Monge-Ampère equation and the Hele-Shaw flow. *Ann. Inst. Fourier (Grenoble)*, **69**(1), 1–30.

Rudi, A. and Rosasco, L. 2017. Generalization properties of learning with random features. In *Advances in Neural Information Processing Systems*. NIPS, pp. 3218–3228.

Rudi, A., Camoriano, R. and Rosasco, L. 2015. Less is more: Nyström computational regularization. In *Advances in Neural Information Processing Systems*. NIPS, pp. 1657–1665.

Sadullaev, A. 1981. Plurisubharmonic measures and capacities on complex manifolds. *Uspekhi Mat. Nauk*, **36**(4(220)), 53–105, 247.

Sadullaev, A. 1982. Estimates of polynomials on analytic sets. *Izv. Akad. Nauk SSSR Ser. Mat.*, **46**(3), 524–534, 671.

Sadullaev, A. 1985. Plurisubharmonic functions. In *Current Problems in Mathematics: Fundamental Directions, Vol. 8*. Itogi Nauki i Tekhniki. Akad. Nauk SSSR, Vsesoyuz. Inst. Nauchn. i Tekhn. Inform., Moscow, pp. 65–113, 274.

Saff, E. B., Stahl, H., Stylianopoulos, N. and Totik, V. 2015. Orthogonal polynomials for area-type measures and image recovery. *SIAM J. Math. Anal.*, **47**(3), 2442–2463.

Samsonov, B. F. and Ovcharov, I. N. 1995. The Darboux transformation and nonclassical orthogonal polynomials. *Izv. Vyssh. Uchebn. Zaved. Fiz.*, **38**(4), 58–65.

Schmüdgen, K. 2017. *The Moment Problem*. Graduate Texts in Mathematics, vol. 277. Springer, Cham.

Schölkopf, B., Smola, A. J., Bach, F. et al. 2002. *Learning with Kernels: Support Vector Machines, regularization, Optimization, and Beyond*. MIT Press, Cambridge, MA.

Serre, J.-P. 1956. Géométrie algébrique et géométrie analytique. *Ann. Inst. Fourier*, **6**, 1–42.

Siciak, J. 1962. On some extremal functions and their applications in the theory of analytic functions of several complex variables. *Trans. Amer. Math. Soc.*, **105**, 322–357.

Simanek, B. 2012. Weak convergence of CD kernels: a new approach on the circle and real line. *J. Approx. Theory*, **164**(1), 204–209.

Simon, B. 2005a. *Orthogonal Polynomials on the Unit Circle. Part 1: Classical Theory*. American Mathematical Society Colloquium Publications, vol. 54. American Mathematical Society, Providence, RI.

Simon, B. 2005b. *Orthogonal Polynomials on the Unit Circle. Part 2: Spectral Theory*. American Mathematical Society Colloquium Publications, vol. 54. American Mathematical Society, Providence, RI.

Simon, B. 2008. The Christoffel–Darboux kernel. In *Perspectives in Partial Differential Equations, Harmonic Analysis and Applications*. Proceedings of Symposia in Pure Mathematics, vol. 79. American Mathematical Society, Providence, RI, pp. 295–335.

Simon, B. 2009. Weak convergence of CD kernels and applications. *Duke Math. J.*, **146**(2), 305–330.

Simon, B. 2011. *Szegő's Theorem and its Descendants: Spectral Theory for L^2 Perturbations of Orthogonal Polynomials.*. M. B. Porter Lectures. Princeton University Press, Princeton, NJ.

Stahl, H. and Totik, V. 1992. *General Orthogonal Polynomials*. Encyclopedia of Mathematics and its Applications, vol. 43. Cambridge University Press, Cambridge.

Stone, M. H. 1990 [1932]. *Linear Transformations in Hilbert Space*. American Mathematical Society Colloquium Publications, vol. 15. American Mathematical Society, Providence, RI.

Suetin, P. K. 1999. *Orthogonal Polynomials in Two Variables*. Analytical Methods and Special Functions, vol. 3. Gordon and Breach Science Publishers, Amsterdam. Translated from the 1988 Russian original by E. V. Pankratiev.

Szegő, G. 1975. *Orthogonal Polynomials*, 4th edn. American Mathematical Society, Colloquium Publications, vol. 23, American Mathematical Society, Providence, RI.

Thomson, J. E. 1991. Approximation in the mean by polynomials. *Ann. of Math. (2)*, **133**(3), 477–507.

Todd, M. J. 2016. *Minimum-Volume Ellipsoids: Theory and Algorithms*. SIAM, Philadelphia.

Totik, V. 2000. Asymptotics for Christoffel functions for general measures on the real line. *J. Anal. Math.*, **81**, 283–303.

Totik, V. 2010. Christoffel functions on curves and domains. *Trans. Amer. Math. Soc.*, **362**, 2053–2087.

Totik, V. 2012. The polynomial inverse image method. In M. Neamtu and L. Schumaker (eds.), *Approximation Theory XIII: San Antonio 2010*. Springer Proceedings in Mathematics, vol. 13. Springer, Berlin.

Tsybakov, A. B. 1997. On nonparametric estimation of density level sets. *Ann. Statist.*, **25**(3), 948–969.

Velleman, P. F. and Welsch, R. E. 1981. Efficient computing of regression diagnostics. *Amer. Statis.*, **35**(4), 234–242.

Vershynin, R. 2010. Introduction to the non-asymptotic analysis of random matrices. arXiv preprint arXiv:1011.3027.

von Neumann, J. 1932. Zur Operatorenmethode in der klassischen Mechanik. *Ann. of Math. (2)*, **33**(3), 587–642.

Vu, Mai Trang, Bachoc, F. and Pauwels, E. 2019. Rate of convergence for geometric inference based on the empirical Christoffel function. arXiv preprint arXiv:1910.14458.

Walther, G. 1999. On a generalization of Blaschke's rolling theorem and the smoothing of surfaces. *Math. Methods Appl. Sci.*, **22**(4), 301–316.

Wang, S. and Zhang, Z. 2013. Improving CUR matrix decomposition and the Nyström approximation via adaptive sampling. *J. Mach. Learn. Res.*, **14**(1), 2729–2769.

Weisse, A., Wellein, G., Alvermann, A. and Fehske, H. 2006. The kernel polynomial method. *Rev. Modern Phys.*, **78**, 275–306.

Widom, H. 1967. Polynomials associated with measures in the complex plane. *J. Math. Mech.*, **16**, 997–1013.

Widom, H. 1969. Extremal polynomials associated with a system of curves in the complex plane. *Adv. Math.*, **3**, 127–232.

Wiener, N. and Wintner, A. 1941. Harmonic analysis and ergodic theory. *Amer. J. Math.*, **63**, 415–426.

Williams, G., Baxter, R., He, H., Hawkins, S. and Gu, L. 2002. A comparative study of RNN for outlier detection in data mining. In *Proceedings of the IEEE International Conference on Data Mining*. IEEE Computer Society, p. 709.

Xu, Y. 1995. Christoffel functions and Fourier series for multivariate orthogonal polynomials. *J. Approx. Theory*, **82**(2), 205–239.

Xu, Y. 1996. Asymptotics for orthogonal polynomials and Christoffel functions on a ball. *Methods Appl. Anal.*, **3**(2), 257–272.

Xu, Y. 1999. Asymptotics of the Christoffel functions on a simplex in $\mathbf{R}^d$. *J. Approx. Theory*, **99**(1), 122–133.

Yamanishi, K., Takeuchi, J.-I., Williams, G. and Milne, P. 2004. On-line supervised outlier detection using finite mixtures with discounting learning algorithms. *Data Min. Knowl. Discov.*, **8**(3), 275–300.

Yoon, G. J. 2002. Darboux transforms and orthogonal polynomials. *Bull. Korean Math. Soc.*, **39**(3), 359–376.

Zhedanov, A. 1997. Rational spectral transformations and orthogonal polynomials. *J. Comput. Appl. Math.*, **85**(1), 67–86.

Zhou, Y. 2016. Asymptotics of L^p Christoffel functions. *J. Math. Anal. Appl.*, **433**(2), 1390–1408.

Index

Printed in the United States
by Baker & Taylor Publisher Services